D0878365

Powers, Principalities, and the Spirit

Biblical Realism in Africa and the West

Esther E. Acolatse

WILLIAM B. EERDMANS PUBLISHING COMPANY
GRAND RAPIDS, MICHIGAN

Wm. B. Eerdmans Publishing Co.
2140 Oak Industrial Drive N.E., Grand Rapids, Michigan 49505
www.eerdmans.com

Published 2018
Printed in the United States of America

2018-11

ISBN   978-0-8028-6405-5

Library of Congress Cataloging-in-Publication Data

Names: Acolatse, Esther, author.
Title: Powers, principalities, and the spirit : biblical realism in Africa
    and the West / Esther E. Acolatse.
Description: Grand Rapids : Eerdmans Publishing Co., 2018. | Includes
    bibliographical references and index.
Identifiers: LCCN 2017039682 | ISBN 9780802864055 (pbk. : alk. paper)
Subjects: LCSH: Powers (Christian theology) | Spiritual warfare. |
    Bible—Criticism, interpretation, etc.—Africa. | Christianity—Africa. |
    Christianity and culture—Africa.
Classification: LCC BT963 .A26 2018 | DDC 235—dc23
    LC record available at https://lccn.loc.gov/2017039682

Contents

Foreword

The world of Christian faith and practice has always been diverse and fluid, but until recently a European framework has afforded the Christian West a fairly coherent, if not uniform, cultural outlook, adding to Christian Europe's self-confident idea of its preeminence. Hillaire Belloc summed it up in his book *Europe and the Faith*: "The faith is Europe, and Europe is the faith." But while many writers continue to speak of Christianity in the spirit of Belloc's Eurocentric assumptions, the ground has shifted radically. The bridge that once spanned the majestic stream of Europe's worldwide hegemony still stands in much theological discourse; but the reality is that the course of Christian history has acquired new momentum and turned in new directions, which has caused tremors in the theological academy.

In few places is the gap between the old-school view of religion and current developments more glaring than in the matter of spirit power and agency, a gap that the charismatic tide has exposed and widened. It has created a Western backlash. There is fear abroad that the post-Western Christian resurgence will overtake the gains of a liberal society and constitute a setback for Western civilization. Yet the pact with secular liberalism that allowed the churches to share in the fruits of Western civilization has exacted a high price in religious adherence: membership decline and theological uncertainty have shrunk the appeal and influence of organized religion. What once were the heartlands of the faith in Europe have turned into increasingly prominent bastions of secular dominance. In the new constitution of the European Union, Europe considers itself to be post-Christian. The enormous resources at its command can now be deployed to support ideas and projects whose impact would hasten the demise of a religion that was once its heartbeat. Yet it is doubtful whether the economic and cultural renewal envisioned in the post-Christian dispensation will be an adequate substitute for faith and commitment—that is, whether economic prosperity is a secure enough firewall against persistent personal disenchantment. And a post-Christian Europe elicits the corresponding prospect of a post-Western Christianity, in the sense that post-Western societies will inherit the religious initiative, with all that implies for the global balance of religious influence.

Esther Acolatse is right to draw attention to an area where that religious influence is likely to be felt quite keenly, where there is evidence of burgeoning theological activity. Charismatic and Pentecostal membership accounts for at least a quarter of all conversions to Christianity during the last half-century. Barely a million strong in the early twentieth century, charismatics and Pentecostals number over 500 million worldwide members today. For these converts, spirit power is a necessary, indeed indispensable, ground of experience and witness.

The paradox, as Acolatse points out, is that theological discourse on the powers and principalities of the spirit world is remarkably scarce in the very post-Western societies that are most deeply immersed in that worldview, while in the West, ideas and theories concerning spirit powers abound, even though there is not as much proximity to or direct experience with the phenomenon. It is not clear here who needs whom most—and why. Theological discourse on spirit power has thrived in the academy without—and indeed sometimes with deep skepticism of—the experience of the spirit world to support it. On the other hand, experience based on the spirit world is teeming in societies without much felt need of intellectual explanation. It is vitally important to hear Acolatse's call for theological exchange across the cultural divide to remedy that disparity.

There is some history to tap into among Western scholars. With echoes of Brevard Childs, the late Lesslie Newbigin, in his treatise *Truth and Authority in Modernity* (1996), alerted us to the modern unwillingness, and perhaps inability, to affirm the Bible as revealed truth, saying it would involve a change in the Enlightenment orientation of the world to alter the picture. That orientation demands that knowledge of the world be split between myth and reality, with religion considered to belong to the world of myth, while objective reality is based in facts.

In his book *The Nature of Doctrine* (1984), George Lindbeck tries to blunt this sharp dichotomy by speaking of myth not as unscientific belief but as a narrative construct through which human experience and understanding of the world are structured and rendered intelligible and meaningful. It is the imaginative language, or the a priori axiom, by which we set the course of our relationship to the world and to others, including our self-understanding; it is the underlying order that animates descriptive life with a conscious narrative intent. Lindbeck was here standing against the Enlightenment's implication that reduces the mythological frame to a subjective norm, while fact and reality acquire an authoritative objective status with power to determine and define the nature and destiny of the world. This Enlightenment perspective has held that human beings, as knowing subjects, must be inducted into the language of rational thought for any claim to knowledge they make to be considered legitimate. This suggests that religion as presented in the language of Scripture is being offered little room in a universe stripped of all nonrational agents and agency. This, critics maintain, strikes right at the heart of what Scripture calls "the powers and principalities of the world"—or spirit agents and agency—and represents a seemingly insuperable cultural obstacle to rapprochement between the children of the Enlightenment and those who embrace the powers of the spirit. The immunity acquired from Enlightenment rationality, critics contend, is an effective antidote to the virus of religion.

The fact of the matter, however, is that spirit-filled religion has not been halted in its march across the world, even as the world has not retracted from embracing the effects of Enlightenment science and technology. From East to West and South to North, the world has become much more complicated than the Enlightenment foretold. In this book Acolatse does not ignore or evade the challenge of understanding these developments. Instead, she simply invites us to encounter again what Scripture has to say to us about the powers of the spirit, bringing in voices from both Africa and the West to ground our encounter in that more complicated, post-Enlightenment world.

In her careful review of the evidence, Acolatse lays out the persisting and persistent impediments and difficulties that dog not only the cause of theological renewal in Africa and elsewhere, but also the pre-shrunk, stripped-down universe that has shackled theological initiative in the West. Given the relatively recent nature of Africa's turn to Christianity, and the fact that the reigning symbols of that society are pre-Christian, the work of reconstruction and reimagining that needs to be done is a fundamental theological task. This book's unflinching commitment to what it would take to do this work should commend it to all who have eyes to see the challenge.

Lamin Sanneh
New Haven, Connecticut

Acknowledgments

The issues addressed in this volume are, on the one hand, about the every-dayness of the theological quest and, on the other hand, about the simple yet complicated ways in which we seek to understand Scripture for life's vicissitudes and also for deep interpretative work for the church and the academy. That art I first learned from my mother, Mercy, who taught me from an early age the value of theological reflection about all things ordinary and extraordinary.

For me, the art of using such lenses aright was also born in the midst of a group of young adult singing evangelists—the Joyful Way Singers, now Incorporated—who, long before we knew what a theologian was, were engaged in ecumenical practical theological reflection through the simple but deep Spirit-led interpretation and application of Scripture to the disciplined Christian life and formation. To these faithful, too many to name, but especially Emmanuel Y. Lartey, whose vision started this group, I offer thanks for company on the journey that gave birth to my theological acumen.

Many thanks to Felix B. Asiedu for several conversations, and to Charles Scalise for his encouragement on this project; the latter read through the draft of some of these chapters and helped me refine some of the ideas I express here.

It is impossible to mention all the friends and colleagues, especially those in the Office of Black Church Studies at Duke Divinity School, who in various ways encouraged me along the way and whose work opens up spaces for thinking imaginatively and daringly about theology in the aid of the church in a primarily research institution. But I am obliged to mention at least one, Judith Heyhoe, who helped shape this work for accessibility and readability. Thanks, also, to Gord Brown, who prepared the indexes.

For Elikem, thanks for gracing my life. For Joshua Kudajie, John Pobee, and James Loder—the men who made a way for a girl.

Introduction

The significant estrangement today between the churches of the North Atlantic/West and those of the global South arises largely from their differing beliefs about the principalities and powers. How are theologians today to understand this language, as well as its attendant mythos? What did it mean in Hebraic thought and in the life and practice of the early followers of Jesus, and what are the implications for ecclesiology in our day? What was their exousiology (as we might call the study of the powers, the *exousiai*), and what should ours be? While we cannot simply assert that belief in and attention to the spirit(s) has led to the numerical growth in the South, while the lack of such belief has caused the decline of faith in the North, the starkly contrasting experience and expression of Christian witness in the two regions of the world at least raises the question. In any event, if the church is to experience and display its catholicity, and if the church is to enact the unity claimed in its affirmation "*One* Lord, *one* Faith, *one* Baptism," then surely its current schizophrenia must be healed.

How? Is there a way to provide parameters within which we can all share a hermeneutical table? Can the North, with its formal, structured liturgical style, which often allows for little affect, and the South, with its often informal and unstructured style, which allows for the affect and charismatic fervor that it equates with the presence and influence of the Spirit, learn from each other?[1] Neither stance is a full expression of the church,

1. Of course, these are generalizations, and references to the West are primarily to the mainline traditions, since there are charismatic and Pentecostal churches in the North Atlantic, as well as many nondenominational churches, that fall under the rubric "megachurch."

and neither can or should be conceived as such. The interpretations of one segment of the church cannot be the standard for all, nor can the spatial and temporal distance between the past and the present be glossed over. In interpreting the language of the powers in Scripture—which also means, especially in the churches of the global South, interpreting miracles and the manifestations of the Holy Spirit—neither the extreme dualism of the South's hermeneutics of the powers, with its extreme supernaturalism of the Spirit,[2] nor the monism or rationalism of the West, characterized by the Enlightenment ideology and its resulting demythologizing project, adequately undergirds pastoral theology and practice in a global church.

The following verses from Ephesians offer us a good composite picture of the language that the scriptures of the Old and New Testaments employ in speaking about otherworldly realities. Paul's words suggest that Christians are embattled creatures who require supernatural intervention to traverse this life. This was the manner of being Christian, a way that was taken for granted, and that somehow today is being variously interpreted across cultural lines and worldviews.

> [10]Finally, be strong in the Lord and in the strength of his might. [11]Put on the whole armor of God, that you may be able to stand against the schemes of the devil. [12]For we do not wrestle against flesh and blood, but against the rulers, against the authorities, against the cosmic powers over this present darkness, against the spiritual forces of evil in the heavenly places. (Eph. 6:10–12, ESV).

This passage, which extends to verse 20, underscores the scriptural message that Christians are embattled and need certain practices to sustain their faith and life in the face of oppositions from otherworldly forces. The writer assumes that the recipients of the Epistle already understand and take for granted the realities addressed. These words instruct about life, not just in general but in the everydayness of navigating familial relationships, indicating that such concepts were in the social imaginary of the Ephesian Christians. And the language of Ephesians, with its references to principalities and powers—its world teeming with otherworldly spirit beings, angels and demons that can traverse the physical world—accords well with the whole of biblical discourse regarding otherworldly powers.

---

2. See Esther E. Acolatse, *For Freedom or Bondage? A Critique of African Pastoral Practices* (Grand Rapids: Eerdmans, 2014).

In the years between Paul's writing of these words and the present, however, there has been an obvious bifurcation in Christian beliefs and attitudes regarding the principalities and powers and the influence of otherworldly spirit beings in the physical world, a bifurcation reflected in such binaries as North versus South, First World versus Third World, modern versus premodern, and so on. On the one hand, there is a belief in and valorization of—and even overinvolvement with—these powers, mainly in the Christian South, and especially where Christianity meets primal religions, and people in general believe in evil spirit beings.[3] On the other hand, in the North and West, people commonly undervalue, disbelieve in, and sometimes flatly dismiss these powers and their ability to permeate and affect what is assumed to be the material world.[4]

In the global South—and in Africa in particular—belief in such powers as real and personal, modern technological advancements notwithstanding, has not diminished or shifted over time. In fact, such belief in the powers and their influence on human life, as well as the work of the Spirit in the church, in the individual, and in human history is well documented in writings on Pentecostalism and charismatic renewal by theologians in both South[5] and North.[6] In fact, in most of the South, one

---

3. A case in point is the recent situation in African-instituted churches in Britain, where children are accused of being possessed by witchcraft spirits and their subsequent exorcisms have attracted media attention. See David Pearson, "How Churches Fight Belief in Witchcraft: African Churches in Britain Are Learning How to Safeguard Children's Rights against Exploitative Pastors," *The Guardian*, July 27, 2010, https://www.theguard ian.com/commentisfree/belief/2010/jul/27/religion-witches-africa-london-exorcism.

4. While much of the demythologizing ethos has been associated with the work of Bultmann, and he is certainly the best-known modern theologian to read for serious consideration of this approach to biblical interpretation, his work is preceded by the work of others, such as William Wrede's work on parts of the Pauline corpus.

5. See J. Kwabena Asamoah-Gyadu, *Sighs and Signs of the Spirit: Ghanaian Perspectives on Pentecostalism and Renewal in Africa* (Eugene, OR: Wipf and Stock, 2015); Nimi Wariboko *Nigerian Pentecostalism* (Rochester, NY: University of Rochester Press, 2014); see also Cephas N. Omenyo, "From the Fringes to the Centre: Pentecostalization of the Mainline Churches in Ghana," *Exchange* 34, no. 1 (2005): 39–60; and "A Comparative Analysis of the Development Intervention of Protestant and Charismatic/Pentecostal Organizations in Ghana," *Svensk Missionstidskrift* 94, no. 1 (2006): 5–22, as well as his earlier "Charismatic Renewal Movements in Ghana," *Pneuma* 16, no. 2 (1994): 169–85.

6. Amos Yong, *The Spirit Poured Out on All Flesh: Pentecostalism and the Possibility of Global Theology* (Grand Rapids: Baker Academic, 2005); Allan Anderson, *To the Ends of the Earth: Pentecostalism and the Transformation of World Christianity* (New York: Oxford University Press, 2013).

would be hard-pressed to make a distinction between liturgical practices in mainline churches and established Pentecostal churches. In both worship and pastoral practice, the various denominations are indistinguishable on the basis of life in the Spirit and belief in the principalities and powers. And while we find an extreme dualism with regard to an understanding of the principalities and powers, as well as an extreme supernaturalism that attends the understanding of the Spirit and his works, there is nevertheless an attempt to uncover and live into assumed biblical teaching.

But we have to grasp that, even in the West, the understanding of these Scripture passages, what is meant by principalities and powers, how they operate, and what their influence on the material world is has undergone changes over time. Before the Enlightenment, belief in the spirit world was a given, and pastoral practice explored and tried to meet such dimensions of care.[7] Theological writings by prominent early-nineteenth-century pastors in North America and Europe indicate that it was common to interpret the above passage in Ephesians as dealing with personal spiritual beings.[8] While a certain psychological and political tenor was seen to accompany much of the interpretation following the Enlightenment, there were nevertheless pockets of resistance to such purely psycho-political interpretation of these passages—resistance from prominent modern theologians such as Johan Blumhardt,[9] Karl Barth (whose insights on the powers and the demonic stem from his engagement with Blumhardt's work),[10] and postmodern theologians such as Gregory Boyd,[11] Walter

7. The arguments about phases of the Enlightenment and its extent are noted but are not essential in this discourse. The reader may refer to Jonathan Israel, "Enlightenment! Which Enlightenment?" *Journal of the History of Ideas* 67, no. 3 (2006): 523–45, for further insights on this point.

8. Among the literature of that period, see William Gurnall, *The Christian in Complete Armour* (London: Printed for Ralph Smith, 1658). Arthur Pierson, *In Full Armour, or the Disciple Equipped for Conflict with the Devil* (New York: Fleming H. Revell, 1893) is a later American version of what is expressed in Gurnall's earlier book.

9. See the account of Blumhardt's experience in Friedrich Zündel, *The Awakening: One Man's Battle with Darkness* (Farmington, PA: Plough, 1999).

10. Karl Barth, *Rechtfertigung und Recht* (1938), is important to note here (Eng. trans.: *Church and State*, trans. Ronald Howe [London: Student Christian Movement Press, 1939]), as well as further engagement of the demonic in *Church Dogmatics*, IV/3 (London: T. & T. Clark, 2009).

11. Gregory Boyd, *Satan and the Problem of Evil: Constructing a Trinitarian Warfare Theodicy* (Downers Grove, IL: InterVarsity Press, 2001).

Wink,[12] and Amos Yong.[13] Sometimes, horrific natural disasters, what Boyd, in an allusion to a poem by Alfred, Lord Tennyson, calls "nature, red in tooth and claw," as well as unprecedented human disasters, mainly in more recent times in the form of nuclear and biological warfare, turn minds toward the possibility of personal evil destructive forces and thus to giving more credence and attention to the biblical language of principalities and powers. The notable books by Walter Wink,[14] whose own work found its impetus in that of William Stringfellow (who in the postwar era was described as the theologian who reclaimed for the church the language of principalities and powers and their implications for social ethics)[15] and biblical scholars of a more conservative evangelical persuasion have led the way in this endeavor.[16]

The discussion so far points to a certain anomaly in the way the issue of how the question of the principalities and powers—and by extension, the Spirit—is to be interpreted; for if what has been portrayed in the literature so far is correct, and I believe that to be the case, then perhaps the argument and the parameters within which it is engaged are flawed. What is at issue is not a question of North/South, First World/Third World, modern/premodern, and so forth, and how belief is to coincide with worldview before humans can make sense of their lives vis-à-vis Scripture, but a question of how to attend to Spirit for the entire church. The Puritans, then, and some of the evangelical Pentecostal denominations of our day (and I will explore those insights in chapters 4 and 2 respectively) are a

12. See Walter Wink's trilogy on the language of powers in the NT: *Naming the Powers: The Language of Power in the New Testament* (Philadelphia: Fortress, 1984); *Unmasking the Powers: The Invisible Forces That Determine Human Existence* (Philadelphia: Fortress, 1986); *Engaging the Powers: Discernment and Resistance in a World of Domination* (Minneapolis: Fortress, 1992).

13. Amos Yong, *The Spirit of Creation: Modern Science and Divine Action in the Pentecostal-Charismatic Imagination* (Grand Rapids: Eerdmans, 2011), esp. chap. 6.

14. Wink's trilogy on the language of powers in the New Testament maps a development of his thought over the years and indicates a rather nominal shift in his position vis-à-vis that of the demythologizing school from which he wishes to distance himself.

15. William Wylie Kellermann, "Naming the Powers: William Stringfellow as Student and Theologian," *Student World* 247 (2003): 24–35, http://www.koed.hu/sw247/william.pdf; see also William Stringfellow, *Free in Obedience* (New York: Seabury, 1964), 51–52.

16. C. Fred Dickason, *Demon Possession and the Christian* (Chicago: Moody Press, 1987); Neil T. Anderson, *The Bondage Breaker* (Eugene, OR: Harvest House, 1990) and *Victory over the Darkness* (Grand Rapids: Bethany House, 1994).

good example of the point that explodes the binary lines along which the current method of interpretation is proceeding.

In addition to trying to interpret the language of the Spirit along the aforementioned false lines of North versus South, in the North Atlantic we have further subdivided the conversation along mainline versus Pentecostal tributaries. The mainline churches, who have perhaps forgotten their Reformed heritage, have ceded all talk about the powers and especially the Holy Spirit and the Spirit's work in history and human life to the Pentecostal and charismatic churches.[17] If and when the mainline churches and theologians talk at all about the work of the Spirit or the principalities and powers, these powers are hardly recognizable as what Scripture describes or characterizes them to be. The language and discourse in many ways offers us an ordinary notion of the Spirit, at once common, real, and indefinable, leading to a domesticated and ordinary mysticism, generic and thus problematic. This account of the Holy Spirit seems appealing and updated to fit the mood of the age: a Spirit that bothers no one and whom no one really need bother with if they do not want to—even though always somehow present.[18] The same can be said of the way in which belief in and theological understanding of the language of the principalities and powers—their definition and function—is framed. The conversation about them usually turns them into sociopolitical structures at best, "the inner spirit of outer structures," as Wink would call them, and to be interpreted psychologically and thus entirely psychodynamically in pastoral practice. These are the powers that good moral Christians stand up to and speak against as they fight for justice for the weak and oppressed. Again, these powers, which are described as operating in "the heavenlies," would be unrecognizable to the early Christians, because they bear no real resemblance to the characterization of their identity and function as described in Scripture.

In pastoral practice, however, the foundations laid down for explaining these powers, as well as the character and work of the Spirit, show their inability to adequately account for human failings and to bear the weight

17. The Holy Spirit has been the most marginalized person of the Trinity in theological work until recently and, as Jürgen Moltmann notes, in Protestant theology the Spirit was no more than the subjective element in the appropriation of the salvation the believer receives via the Christ event. See Moltmann's *The Spirit of Life: A Universal Affirmation*, trans. Margaret Kohl (Minneapolis: Fortress, 1992), 83.

18. The work of John Levison on the Holy Spirit is a good example of this point. I will explore his concept of the Holy Spirit in the final chapter, but it is worth noting some of his thoughts here. See especially his *Filled with the Spirit* (Grand Rapids: Eerdmans, 2009).

of the cares people carry, and they begin to crumble. When people, especially those in need of comfort, direction, teaching/instruction, come to Scripture, what they come to, and hope for, are the stories of the God who has demonstrated power on behalf of God's people in acts of healing and deliverance in the Old Testament, and especially in the New Testament through Jesus's numerous exorcisms, healings, and other miracles—and ultimately the promise of the resurrection and eternal life. They come to a God who acts in the *now*, not one who, it is claimed, did something in the past that they can grasp and know merely historically and cerebrally; they come to a God who continues to be a part of lives today as Immanuel.

People for whom the Bible is important are seeking a Savior who continues the promised salvific work of Jesus through the presence of the Holy Spirit in the church and in the world: in short, a God they can know both noetically and experientially. At the feet of pastoral practices, then, the carefully laid-down assumptions about how to parse these Scripture passages, either in the South or North, crumble. We are made aware that there is not a North/South issue when we observe the kind of ambivalence in Walter Wink's work. It is almost as though his training and what his mind knows attempt to disbelieve what his eyes are observing, especially when he speaks about experience of the Spirit and the powers in South America.[19] At the same time, people often ignore the fact that the history of Christianity in America is filled with experiences of the Spirit and belief in the powers as personal beings; in our day we can observe this fascination with evil at an unredeemable level, in literature, movies, and other media.

In pastoral practice we find the limits of both approaches to defining and understanding the powers and work of the Spirit. Here we quickly note that neither the extreme dualism of the former, that is the Christian South (notably Africa,[20] and, to some extent, Latin America), or the lackadaisical monism of the latter, the North, bode well for exploring and understanding Christian belief and life according to the Spirit. How do we explain not only purposeless personal pain and suffering or general evil on a cosmic scale without adducing the powers or calling in the aid of the Spirit of grace? This is the one who is named Comforter, who shores up individuals and communities with strength, but also the one who is

19. Wink, *Naming the Powers*, xi.

20. I have already given an extensive account of what happens in pastoral practice when we valorize a particular worldview in our interpretation of the language of the powers or fail to heed the real nature of the Spirit. See Ecolatse, *For Freedom or Bondage? A Critique of African Pastoral Practices*.

described in Scripture as the Spirit of truth, who appears "to convict of truth, of righteousness and of judgment" (John 14:17; 16:8–11), and can dismantle oppressive arguments and forces.

Accounts of evil from the global South currently lack appropriate attention to personal complicity and guilt, as well as structural dimensions; but accounts from the global North also emphasize the individual and structural dimensions without giving sufficient attention to extra-human components. Without a thoroughgoing scriptural account of the powers and the Spirit, our explanations of evil in this world will lack the texture that adequately accounts for the collusion of individual sociopolitical structures and otherworldly evil spiritual forces—and thus forms a comprehensive account. It could also not mediate among or ameliorate the devastation left in the wake of the trauma from the assault of evil on a large scale. As long as the South reads these texts in ways that valorize the powers and reads the Spirit with an extreme supernaturalism that separates the Spirit from the triune God, or even as the one who infuses humans with life, it is not speaking biblically. Conversely, as long as the North refracts the works of evil in a way that favors monism as though the principalities and powers are too inebriated to affect humans in any way, as long as it succumbs to the rationalism that attends conversation about the Holy Spirit in a way that merely reifies the Spirit within a human form, it is also not speaking biblically. Therefore, neither the South nor the North is speaking with a thoroughgoing understanding of the picture cast by Scripture on the Spirit. We have to be vigilant against falling into either of the traps set for navigating the hermeneutical issues attendant on what Scripture means by the powers and, by extension, the work of the Spirit.

Furthermore, not only does such bifurcated interpretation hinder the unity and witness of the church to the one gospel and its one Lord of the faith, ceding the life of the Spirit to either the African/South or Pentecostal-charismatic traditions in the North, it is also problematic, as the general tendency in theological discussions today demonstrates. In its reading of the African perspective, what we observe in the academy are the marginalized Pentecostal studies or the phenomenological approach under the rubric of religious studies in theology and religion departments. There is general admiration for the African church's enthusiastic worship, spiritual fervor, and dynamic and expansive growth.[21] But the theology

---

21. Philip Jenkins, *The Next Christendom: The Coming of Global Christianity* (Oxford: Oxford University Press, 2011).

that accompanies this expression of Christianity is not engaged on a par with that of mainline theological discourse. The result is a ghettoizing of African Christian theology while its fervor in worship and its numerical growth are seen as exotic.[22] Even in the North, the churches that are growing are those with a charismatic ethos, while the mainline churches continue to lament their numerical decline, seemingly failing to see that their decline might be linked in part to their lack of interest or belief in the life and work of the Spirit as anything other than a myth. Yet, while mainline churches hold a monistic view of human existence vis-à-vis the principalities and powers and the work of the Spirit, there is an imaginary that apprehends a pornography of evil that is dark and almost dangerously unredeemable.[23]

But we cannot relegate the New Testament concept of the powers to primitive myths without serious consideration of the implications of such a move to Christianity as a biblical and apostolic faith. The faithful are invited to *a particular* kind of faith that entails believing with a community before us—the disciples, the early apostles, and the *abbas* and *ammas* of the church. There is a need for—in addition to the possibility of bridging what appears to be an enormous hermeneutical gap between the New Testament and the early church's concept of the powers—modern critical

---

22. This is an attitude toward Africa by the North that stems from its primitivization ethos inculcated in its approach to the study of religions as far back as the nineteenth century, which culminates in the work of Arthur Lovejoy and George Boas. See the citations to Lovejoy and Boas (pp. 12–15) in Armin W. Geertz, "Can We Move beyond Primitivism? On Recovering the Indigenes of the Indigenous Religions in the Academic Study of Religion," in *Beyond Primitivism: Indigenous Religious Traditions and Modernity,* ed. Jacob K. Olupuna (New York: Routledge, 2004). Additionally, I need to mention that the sensibilities that propelled the early missionary activities of the nineteenth and twentieth centuries were not just due to the theological norms but, more importantly, due to the philosophical and intellectual and even religious environment of Europe following the Enlightenment. Christianity and the church were losing ground as the favored domain of ultra-existence, and the impetus to find other places where it might claim prime position again fueled some of these missionary enterprises.

23. Stories in every medium, especially on the large screen, show this fascination for the otherworldly, the supernatural in even its goriest form, to the extent that previous childhood fairy tales have taken on the specter of fearful evil. What we refuse to name in our day-to-day life, psychologically speaking, finds its way out in other forms as a requisite for the individual health of the unconscious. However, it transcends the individual sphere to that of the "soul" or collective psyche of the society. Evil has to be placed outside, otherwise it is absorbed. At the same time, a purely psychodynamic account of evil falls short of the kind of cosmic evil we are faced with in our world today.

9

approaches to Scripture. It has to be acknowledged that this seems to be a daunting proposal that raises very serious questions of what may easily be seen as a call to intentional bilateral existence. Bultmann's invitation to demythologize Scripture is based precisely on the incongruity of such an expectation and strategy: that is, to live in a scientific one-tiered world with a faith that holds to a primitive three-tiered world: heaven above, hell beneath, and earth in between. To live on these two seemingly parallel planes, with their differing assumptions regarding existence, with integrity and faithfulness poses very difficult questions for modern people of the North. At the same time, it is curious that there are many in the so-called third world, such as in Africa, who navigate the tensions well, since globalization has brought a modern ethos to African city-states yet has not squelched belief by some in what is assumed to be the mythic language of Scripture.

The difficulty is exacerbated by modern theology's insistence on basing the meaningfulness of Christianity on rational grounds that make it intelligible and accessible to human minds. For instance, Bultmann's popular existentialist framework, which characterizes the North Atlantic approach to truth as we experience it through the use of mainly form-critical methodology to biblical studies (as though any subjectivity can be transcended through the use of scientific tools), continues to pervade biblical exegesis. An indiscriminate use of this approach as a standard for scholarship and understanding of Scripture is a move away from the individual knower within its primary domain—the church—toward the realm of the purveyors in the various academic guilds that sprang up in the nineteenth and twentieth centuries.[24] But in its strict adherence to this method of biblical interpretation, it relegates its most important and unique features of the faith to the realm of myth, which it then jettisons even as it ignores the insights of individuals or communities who are reading devotionally.

For both the West and the global South, then, a particular worldview has become the framework for accessing and interpreting Scripture, especially as it relates to understanding the language of powers in the New Testament—and even the work of the Spirit. Often these Scripture passages are subordinated to the competing worldviews rather than allowing Scripture to disrupt and transform the worldviews and thus the cultures

24. See Edward Farley, *Theologia: The Fragmentation and Unity of Theological Education* (Philadelphia: Fortress, 1983), for a brief description and history of these guilds and their inception and aims.

that read it. It is true that Scripture itself comes to us through a particular worldview; nevertheless, a reading that privileges worldview over Scripture and interrogates it to the point of dismembering its validity for kerygma and practice, renders it otiose as the basis of revelation and religion. It is in this way that we may ask the question whether we are fleeing from the Spirit when we are faced with biblical realism, the world picture that the Bible paints for us about the reality to which the prophets and apostles and martyrs attest.

What is becoming obvious as we continue to grapple with the language of the principalities and powers and how to define and appropriate them in theology, teaching, and pastoral practice, at the same time as considering the role of the Spirit in human life, is that the conversation is taking an unbiblical turn that fractures the church. Belief in these powers as personal spirit beings has traditionally figured as part of the Protestant faith, as evidenced in the confessions of the church. But now many mainline churches seem to be forgetting their Reformed heritage and its discourses about the Spirit and "principalities and powers" as tangible sources of inexplicable ills (a point I shall explore in chapter 5 as part of my account of the history of interpretation of the language of the powers).

The objective of this book is primarily to review and refine current theologies—and by extension, pastoral practice—as they relate to belief about the principalities and powers and the Spirit in the light of contemporary global Christian questions. It does so by exploring the larger question of what occurs when those acculturated in significantly different ways encounter a world picture painted by Scripture in which humans seemingly live in a liminal space between the physical and spiritual domain. How may a particular worldview facilitate and/or hinder faithful understanding and interpretation of the Bible and the role of the Spirit? I will argue that the current norm of interrogating Scripture with the strong arm of a particular worldview devalues the scriptural import in practice and offers little hope to careseekers who need the God that is theologized about in the interpretive task: on the one hand, a God who is a superhuman—with equal emphasis on both parts of the word—and, on the other hand, a nonpersonal being who is thus not affected by, nor can affect, human affairs.

This book also seeks to heal the current bifurcation between the Christian West and global South by bridging the hermeneutical gap in the understanding and interpretation of the language of powers in the New Testament, thereby strengthening the church's witness as one holy and apostolic church. Indeed, two instances of this hermeneutical gap are clearly apparent when we consider both the way in which belief in the Christian South differs from that of the earliest centuries of the faith and how belief in the North American space differs from that generally held in the not-so-distant past. Although there remain pockets of resistance to modernity, historical-critical approaches to the interpretation of Scripture, and scientific/technological ways of reading the world in the latter context, vestiges of belief in supernatural beings and otherworldly powers continue, a fact that pastoral practice cannot and should not ignore.

If what I have noted so far is the case, how do we chart a way forward so that the global South (especially Africa) and the West (especially the North Atlantic academic and ecclesial spaces) may engage each other in mutually respectful and beneficial ways for the church and the world? An intercultural hermeneutics is a viable approach to a dialogical encounter in biblical interpretation so that the different ways of knowledge and knowing may be brought into conversation. This kind of approach, reframed within a postmodern ethos, eschews any assumed normative metanarrative and facilitates an intercultural approach to hermeneutics that is at once *global*—acceptable to all Christian contexts, *biblical*—believable according to Scripture, the faith book of the church, and *creedal*. This is not to say that context does not matter in the way in which belief is refracted, experienced, and expressed; rather, it is to say that because context matters we bear all contexts in mind when we mind our contexts. The global focus takes into account the diversity or pluriformity of the Christian witness in each spatial and temporal context without losing sight of one's own context and reading. Reading Scripture in communion with fellow Christians demystifies these identifying markers of particular contexts so they are not so peculiar as to invite the kind of study that currently occupies the discipline of world/global Christianity. Christianity will continue to be recognized and believed in both its particularity and universality as that which is the norm for the people "called Christian" rather than a faith of many versions or strands with different adherents of its various parts. In light of the kind of approach to globally experienced and biblically rooted intercultural hermeneutics that I am proposing here with regard to biblical realism reflecting a particular context, I turn to my own context as a starting point for what I hope will engender a rich conversation and lay out the parameters for the kind of intercultural hermeneutics and contextual relevance with a global ethos that I propose.

Thus I begin the first chapter with an engagement of the seminal work of an African theologian who embodies the kind of approach and goal of theological endeavor I am seeking to express here: Kwesi A. Dickson, an Old Testament scholar in the academy and a churchman at the local and continental levels. Dickson's account of and engagement with the African religiocultural basis for understanding Scripture is one that takes serious note of the continuities and discontinuities between African and biblical cultures and is thus an ideologically appropriate place to interrogate the relationship of worldview and biblical hermeneutics, as well as to forge a viable intercultural hermeneutics for the church in our time—with particular reference to Africa, which is fast becoming the center of Christianity. Beyond the obvious contribution to African biblical hermeneutics is the benefit that paying attention to the ecclesial space in Africa offers the global church. The importance of African Christian thought for Western Christianity, as Thomas Oden artfully states, has historical roots from the beginning of Christian history.[25] What the Western church was in its momentous days may well have its seedbed in African Christian minds, the earliest church fathers, whose works have in profound ways shaped and sustained the core tenets of the Christian faith, not only in Africa but around the world.[26]

Africa, then, is of vital interest to—and needs to hold an important place in—the history of Christianity, not just for Africans but for all Christians. Beyond the significance of the explosion of growth in the region, the place and part of Africa in the history of redemption is already anticipated in the New Testament. The growth of the church in Africa and the prospects it provides for the future of the global church is often observed in the optimistic voice of African theologians, as well as historians and sociologists of religion from the West. Such well-known historians of religion and world Christianity as Andrew Walls, Philip Jenkins, Kwame Bediako, and Cephas Omenyo, to name a few, give glowing and fascinating accounts of

25. See Thomas Oden's trilogy, *How Africa Shaped the Christian Mind: Rediscovering the African Seedbed of Western Christianity* (Downers Grove, IL: InterVarsity Press, 2007); *The African Memory of Mark: Reassessing Early Church Tradition* (Downers Grove, IL: InterVarsity Press, 2011); and *Early Libyan Christianity: Uncovering a North African Tradition* (Downers Grove, IL: InterVarsity Press, 2011). While some of his insights, especially in the last book, are arguably plagued by lack of sufficient citations to buttress his findings—and many of his conclusions are tenuous and modest at best—we catch a glimpse of Africa's part in the formulation of Christian doctrine, even if part of its role was to refine and refute heresy.

26. See Kwame Bediako, *Christianity in Africa: The Renewal of a Non-Western Religion* (Maryknoll, NY: Orbis, 1995), for a more extended insight on Africa's contribution to Christian faith during its first centuries.

the growth of Christianity in Africa. Christianity is suddenly looking less and less like a Western religion that has been exported to other parts of the world through the conquest and expansion of former European empires. It has, as it were, come to roost in its nascent soil once again as a primarily Afro-Asiatic religion.

Therefore, it is more than appropriate to begin this inquiry with an African biblical scholar trained in the North, Kwesi A. Dickson, because he brings a perspective garnered from a faith lived in both cultural spaces. I engage his work and lay out his thinking on the issues of hermeneutics, but also provide a short biographical sketch of this scholar/churchman to situate him as a key interlocutor in our discussion of how we should understand the powers and the Spirit in Africa. His work, however, also reaches into the context of the North and helps bridge the gap between interpretative frameworks of South and North perspectives. I examine his insights side by side with those of Bultmann, whose approach to interpretation still carries the day in contemporary biblical hermeneutics.

Dickson's analysis of the African religiocultural world and how that influences Christian theology in Africa brings out two important aspects of contextual biblical interpretation that indirectly critique Bultmann, whose approach is the most favored in biblical interpretation and theology today. First, as an Old Testament scholar, when he writes about scriptural interpretation he engages both testaments, affirms the reality of the Old Testament, and asks that the Old Testament world and its realism be brought to bear on whatever we do and think in Christianity. The Old Testament reality is also something that Christians in an African context cannot ignore, nor should Christians in any context, since it is part of the heritage of the faith and the Scripture of Jesus and the earliest churches.

To begin with Dickson's account of how culture intersects and interacts with Scripture and the indispensability of the Old Testament for Africans is also a way to deal with some of the polarities in the current conversation about the powers and the Spirit. Africans cannot be fully persuaded by the Bultmannian project insofar as it omits the Old Testament from his account of myth. Dickson's work performs a critique of Bultmann and at the same time forces the issue of the split Bultmann brings to the New Testament study, in which the New Testament is vitiated and disconnected from its Hebrew scriptural moorings. Thus Dickson helps us acknowledge the relationship between the Bible and myth. He also forces us to take another look at the social context of Christianity in the North, where ideas about spirits do exist, even if certain biblical scholars might write as if they do not.

When we place Bultmann's approach side by side with that of Dickson, it becomes clear that the latter's work uncovers the fact that Bultmann's demythologizing dispenses with the Old Testament and its world of myth; this dismissal is something Christian theology should find worrisome, considering how far Bultmann's demythologizing has penetrated into Christian theology today. There is no reference in Bultmann's entire project to what Israel understood and meant by the mythic language through which it described its faith and its encounter with the *Real*. In a very crucial sense, Bultmann's demythologized Christianity has almost no Hebraic consciousness, historical or otherwise, thereby making it inadequate for the kind of global and intercultural hermeneutics I am proposing as a faithful way to read Scripture, especially the biblical passages that pertain to principalities and powers. Bultmann has, by and large, designated these passages as myth. Although he shows interest in the Old Testament and writes about it in several volumes, it does not appear to have affected his view that the Old Testament needs to be demythologized; he is still engaging the Old Testament largely with Form Criticism.[27]

In chapter 2, I uncover what prompts the demythologizing posture and its popularity by exploring how shifts in the Western worldview have affected the *episteme* that undergirds biblical interpretation. I also interrogate Bultmann's claim to make Scripture accessible to modern human beings and, wondering which "modern" human beings he may have been considering, go on to ask whether the current trajectory of shifts in Western *episteme* can be sustained given the global expression of Christianity, especially in the vibrant heart of Africa. Bultmann claims to be protecting the *kerygma* and allowing Christian faith to stand on its own without the props of what he terms "myth."

At this point, Bultmann's view of myth has to be critiqued because it surely fails to offer an adequate theology that accounts for the trajectory of belief over the centuries of Christianity. This is because his understanding and use of myth seem almost like a smokescreen to obscure what he deems embarrassing in the New Testament. Chapter 2 below further presses the issues at stake by exploring the contours of biblical and extrabiblical un-

27. See Rudolf Bultmann, *Theology of the New Testament*, vol. 1, trans. Kendrick Grobel (Waco, TX: Baylor University Press, 2007). See esp. his discussion of Jesus in relation to the Old Testament and also the early church's self-understanding in relation to the Old Testament, pp. 1–62. See also David Congdon, *The Mission of Demythologizing: Rudolf Bultmann's Dialectical Theology* (Minneapolis: Fortress, 2015) for an extensive exploration of Bultmann's engagement with the Old Testament in several of his writings.

derstandings of the demonic and exorcism (the main character of what is assumed mythic in the New Testament) with attention to Jesus's life as exemplar. Here I argue that the hermeneutical barrier Bultmann assumes is posed by the mythic content of the New Testament for hearing and believing cannot be borne out by the evidence of the history of belief across the Christian era—even into modernity and postmodernity. The issue of myth, then, is banal at best, but is also too amorphously defined and used in Bultmann's demythologizing and has to be deconstructed, refined, and reconstructed. The understanding of myth in his operation of biblical criticism stems from the assumption that there is *one* ancient worldview that can be replaced with *one* identifiable modern worldview, which is an unrealistic, if not false, assumption because Scripture itself displays and speaks from many worldviews, and surely there are, in our modern world, more than one worldview. Bultmann's hermeneutics is, in the end, significantly at variance with traditional Christian belief and is not useful for an adequate theology that accounts for what the Bible and Christian theology over the centuries say about the powers or the Spirit.

Accordingly, the third chapter appropriately begins with a comprehensive approach to the understanding of myth and how it has been conceived in theological and psychosocial literature in premodernity, modernity, and postmodernity. What is the nature of myth and mythos—and their relationship—and what, if any, are the benefits of myth and even *mythopoesis* for hermeneutics and reclaiming the powerful myths, indispensable to Scripture, for a life of faith then and now? Thus, in part of the third chapter I attempt to provide a credible working construction, or definition, of myth, especially as it relates to understanding and articulating what are named "principalities and powers." This understanding is, in general, the form in which the biblical narrative uses and dispenses of myth, what Old Testament scholar Brevard Childs calls "broken myth."

In tracing the history and contours of myth across the various disciplines, I seek to make a case for the appropriateness of the mythic language of Scripture. I argue that the thrust of the message of the Bible—the lordship of Christ, the God/man—is best apprehended by means of myth, with its timelessness and fluidity. When coupled with imagination, myth becomes indispensable for the life of faith for the Christian believer. It is a turn toward remythologizing for contemporary ecclesial spaces, and for a pastoral ministry that transcends specific cultural boundaries, and ultimately for bringing to fullness (completeness) the body of Christ in its unity.

Thus the focus here is to find a dynamic dualism that undercuts and corrects both South/North approaches to interpretation and practice and yet is robust enough to engage the unique situations in each ecclesial space and time.

Then, in the fourth chapter, I turn to Karl Barth, who holds an eminent position in Protestant theological thought and who offers, in my view, substantial theological insights into the complexities of the "powers" language, especially how worldview functions in the interpretive framework. Barth's teachings on demons, framed by his understanding of creation based on his exegesis of Genesis 1 and 2, as well as his understanding of sin as the "impossible possibility" and evil as "nothingness," are particularly important here. His insights on these issues all bear on how we think about the relationship between the principalities and powers and human affairs, and whether or not belief in evil spiritual powers characterizes common life. Robust as Barth's thinking is, however, his insights need further framing for a global church; Therefore, I will bring him into dialogue with other voices, especially from the global South. Thus the works of William Abraham,[28] Kwame Bediako,[29] Nimi Wariboko, [30] and Amos Yong[31] offer us the opportunity to probe and extend the limits of Barth's insights on the powers and the Spirit.

The fifth chapter considers how we should properly understand the language of the powers in the New Testament. Here I seek to uncover the ways in which interpretation has been done in past Christian eras, within the parameters of the specific cultural context, and yet without allowing the context or worldview to crowd out the scriptural teaching for the life of the church. To do this, I look at how a representative scripture passage— Ephesians 6:10–20—has been understood and exegeted and used in Christian practice over the life of the church, starting with the Pauline literature and moving through the earliest church fathers, the Ante-Nicene and Nicene fathers, to the theologians of the Reformation; I then examine the era of the Puritans through the modern and postmodern periods; finally, I ask how the Christian South, particularly African theologians and pastors,

28. William J. Abraham, *Divine Revelation and the Limits of Historical Criticism* (Oxford: Oxford University Press, 1982).

29. Bediako, *Christianity in Africa.*

30. Nimi Wariboko, *The Pentecostal Principle: Ethical Methodology in New Spirit* (Grand Rapids: Eerdmans, 2012).

31. Amos Yong, *Spirit-Word-Community: Theological Hermeneutics in Trinitarian Perspective* (Eugene, OR: Wipf and Stock, 2006).

interpret these pertinent verses. Ultimately, I seek to probe the basis of interpretations across the eras and to determine how much the understanding, interpretation, and use of the language of the principalities and powers were determined by context. Were interpreters able to transcend their cultural contexts when engaging these passages? If so, why? And what can we learn from such approaches? It is the case that the approaches until the Enlightenment were consistent with minute differences in emphases according to the pastoral tenor of each representative expositor. What is also significant is that each one of these insights was born in pastoral practice, as were the original contexts of the verses under investigation. That theology is born at the confluence of Scripture and pastoral concerns cannot be overlooked, for this has been the model across the Christian landscape. Above all, I attempt to address, through the examples left by the apostles and the earlier churches, how worldview can be appropriately transcended in hermeneutics in our day with theological and cultural integrity.

Ultimately, the interpretative framework should be grounded in historical precedents that point forward eschatologically. That is, it should look to the past insofar as it is future-directed and dependent on the mediation of the Holy Spirit, who is the harbinger of truth and who also takes the words of Jesus and points his followers to it (John 16:13–15). This same Spirit is also the communion-forming character of the triune God (2 Cor. 13:14), upon whom the Christian community is dependent for its unity, a unity inscribed into its being from its inception. This unity is both the ground of its identity and function in the world, which in turn is predicated on its reading and interpretation of Scripture—readings that need to be mediated by the Spirit, who alone can lead in excavating truth from Scripture.

The final chapter, then, makes a pneumatological turn in addressing the issue of how to understand and apprehend the language of the principalities and powers portrayed in Scripture and attempt to press the issue of how both the Christian South and North, in their respective perspectives, are in a sense fleeing from the Spirit. Those in the North and South are reading Scripture existentially, allowing their contexts to determine their hermeneutics, rather than adjusting their existentialist assumptions to the kerygma.

A turn to the pneumatological is, however, usually fraught with its own challenges, since many more questions are raised by the turn toward the Spirit due to the differing attitudes across the Christian theological landscape. The issue of the apprehensiveness that attends any talk of the Holy Spirit, especially in the mainline churches, cannot be ignored in any attempt and/or proposal to turn toward pneumatology in addressing the current state of the church. This is even more pressing since the place and work of the Holy Spirit in interpretation are at the heart of the arguments in this book. Over the course of the church's existence, it seems that the communion-forming Spirit (for both the Godhead and the church, of which the Son is the head) has somehow come to be thought of as the source of major divisiveness, to the point that many Christians walk on tenterhooks around any reference to the third person of the Trinity. At the same time, as the biblical records show, the church has always existed in the midst of the competing, divisive response to the presence of the Spirit, and the church has also always heeded the Spirit's voice through prophetic teaching in the ferment of disagreements.

Therefore, the twenty-first-century church can be persuaded to attend to what the Spirit is saying to the churches in spite of the hesitancy and even reluctance with which some denominations might approach the subject of the Holy Spirit as arbiter/advocate in matters of discernment and interpretation. To this end, through the work of John R. Levison, I explore how the Spirit is conceived in our day. Levison is one theologian who, in both his academic work and his writing for lay readers, has adopted a wider lens with which to examine who the Holy Spirit is and what the Spirit does in both private and public life. His work shows that even the best efforts can fall short of a thoroughgoing biblical account when we let the worldview shape and define the parameters within which we interpret pertinent Scripture passages about the spirits. In spite of how close he stays to the biblical narrative in his analysis of the Spirit—an analysis that covers Israelite, Jewish, and early Christian ideas, and has been acclaimed by Pentecostals and non-Pentecostals alike—Levison demonstrates that he is a product of his times. On a long journey through the foundational, post-foundational, nonfoundational, and postmodern approaches to Scripture, he lands right back at modernity, with its insistence on weeding out the supernatural from biblical accounts by reifying the Spirit within a natural form. In the end, his analysis demonstrates an affinity for the modern agenda at several points. This is because, ultimately, worldview determines the direction of interpretation and, while at first blush his work helps us overcome the extreme dualism of the Holy Spirit's work in and through humans, it stops short of being a comprehensive biblical understanding of the Spirit.

In charting the way forward, I make a modest proposal as to how to understand and interpret the world perspective offered by the Bible in a way that allows for belief in Scripture and its language about the powers and the Spirit in a way that halts the march toward the bifurcation of the church North and South. This proposal involves a return to biblical realism as the proper interpretative framework for exegesis: it is an approach that is cognizant of the context of interpretation, but because of its fluidity and resistance to being a kind of approach that is wedded to *a particular* school of interpretation (form criticism, historical criticism, textual criticism, etc.), it can, while utilizing them, still follow the Bible's own inherent character and pattern by resisting systematization and by being its own interpreter. In biblical realism, Scripture aids in interpreting Scripture, with an aim to presenting its reality and the *Real*. In the words of one of its proponents: "It does not ask for agreement with world-and-life-views, not even Christian views of life and the world."[32]

This project, finally, is an experiment in theological method for the work of pastoral practice. It is a prolegomenon to practical theology for a global church, in its methodology, and especially when the cross-cultural context is brought to bear on it. It expands the shepherding, healing, guiding, sustaining function—the core of pastoral practice—from the individual, personal setting to the corporate body, even as it theologically imagines a new vision of African Christianity in relationship to the North/West and thus a new theological vision of the global church.

32. Hendrik R. Kraemer, *The Christian Message in a Non-Christian World* (New York: Harper and Brothers, 1938), 65.

A Question of Perspective

CHAPTER 1

Kwesi Dickson and Rudolf Bultmann

This chapter engages the work of an important African theologian, Kwesi Dickson, a churchman, biblical scholar, and academic theologian whose works, career as a professor of Hebrew and Old Testament, and vocation as a pastor have compelled him to grapple with African religiocultural reality and its relationship to the biblical world in order to formulate a viable theology for Africa. Dickson's theology has sought to be authentically African and deeply orthodox. He was deeply committed to a basic premise that traditional Christian doctrine should be able to address the African in particular and humanity in general.[1]

Churchman

Dickson was born in Saltpond, Ghana, in 1929. He was educated at Mfanstipim School, a Methodist boarding school for boys at Cape Coast. Following completion of the General Certificate of Education (GCE) via the Ordinary-level exams, he entered and completed ministerial training at the then Trinity College at Kumasi in the Ashanti region. He continued his studies at the University College of the Gold Coast (now University of Ghana) and successfully gained entrance to Mansfield College at Oxford University.

Following his postgraduate work at Oxford, Dickson was ordained into the ministry of the Methodist Church, Ghana, at the British Conference

---

1. By "address" here, I mean to hear oneself called and invited into life with God and obedience to concrete tenets that, though framed within differing values and meaning based inside different cultures, is yet recognizable as godly and Christlike virtue.

of 1957. During his three-decade tenure as professor of Old Testament and Hebrew in the department of religions at the University of Ghana, he also taught at Trinity Theological Seminary, an affiliate of the University of Ghana, and formed seminarians in an ecumenical setting while fulfilling the role of resident pastor for the Protestant congregation at the university.

Dickson served two terms as the president of the Methodist Conference–Ghana, and was concurrently chairman of the Christian Council of Churches during the second term of his presidency of the Methodist Conference. He also occupied various positions for the World Council of Churches (WCC), and at his death in 2005, Dickson was the immediate past president of the All African Council of Churches. Thus, like a few of his peers within the African theological guild, he combined extensive ecclesiastical service with an academic life.

A Professional Profile

Dickson's scholarly publications spanned a number of related fields of interest: Old Testament studies, church and society, Christian mission, ecumenism, and African theology. When his British colleague, the Rev. Dr. Sidney G. Williams died in October 1959, Dickson took on the task of editing Williams's dissertation and publishing it under the title *Akan Religion and the Christian Faith* (1965, 1974). That publication was followed by a nineteen-page introduction to the pioneer Ghanaian philosopher J. B. Danquah's seminal work, *The Akan Doctrine of God* (1968), which was to be reworked as his inaugural lecture in 1976 as professor in the department for the study of religions in the University of Ghana. This lecture, published under the title "The Human Dimension in the Theological Quest," points to the need for theology to be engaged in and through a person's dispositions and values, for "a theologian is one who has thought through religion in terms of his existence."[2]

2. Kwesi Dickson, *Theology in Africa* (Maryknoll, NY: Orbis, 1984), 12. In this regard, he is not that different from the other African theologians, such as John S. Pobee, who point to the African's theology as stemming from lived experience and as one that goes beyond propounding a body of knowledge. It is in this sense that knowing leads to doing, understood in Jean-Marc Ela's terms as acquired "through the primordial symbol of their existence." See Jean-Marc Ela, *My Faith as an African* (Maryknoll, NY: Orbis, 1988), 44.

Dickson's university career in Ghana, as a member of the department for the study of religions and in the Institute of African Studies, and as a teacher of Old Testament and Hebrew, as well as of African traditional religions, demonstrates the breadth and depth of his scholarly enterprise. The Institute of African Studies, an interdisciplinary center for humanities and social sciences, is an important arm of the University of Ghana, which serves several countries on the continent. It was established in 1962 by the first president of Ghana, Kwame Nkrumah, to encourage African studies and to promote an African approach to the acquisition and attainment of knowledge.

Theologian

In his inaugural address as professor of Old Testament and religious studies at the University of Ghana, Dickson raised a number of important issues that formed the basis of his influential work *Theology in Africa*, which will occupy our attention in the following pages. In 1991, at the beginning of the first term of his presidency of the Methodist Conference–Ghana, Dickson addressed the congregation on "The Uncompleted Mission: The Christian Faith and Exclusivism."[3] He provided in outline an indication of his conception of the kingdom of God beyond the borders of the church.

Many outside the church encountered his work as the author of books for secondary education. For most secondary-school students in West Africa, the name Kwesi Dickson became synonymous with the religious studies curriculum that formed the basis of the GCE at the Ordinary and Advanced levels in religious studies, which students took at the end of their fifth and seventh year of secondary education, respectively. His series of textbooks for both levels of exams have been in use since the late 1960s.

As an educator at the University of Ghana, an author of textbooks for secondary education, and a churchman, Dickson was able to combine his academic career with visionary ecclesiastical involvement on a global level. Part of this derived from the education he had received at Mfantsipim and thereafter. Invariably, he came to his theological and academic calling on the way to becoming a pastor. The issues surrounding the problems of theology and culture were not theoretical for him.

3. This would later become the basis of a book with the same title: *Uncompleted Mission: Christianity and Exclusivism* (Maryknoll, NY: Orbis Books, 1991).

The very nature of the Wesleyan mission in Ghana, West Africa, and elsewhere made this an essential consideration for those who were educated by the various outgrowths of that mission. Dickson had to think about the implications of their relationship not only as churchmen working with other Africans but also as ordinary Africans in other broader ecclesiastical and ecumenical settings. For an African with his particular biography, he was bound to ask questions about the authenticity of Christian expression in African society. The fundamental questions and his attempts at addressing them have had a profound effect on the thinking of other Africans who have found his way of grappling with questions of theology, culture, and identity germane to their own education and personal lives.

A signal moment in this history was the All African Council of Churches (AACC) conference held in Accra, Ghana, in 1977. The meeting had all the power brokers of African theology present, including Archbishop Desmond Tutu. The proceedings of this important meeting were later published under the title *African Theology en Route*,[4] and the article contributed by Dickson would later become the foundation of *Theology in Africa*.[5] Indeed, it is to this article that many African theologians and others engaged with African theology have often turned in order to grapple with the problems and prospects of African theology.

African Religiocultural Reality and Biblical Hermeneutics

The question of the relationship of African religiocultural reality with that of the biblical worldview, and how that relationship impinges on the interpretation of biblical texts in the context of Africa, has been a thorny one. Kwesi Dickson identifies this problem as one of the fundamental questions of Christian experience in Africa.

Against the backdrop of those who take an adoptionist approach— seeing similarities in the concepts of aspects of the two cultures and making "erroneous equations"[6]– Dickson, the professor of Old Testa-

4. Kofi Appiah-Kubi and Sergio Torres, eds., *African Theology en Route: Papers from the Pan African Conference of Third World Theologians, December 17–23, 1977, Accra, Ghana* (Maryknoll, NY: Orbis Books, 1979).

5. Kwesi Dickson, *Theology in Africa*. Hereafter, page references to this work appear in parentheses within the text.

6. J. J. Williams, *Hebrewism of West Africa: From Nile to Nigar with the Jews* (Lon-

ment, calls for attention to both the continuities and discontinuities between African religiocultural reality and the biblical worldview. Dickson insists that the Old Testament must be conceived of as a "Hebrew phenomenon" about a "particular people" in a "particular time" (98) even though it "contains seeds of universality" (99). Assumed places of similarity (which are obvious to the ordinary observer), such as a sense of community, theology of nature, concept of death and the afterlife—coupled with the African "predilection for the Old Testament"[7]—do not necessarily imply "a correct understanding of . . . meaning" (98), as if the similarities in aspects of cultural phenomena could be equated with similarity of meaning and hence belief. To make this leap is to ignore what scholars who study the Old Testament in its Ancient Near Eastern context point out:

> That there is no proto-Semitic religion of which the ancient Israelite tradition is merely an expression and that what most characterizes the Old Testament is not what it had in common with other traditions in the world and that the relevance of the Ancient Near Eastern traditions for understanding the OT must not be allowed to detract from the distinctiveness of this collection of documents from ancient Israel. (99)

Revisiting the Parameters

Dickson's reflection on African cultural reality and its place in doing theology begins with an exploration of the key components of what he believes to be the theological task in light of his understanding of theology. He does this as preparation for engaging African religion from a theological perspective, a necessary move, since a certain ambiguity continues to hang over the status of African religion as "religion" in the sense in which other religions are understood. This provides another layer of context for Dickson's descriptions and analysis in articulating a framework for a proposal for African Christian theology.

---

don: Allen and Unwin, 1930), 96. Also available online at: https://archive.org/details/HebrewismsOfWestAfricaFromNileToNigarWithTheJews.

7. Even today, one is more likely to hear sermons based on OT texts, especially in the African Initiated churches and Independent Evangelical Charismatic churches, both on the continent and in the diaspora.

For Dickson, theology, properly conceived, has three basic aspects: reflection, the situational reality of the reflection, and the communication of that reflection, which can only be meaningfully done in context (15). Yet the dangers associated with situational interpretation are always present.[8] The Christian theologian might easily be tempted into interpreting situational reality so narrowly that it not only becomes (a) the reality into which all others are situated, but also (b) can occur without the interpreter's awareness "that by his own mode of life he might be contributing to that very situation," and (c) that sometimes the very situation to which theological analysis or action is aimed might be akin to the one in which he exists and takes pleasure (15). Dickson then explores the situational reality that guides his theologizing and the communication of that reflection about African religiocultural existence and the overall contribution to understanding Christian theology in Africa.

Dickson's dictum about the pitfalls that accompany interpretation of situational reality (in his case the African context) suggests that we take seriously the case for the three-pronged means of Christian revelation and theologizing—Scripture, experience, and tradition—that are the theologians' working tools (29). A brief summary of how he understands and uses each of these tools will be useful.

Scripture

For Dickson, not only is Scripture the beginning point for the consideration of all theology, but for the Christian African in particular, it is the primary formative factor.[9] Dickson, however, finds the overemphasis on the primacy of Scripture to be problematic, that is, Scripture as the inspired word of God, to which some (particularly those in the Reformed tradition) have ascribed the character of inerrancy, not just in the essence

---

8. And this is an obvious fact and is the main concern of this project as reflected in its subtitle—the demands of contextual theology—which dogs all theological enterprises, especially practical theology, because by its nature it operates within the tensions of text and context.

9. One can more fully appreciate this point if one understands that the primary literacy tool in most homes is the Bible, and that biblical commentaries and other study aids are not readily available to some church leaders and pastors. The work of Bible translation, an embedded aspect of the gospel, has afforded many the opportunities to read and hear in their own tongues God's Word to them.

of the message but in the actual transmission of the words. According to Dickson, the assumption that "the Hebrew manuscript of the Bible was inspired, not only with regard to the consonants but also with regard to the vowel point" is dangerous because it runs the risk of constricting theological vision.[10] Rather than exalting God's word as it intends, an insistence on inerrancy "may diminish the breadth of that word."[11] It may also suggest that God, especially if Scripture claims him as Creator of all the peoples of the earth, is more for Israel than for other peoples, a fact negated in the Old Testament, Israel's own historical annals.

Dickson cites Malachi 1:11, which he notes could be interpreted in two different ways: 1) that the passage speaks to the situation of Jews in Diaspora, or 2) that it is a commendation of heathen worship as acceptable— indeed, perhaps more acceptable—to Yahweh than Israel's worship. The tension between these two possible interpretations is seen as enduring throughout Israel's religious history, and was still going on at the time of the apostles, and forms the basis of the argument that led to the dispute brought before the Jerusalem Council in Acts 15.[12] The importance of these considerations in the pursuit of a theology germane to the African context is to point to God being for *all* peoples, in order that every individual may be addressed by the vital question to Adam and humanity: "Where art thou?" For "this is a biblical fact of which theology must take account; for

10. *Formula Consensus Ecclesiarum Helvitiarum Reformatorum*, 1675; cited by Dickson, *Theology in Africa*, 16.

11. One could think in this instance of the numerous contexts in which the Bible has been translated, including Africa. Such translations, which make the Word of God accessible, would also indirectly be offering only a portion of, rather than "the whole counsel of God." While it is possible to think of this strict adherence to inerrancy of the Scriptures as being tied to the original languages as being dated, one suspects that traces of such assumptions may underlie the insistence by some denominations for knowledge in the biblical languages as prerequisite for correct understanding and right exegesis. On this point see also Mugambi's crucial note on the ills of both literalism and its obverse, liberalism, as hindrances to proper hermeneutics, in his essay "Challenges to African Scholars in Biblical Hermeneutics," in *Text and Context in New Testament Hermeneutics*, ed. J. N. Kanyua Mugambi and Johannes A. Smit (Nairobi: Acton Publishers, 2004), 6–21, esp. 15–17.

12. Dickson's discussion on this point is more nuanced than can be contained in this chapter, and the interested reader may read Dickson's whole chapter, esp. pp. 15–20, for a fuller development of these ideas. Dickson explores the OT view of the relationship between Israel as the covenantal people of God and the rest of the *goyim*, noting their special place, that is, their particularity within the general, without losing sight of either.

if God is indeed concerned with all peoples, then there is a theological continuity between the people of Israel and the *goyim*" (17), the other nations. Otherwise, Israel's own calling to be the people "through whom all the nations of the earth—*ha eretz*—would be blessed" (Gen. 12:1–3) would not be possible, thus nullifying Israel's existence and self-identity as a called and destined people of God.

If the above claim to theological continuity between Israel and the people is as Dickson states it (and we will return to his assumptions below), then we might be more persuaded by his suggestion that theological continuity has to be followed with an assumption of "a hermeneutical and interpretive continuity between Israelite traditions in the scriptures, and the life and thought of other peoples" (20). It is the only possible assumption if indeed God is for all peoples and the Word of God is to be an active and living agent in the experience of all peoples, regardless of the cultural and temporal distance between Israel and other peoples. If Scripture as a *living word* is to hold the same expectations and life-changing effect for all peoples, then its hermeneutics needs to be guided by the "Spirit of Truth" that Jesus promises to his disciples (John 14).

Here Dickson makes an important observation about the hermeneutical imperative for interpreting Scripture and calls our attention to the role of the Spirit. In the Gospels and Epistles, the "Spirit of truth" is in a sense already at work translating the scriptures of a particular people— that is, Israel—made through particular events, across temporal and spatial dimensions different from those of the original recipients. Further, the example had already been set by Jesus, who manifests his "Spirit of Truth" in the way he interacted during his own ministry with Jew and Gentile alike. And insofar as the Gospels that came to us were shaped by the various communities of faith and their memories of Jesus (hence the diversity among them), we are given a primary example of the workings of the Spirit. In spite of the possible misuses of "the leading of the Spirit" in ecclesial history, notes Dickson, "no confessional statement on the scriptures is complete without reference being made to the Spirit who renews" (22).[13] It is in this sense that a response to Christ, in whose name and on whose account the Spirit of Truth is sent, always preceded an articulation

---

13. The importance of this statement, especially in the African context, is observed in the dimensions of African Christian theology and pastoral practice within the growing Independent Charismatic churches. See Esther Acolatse, *For Freedom or Bondage? A Critique of African Pastoral Practices* (Grand Rapids: Eerdmans, 2014) for a thorough critique of this phenomenon.

of faith. As Dickson points out, it is this process of encounter leading to belief, then leading to articulation of faith that gives the Gospels the multifaceted portrait of Jesus and the lack of homogeneity in the accounts of the one redemptive encounter with the one Jesus of Nazareth. In a sense, Dickson is suggesting that the articulation of the faith engendered by *each* new encounter with Jesus be allowed to emanate from the *experience* of the encounter. Clearly, Dickson, by this statement, which he suggests finds support in the New Testament, is positioning himself to offer a credible account of an African theology born out of the experience of Africa's encounter with the gospel. Experience, properly understood and expressed, is thus important in any theologizing.

Experience

The second of the essential working materials of the theologian—and perhaps the most subjective—is experience. But as I have noted above, it is born of encounter and is thus key to authentic articulation of faith, which in short is theologizing. And Scripture is laden with the accounts of experiences, many with revelatory dimensions (think, for example, of the experiences of the Old Testament prophets). In spite of the arguments about the subjective nature of experience and necessary cautions about their place in revelation, the subjective elements may be kept in check by the appropriate balance of the primary component, Scripture, and the third, tradition.[14] Of course, any reference to tradition asks the question of whose tradition, and raises further issues of authority, which is in turn based on interpretation and is also bound by tradition, which, as we know, functions differently between—and even within—strands of the various Christian denominations. Even those for whom tradition holds a high place in interpretation and valuation of experience, there is not "an unimaginative attachment to tradition" (27), as demonstrated in periodic reconstructions of doctrines and creeds.[15] Additionally, notes Dickson:

14. The kind of suspicion of subjectivity attached to experience is itself currently under suspicion, as it were, as possibilities of pure objectivity continue to be questioned even in scientific endeavors.

15. Consider Conciliarism in the Catholic Church and the various reforms it birthed, as well as the various new declarations (e.g., the Barmen Declaration) that seek to modify previous ones in the Reformed tradition. See, e.g., Francis Oakley, *The Conciliarist Tradition* (Oxford: Oxford University Press, 2003), for a historical account of the Catholic issues.

[N]o formulation of teaching may be considered *definitive* in the sense that there will never be any need of further re-interpretation in a new social and cultural situation. It must be explained that this is not to suggest that interpretative exercises should never start from the possibility of particular formulations having relevance in another context, for often the problems of one society may be a fair reproduction of those of another society, even of another era. Nevertheless, different societies will have *specific concerns* which will make the re-interpretation of Christian doctrinal formulations necessary. (27)[16]

With these insights, Dickson paves the way for negotiating the interpretive space between what may be considered normative and translatable *en bloc* to other cultures across time, and those that have to be reframed, it seems, not just for the new contexts but for the entire Christian landscape. In other words, Christian "things" will and must remain Christian things across time and space, a point that will become relevant for the proposal this book makes about hermeneutics and the undergirding assumptions, and which will be taken up in further development in a later chapter. Thus, while tradition is important, it is equally important not to allow it to bog down interpretation and quench the imagination, which is an essential element that attends all epistemology in religious endeavors.[17]

Culture

Culture, observes Dickson, is the lynchpin for putting the other three essentials of interpretation together. He cites an anecdote about Paul Tillich's bewilderment when confronted by Japanese culture, a culture so distinct from his Western one that "his bewilderment turned into a sense of depression at the thought of his having to rewrite his theology in order

16. Andrew Walls also has an extensive discussion on this point—a necessary aspect of being church and the need for the gospel to traverse cultures—and the benefits to the church of being engaged with grace. See Walls, *The Cross-Cultural Process in Christian History: Studies in the Transmission and Appropriation of Faith* (Maryknoll, NY: Orbis, 2002), 72–81.

17. See, e.g., Paul Avis, *God and the Creative Imagination: Metaphor, Symbol and Myth in Religion and Theology* (New York: Routledge, 1999), on the importance of imagination for belief and apprehension of the divine.

to make it truly catholic" (28–29).[18] Dickson notes that this yearning for catholicity is a "necessary function of theology," and he points to the one transcendent meaning with varying parts, of one salvific event in Christ embraced and expressed in and through different peoples (29). His summation of culture's place in African reality underscores the need to give it a place of importance in framing questions and issues, and to provide direction for and critiques of African Christian Theology.

Many aspects of African culture subsume religion. As Dickson notes, "religion informs the African's life in its totality," an observation indicative of the mutual dependence of religion and culture in an African worldview. This interdependence between culture and religion, Dickson suggests, makes the African experience the epitome of the definition of a culture that, according to Christopher Dawson, is "a theogamy, a coming together of the divine and the human within the limits of a sacred tradition," and "a man's way of life by which he apprehends reality."[19] The almost undifferentiated unity between religion and culture, and the fact that within this very interpenetration of the two is the space where divine and human meet, allows Dickson to broaden (and possibly make more complex) his discourse on African reality by introducing the question of the place and importance of African Traditional Religion (ATR) in theologizing in the African context.

I note that this is complex because Dickson is very aware of the problem ATR already presents as not being, strictly speaking—or, perhaps more appropriately, religiously speaking—a religion (having been set aside in the taxonomy of religions), partly because of the interplay between religion and culture, but more because of the strong belief in the mutual interdependence of all created entities, which is portrayed in the deferential treatment of aspects of nature by the African.[20] However, ATR

18. See also a fuller account of Tillich's experience with Japanese culture in Tomoaki Fukai, ed., *Paul Tillich: Journey to Japan in 1960* (Berlin: De Gruyter, 2013).

19. Christopher Dawson, *Religion and Culture* (New York: Meridian Books, 1952), 54, 58; cited in Dickson, *Theology in Africa*, 29.

20. Dickson notes, however, that these aspects of African Traditional Religion (ATR)—what he terms "its positive attitude" toward nature—have unfortunately made it seem infantile to theologians of a certain ilk, "particularly those brought up on the theology of Ernst Troeltsch or on the dialectical theology of such scholars as Karl Barth" (*Theology in Africa*, 30). For a religion without a founder and creed, in the minds of Westerners who first encountered the African in what was assumed to be "natural" or "primitive" religion, did not find it necessary to include ATR in a taxonomical study of world religions. He notes, esp., a book edited by Harold A. Guy (whose books on the

is such an integral part of African culture that no real theological encounter with African culture can take place without taking ATR seriously. How, then, does one expect a viable interplay between Christianity and ATR in a construction of African Christian theology without in any way engaging in translating the gospel using certain cultural prompts and props? How does one do the hard work of articulating African Christian theology without also referring to ATR's sense of created existence and its sense of a Creator? At the same time, how does one avoid conflating African traditional religious belief in a creator with the Christian belief in the same? Can Africa and the experience and expression of Christianity that is refracted through African religion contribute to shaping the Christian mind in the same way that Hellenistic Christianity and its worldview shaped the Western world and, via colonialism, has been translated into other parts of the globe?

These are questions, I hope, that Dickson's forays raise and to which some answers are possible if we are to take African Christian theology and the reality it presents as serious and equal conversation partners for deliberating on a reality that the Old Testament and New Testament attest. I refer here to the aspect of Christian belief and practice that was normative for the entire Christian communion until as recently as the eighteenth century (and perhaps currently for certain denominations). This is the belief in the reality of the spirit, the reality enshrined in the language of the "principalities and powers," and by extension the Holy Spirit.

Part of Dickson's own answer lies in the hope he holds for the future of this enterprise especially in light of the observations about social scientific studies in religion and new approaches in biblical scholarship. If the evolutionary view of religion that places religions in hierarchical relationship to each other is being called into question, as in Troeltsch's assessment and repudiation of Hegelian evolutionism, if the tying of Christianity to culture has now been made vacuous by postcolonial biblical and theological studies, then the way has been paved for taking seriously what contribution ATR makes to African Christian theology.[21] This means that it can

---

NT feature prominently in the required texts for West African students in prereligious studies programs), *Our Religions* (London: Dent, 1973).

21. Dickson faults Troeltsch for duplicity in his own criticism of Hegel, whom the former notes as harboring the evolutionary theory of religions in his writing, while at the same time evidencing traces of evolutionism in his own hierarchical structuring of other religions in relation to Christianity, and also tying Christianity so closely to Western culture as to make it impossible to allow one to be Christian outside the Western

be incorporated into Christian theology in general without any accompanying tendency to first contextualize, then localize and marginalize, or ghettoize it as a species of theology designated African theology.[22]

It is in light of the above considerations that we turn now to an account of African religiocultural reality and examine closely its interrelationship with ATR as a lived religion of a "flesh and blood people who practice this religion" (38). Theologians *qua* theologians, Dickson suggests, ought to begin their work with a "deep sense of commitment to the world of their day," see "the reality of the revelation of God into the particular circumstances either of their own or their society," and be compelled to engage the religions of the world, since the hopes and dreams and fortunes of real people are tied to these religions. It behooves the Christian theologian to approach the variegated contexts of African Christian lives and the realities that give it impetus with the same hospitality and commitment that characterizes all theological endeavors (45–46).

African Culture and Reality in Outline

For Dickson, the obvious markers of the African religiocultural reality that demand attention center on understanding 1) the physical world and its relation with humans; 2) belief in God, the gods, and their interrelationships with humans; and 3) humanity as co-humanity—that is, humanity and community. These constitute what might be termed the spiritual aspects of African reality or the sociospiritual reality of African lives.

Religion and Created Existence

The most salient feature of African religiocultural reality is the mutual interdependence/interrelationship of all created entities. Human beings live in mutual obligation to nature, what Dickson terms "a kind of fellow-feeling with nature," on account of which African sociospiritual reality

---

world. See Ernst Troeltsch, *The Absoluteness of Christianity and the History of Religion* (Atlanta: John Knox, 1971).

22. African NT scholar John Pobee, with an extensive tenure in the WCC, makes a similar observation and plea for African theology to transcend itself and its cultural boundaries and become truly ecumenical; see Pobee, *Towards an African Theology* (Nashville: Abingdon, 1979), 21.

and the religious practices pertaining to it have been described and labeled as animistic or as composing a "'nature' religion" (48).[23] In view of this interrelatedness between all created entities, there is no sharp distinction between animate and inanimate, physical and metaphysical, sacred and secular, and natural and supernatural realms. The world is experienced as holistic and dynamic, and this sensibility is at the heart of all life affecting every function at individual and cosmic levels. The natural and spiritual, this-worldly and otherworldly, interpenetrate at the junctures of human existence—birth, life, and death—which themselves are believed to be cyclical phenomena. The assumed interrelationship, and the interpenetration of the two worlds, does not mean that people are not aware of the distinctions between the two; it is more that "the distinctions are not as meaningful as one might expect, for the unseen powers are held to be active also in the natural order" (49). And the working of this interrelatedness is most notable in the area of causation, and especially regarding the causes of disease and death. Here Dickson cites Horton's observations from his studies of African traditional life:

> Through the length and breadth of the African continent, sick or afflicted people go to consultants as to the cause of their troubles. Usually, the answer they receive involves a god or other spiritual agency, and remedy prescribed involves the propitiation or calling-off of this being. But this is very seldom the whole story. For the diviner who diagnoses the intervention of a spiritual agency is also expected to give some acceptable account of what moved the agency in question to intervene. And this account very commonly involves reference to some event in the world of visible, tangible happenings.[24]

23. Dickson refers to works such as Lévi-Bruhl's *Primitive Mentality* (London: Allen and Unwin, 1923).

24. Robin Horton, "African Traditional Thought and Western Science, Part I, From Tradition to Science," *Africa: Journal of the International African Institute* 37, no. 1 (1967): 50–71, cited in Dickson, *Theology in Africa*, 51. It is worth noting that Evans-Pritchard's observations of such causality in his seminal work on witchcraft among the Azande confirm Horton's observations. In his analysis he makes note of the commonplace attitude that frames the concept and belief of witchcraft and distinguishes it from Western constructs in a historical perspective. The Zande, like most primal religious peoples, use witchcraft as a frame for articulating causality much in the same way that, say, the Westerner uses a theory of bacteria to account for disease. Thus, while the Zande may blame witchcraft for failed crops, she or he is also aware of the blight that is the

What is important in the observation of the interrelatedness of all created entities, of the kind of fellow-feeling Africans have with their world, the understanding of causality with which they make meaning of their world, is that in a comprehensive way "it coheres for [them] . . . for the universe is for [them] a living universe, and [they are] part of it" (52). Thus it seems that the African in this sense "interprets his world theologically" rather than scientifically (51).

Dickson foregrounds the kind of misinterpretation and mislabeling of this at-home-ness, or fellow-feeling, with the universe that most Africans possess, and that is sometimes demonstrated in religious practice. To use "nature religions" as nomenclature for African religions is not only a misnomer, since the religious African is not really worshiping nature or ascribing ultimate power to nature, but also because Dickson sees the same attitude toward nature and created reality expressed in Israel's religion.

Not only is Israel's religious history one that displays a constant treading toward the cults of nature often belonging to their neighboring nations, Israel also needed to be constantly summoned back by one prophetic message after another. In another respect, the way in which the Old Testament describes Israel's God, Yahweh, is often couched in language that suggests that their god is "conceived as a Nature deity," whose voice is in the thunder (Ps. 29:3–9). As the poetic rendition of "the victory of Barak and Deborah over Sisera on Mount Tabor" depicts it, Yahweh comes to the aid of his people "in a storm which resulted in the enemy's chariots being bogged down in mud" (163).[25]

In addition, the sacrality ascribed to certain objects—such as the Oak of Moreh, situated in a Canaanite sanctuary, which Abraham appropriates as the place for an altar for Yahweh (Gen. 12:6) and which later becomes the burial place for Jacob's family idols (Gen. 35:2–4); Beersheba, so named by Abraham after he has made a covenant with Abimelech (Gen. 21:25–32), at which he would later call on the name of God (Gen. 21:33); and the place where Isaac will later set up an altar to God after a the-

---

immediate cause of the diseased trees. See E. E. Evans-Pritchard, *Witchcraft, Oracles, and Magic among the Azande* (Clarendon: Oxford, 1976 [1937]).

25. Dickson refers to such examples as the Elijah contest with the prophets of Baal on Mount Carmel and his flight to Sinai, noting the association of Yahweh with the latter, the appearance of God to Moses in the burning bush, and how the tradition depicts Yahweh going before the Israelites during the exodus as a pillar of cloud by day and of fire by night to give light and direction for the journey.

ophany (Gen. 26:23–25)—all these suggest the tendency of Israel toward nature worship (162).[26]

If monotheism is gleaned from Israel's religion (and Dickson is not arguing that case for African religion), in spite of the instances of attachment to sacralized natural places and the conceptions of their deity as a "Nature God," why ascribe "Nature" religion to one that shares the same traits and not the other? If Israel is not worshiping nature by its attitude and stance toward how they conceive of God's workings through nature and have attachments to sacred natural sites, why is the African's attitude and stance described in such a manner as to suggest that the African is incapable of differentiating the acts of the deity via nature from nature through which the deity's power is manifested? To ascribe "nature" religion to one and not the other is only possible in the hierarchical religious landscape and the theories that undergird it. It belongs to an era in which "primitive" and "pre-logic" were erroneously attributed to certain religions by a measuring standard foreign to it, notes Dickson (50).[27] Yet this same line of reasoning continues in other forms of description for African religions as animistic. There is no doubt that there are elements of the animistic in African religions, but that alone need not qualify it for labeling as animism any more than it would Christianity and a host of other religions with animistic elements (49).

It is clear that Dickson is making more than an observation in his detailed comparison of African religions and Israelite religion. In fact, he is making the claim here, as well as elsewhere, about the continuity he sees between biblical and African worldviews.[28] He is calling attention to taking African religious views seriously in the shaping of Christian theology, perhaps as seriously as Israelite religious perspectives have had an impact on, not only Christian theology and Christianity, but Western civilization.

---

26. Dickson also notes a possible conjecture that can be made regarding the possibility of the well water from this site being used as sacred water, like what pertains in some Independent African Churches. The broad insight, however, is part of a larger claim that Dickson makes for African cultural continuity with the Bible (to which I will return later in this chapter).

27. Dickson refers, in particular, to Lévy-Bruhl's *Primitive Mentality*, as well as *How Natives Think* (London: Allen and Unwin, 1926).

28. See his edited volume with Paul Ellingworth, *Biblical Revelation and African Beliefs* (London: Lutterworth, 1969), as well as his "Continuity and Discontinuity between Old Testament and African Life and Thought," in *African Theology en Route*, ed. Appiah-Kubi and Torres.

But it is also clear that he understands the problematic nature of the moves he is making in this regard, particularly in the conclusions he draws about the religiocultural reality of African peoples, and that of ancient Israel as depicted in the Bible, especially in light of other aspects of African religious reality—God, the gods, and humanity—to which we now turn.

God, the Gods, and Humanity

It is common knowledge that many Africans understand their world as a hierarchical ordering among all existing entities, both natural and spiritual, and it is this that gives structure and stability to their world. Moreover, the belief in the stratified coexistence of such spiritual entities is assumed to be patterned on African social structures.

The spiritual hierarchy has at its pinnacle the Supreme Being, or God.[29] Called variously by different names in different languages, God is Creator and General Overseer of all creation and yet one whose transcendence allows for relegating oversight of the world and human affairs to lesser gods or deities. No one today needs to argue the point that such a concept or belief in God is a borrowed one, notes Dickson, for as an Akan (Ghanaian) saying goes: *Obi nnkyere abɔfra Nyame*, meaning that "no one points out God to a child." The reality of God is self-evident, intuited, and acknowledged as such. What is important is how God is viewed across the African landscape and what the implications are, especially for the task of African Christian theology.

God and the Gods

The names given to God among several African peoples depict God as transcendent and associated with the sky, suggesting that God is thought of

---

29. It is worth noting that in missionary activity in sub-Saharan Africa and in translation work across the region, the name given by the locals to the deity known as the Supreme Being, who in many ways was one among many other deities, was retained and appropriated for the new Christian religion. In some instances, as among the Ewe-speaking Fon (Benin) and Anlo (Ghana), the pair *Mawu-Lisa* was split and the Christian God became *Mawu*, obliterating the idea and understanding of conjoined maleness and femaleness of the traditional High God, a concept perhaps closer to the Hebraic understanding of YHWH, who is described in male and female gender terms.

as being far from the world of humans. Several creation myths, however, imply that God was conceptualized as being formerly closer to the world of humans and only moved further away on account of the behavior of humans.[30] The presence of other divinities—lesser gods, as they are normally called—and their relationship to God, pose not only questions but a problem for any attempt to use African spiritual reality in formulating an African Christian theology. It is not entirely clear whether the concept of an inaccessible God is merely an explanation for the presence of the lesser gods, or whether, indeed, the inability of humans to reach God to understand and access his power necessitated the presence of these intermediaries. Whatever the reasons adduced for the presence and belief in these lesser gods/intermediaries, it makes redundant any attempt by some African theologians and philosophers[31] to ascribe strict monotheism to African religions as opposed to the tendency of others, mostly non-Africans, to describe them as polytheistic.[32]

For Dickson, both approaches are problematic. He submits that the plethora of gods in African religions belies monotheism; however, "polytheism . . . does not quite do justice to the deep respect Africans have for God . . . evident from the study of the praise-names and attributes to him as well as how his relation to man is conceived" (54). As descriptors for African religions, monotheism and polytheism are both inappropriate. Neither term sufficiently attends to the relationship of God to the gods, and, in turn, the relationship of the two to humanity.[33] If African religions

30. One such story involves the action of women pounding yams in a mortar with a long pestle that kept hitting God. God, who was associated with the sky, which was then quite low, had to keep moving farther and farther away from the intrusion of the pestle.

31. See, e.g., J. B. Danquah's arguments in his *Akan Doctrine of God* (London: Cass, 1968); see also Harry Sawyerr, *God: Ancestor or Creator* (Harlow, UK: Longmans, 1970), both of which are arguments against the position taken by anthropologists such as R. S. Rattray in his classic work *The Ashanti* (Oxford: Clarendon Press, 1923).

32. See E. B. Idowu, *Olódùmarè: God in Yoruba Belief* (Plainview, NY: Original Publications, 1995), for an extensive argument for considering African belief as primarily monotheistic despite the plethora of other divinities, whom Idowu considers merely mediatory.

33. John Mbiti's more recent comparative studies in his two well-known books, *African Religions and Philosophy* (Oxford: Heinemann, 1990) and *Concepts of God in Africa* (Nairobi, Kenya: Action Publishers, 2012); both suggest that the questions are still rife. He proposes a solution that might still seem problematic to both anthropologists and theologians of religion, that is, the unity and plurality of God in African thought, a plurality within unity that he finds present in other monotheistic religions in which the plurality merely defines aspects of divine activity.

are neither monotheistic nor polytheistic, as Dickson hints, then exactly what is the relation between God and the lesser gods (not to mention the other spirit beings)? This presents a key to the defining, describing, and understanding of African religions.

In most African contexts, it is assumed that the lesser deities are the frontline messengers between God and the rest of creation. The gods are the intermediaries between humans and the Supreme Being and in most instances act on behalf of the Supreme Being to the point of being worshiped and propitiated to ensure good will in one's behalf and for evil on one's enemies. Some cultures make a further distinction between good lesser gods and evil lesser gods: they often do not ascribe divinity to the latter and tend to speak of them periphrastically as supernatural powers.[34] Thus, among the Yorùbá of Nigeria, for instance, it is believed that the supreme being, or high god, is Olódùmarè, and underneath him in hierarchy are the Òrìsà (all the Yorùbá divinities), the Ajogun (anti-gods or the malevolent supernatural powers), the Àjë (inadequately translated into English as "witches"), and the ancestors. Among the Akan of Ghana, West Africa, we find yet further distinctions among the supernatural powers. The lesser gods are sometimes referred to as children of *Nyame* (the sky god) and a place is found in this cosmology for good spirits as well as malevolent spirits. Witches, for example, can be good or evil, and many seek the powers of "good witchcraft" in hopes of finding success in their affairs, whereas "bad witchcraft" is believed to be used to destroy one's enemies and thus is inherently antisocial. Apart from ancestors, who are revered and sometimes worshiped,[35] there are other supernatural beings/

34. Parallels between this concept and that of other religious traditions, such as Judaism, with its belief in the existence of both a good and evil being such as God and the devil (or Satan) can be easily drawn; so also is depth psychological assessment of such belief as no more than splitting the God image into good and bad objects.

35. The debate about whether the appropriate terminology to describe the attitude toward the ancestors is veneration or worship is very much current. Proponents of veneration, largely African Christians who need to maintain the valid place of ancestral cultic practice vis-à-vis the Christian religious practices, insist that what pertains is veneration; others (more evangelical voices) who disavow syncretism, and who need to separate ATRs from what they consider as pure and true Christianity, observe that while there is veneration accorded ancestors, the rituals of sacrifice pertain to worship, and that accords worship to the ancestors. For more on this debate, see Dickson and Ellingworth, *Biblical Revelation and African Beliefs*; Mbiti, *African Religions and Philosophy*; Kofi Asare Opoku, *West African Traditional Religion* (Accra, Ghana: FEP International, 1978); and Idowu, *Olódùmarè*.

powers, including *mboatia*, dwarves and witches (mainly female) who, because they traverse the world of humans and the superhuman, bear the brunt of all mishaps that befall humans and other living things. It appears that part of the reason for the plethora of gods and other spirit beings is the seeming inaccessibility of God, whether for good or for judgment or justice (e.g., in punishing transgressions).

Dickson suggests that these assumptions and conclusions are rather hasty and do not bear the weight of how the practitioners live their religion. In the first place, the absence of direct reference to God in the worship, sacrifice, and other rituals of African people in no way suggests that these Africans assume God as redundant and unconcerned about their affairs. While there are indeed no temples and formal worship spaces for the Supreme Being, the Akan of Ghana, for example, have the "*Nyamedua*, a three-forked branch supporting a pot in which food items are put as offerings to God" (53).[36] Additionally, the Igbo of Nigeria make sacrifices to God, however infrequent they may be. This is some indication that these Africans think of God as close enough to be worshiped.[37] Additionally, the various praise-names given to God, often demonstrated in the choice of names for their offspring, as well as "informal, ejaculatory statements featuring the God-name," especially in times of stress, all point to the fact that the God they have in mind or appeal to is never far from them (53).[38]

At the same time, as noted earlier, the presence of so many gods and their respective functions and relationship to the supreme God in the practice of African religions sometimes belies the aforementioned belief in the

36. *Nyamedua*, literally God-tree, is dotted over the Akan landscape, as noted by Geoffrey Parrinder, whom Dickson cites in this case. See Parrinder, *West African Religion* (London: Epworth Press, 1961), 15.

37. Here Dickson cites Francis A. Arinze, *Sacrifice in the Ibo Religion* (Ibadan, Nigeria: Ibadan University Press, 1970), 54ff. Arinze notes, however, that these sacrifices are so infrequent that the average Igbo may not be aware that they even exist. It is worth noting that C.R. Gaba (with whom Dickson disagrees), who has written about the Anlo Ewe of Ghana, observes that sacrifices seemingly made to the deities or lesser divinities are actually being made to the supreme being, because he is usually referred to first in all oratory pertaining to libations; see Gaba, "Sacrifice in Anlo Religion," *Ghana Bulletin of Theology* 35 (1968): 10–15.

38. Examples of such praise-names indicate God as provider, as advocate, as hearer of prayer, and so on. It needs to be noted that these are like the names ascribed to YHWH, often in times of need or answers to prayer, reflected sometimes in the names of places where such deliverance occurred, or in persons who were seen as the direct answers to the prayers.

acknowledged presence of God. And while the necessity of these gods has been explained largely in terms of their role as intermediaries, Dickson says that the practices of people do not entirely bear out the assumptions and theories entailed in this conception. He notes, citing the case of the Akan of Ghana, that there are three distinct ways of conceiving of the relationship of God to the gods tied to three different functions that they are said to perform.

There are divinities referred to as *Nyankopɔn ne mba* ("sons of God"), used specifically for certain water deities related to particular rivers of the Asante, among whom one name for God is *Amosu*: one who gives rain. In this respect, the giver of rain, the one who fills the rivers with water, implies that other gods derive from this rain-giver: they partake of his nature and hence are his children. These divinities are thus considered intermediaries who serve in a delegated role of ministers of a sovereign. It is important, however, as Dickson points out, that the reference to "sons" be assumed to mean, in Akan terms, not only one's own progeny but anyone younger than the user (55–56).[39] It also means that the "cult of the gods" came later in Akan belief, even though Dickson is quick to point out that it does not in any way suggest that monotheism was the original worship of the Akan, as some, such as J. B. Danquah and B. Idowu, have proposed (56, 54).[40] *Abrafoɔ* ("executioners") is the second term used to describe these divinities, indicating their interest in the moral lives of the people, a reference perhaps to the Creator's interest in morality. In the same way as the Supreme Being eschews evil, so do these gods, and consequently they punish evildoers with calamity. Again, as with the sons of God, these executioners are limited largely "to the medicine cults" and not related to or referred to by all the gods (55–56).

The third description, the most problematic of all in Dickson's assessment, is that of *akyeame* ("linguists or spokesmen"). The linguist is

39. Perhaps the "sons of God" used here might recall for some the expression in the Hebrew Bible, as in Gen. 6:2, the *benei elohim*, where "sons" have sometimes traditionally been conceived of as angels, that is, messengers of God, or claimed to be Nephilim, "demigods" fallen from heaven. While the point is still debatable, a new insight in a recent article suggests, in light of recent scientific data, that the *benei elohim* are the Homo sapiens of that prehistoric era recorded in Genesis and thereafter, those who intermarried with female Neanderthals—the *benot ha-adam* (daughters of men). See Shubert Spero, "Sons of God, Daughters of Men?" *Jewish Bible Quarterly* 40 (2012): 15–18.

40. See their accounts in Danquah, *Akan Doctrine of God*; also Idowu, *Olódùmarè*.

an important personality in the Akan king's court because he speaks for the king, receives requests from the people for the king (as the king is not customarily addressed directly in court), and sometimes acts on his behalf in his absence. While a case can be made for the first two sets of gods as possible intermediaries, it seems less clear that this is how one should understand the third set. With *akyeame,* one may still think that the role indicates God as the ultimate power, without whom the intermediary cannot fully function. However, Dickson urges caution. He believes that this latter understanding may only be theoretical, not fact, because "unlike the two other expressions this one is not experientially and ritually exemplified in Akan religion" (56).

Experientially—and this is evinced across the traditional African religious landscape—prayers and ritual sacrifices, whether private or communal, are offered to the gods almost as ends in themselves. They are the addressees, and blessings are asked of them for oneself and loved ones, and their names are directly invoked in curses on one's enemies. On the other hand, threats are made to these lesser divinities from devotees if they fail to deliver on bequests made to them—action that would never be taken toward the Supreme Being, and so pointing not only to the high esteem in which the Supreme Being is held, but also to his indispensability compared to the dispensability of these lesser gods in the life of these Africans.[41] It might suggest, then, that these divinities are conceived of as merely intermediaries, even though ritual practices may not always bear out that fact. There are no easy answers here, and the Christian theologian, as Dickson notes, cannot easily ascribe monotheism or polytheism to African religions, for these terms are less than enlightening, given the facets of the religious expression just outlined (58).

While Dickson's insights from Akan religious practice throw further light on the relationship between God and the lesser divinities, they also complicate matters: first, they make clear that the relationship between God and the lesser gods in African religions is not as simple to ascertain as some tend to think; second, they raise questions about how to conceptualize African religions and how that conceptualization affects attempts at constructing an appropriate Christian theology for Africa; and third, how such a Christian theology relates to the rest of the Christian world.

41. This point is noted by Dickson and other African theologians, such as C. Gaba and Idowu, who disagree with Dickson on whether these divinities are merely intermediaries or worshiped in their own right.

Humanity and Evil

It is taken for granted in most African cultures that human beings are created by God as moral beings who know right from wrong. The ability to know right from wrong is what sets humans apart from the rest of creation. African cultures may be thought anthropocentric; but that does not imply that they are "humanistic in a sense that is antithetical to religion," because all reality, as already noted, is religious (60).[42]

Because humans are believed to be created by God as moral beings with the inherent capacity to know right from wrong, it is not always clear how evil and its ramifications are to be understood in the relationship of God to the gods. The Akan, for example, believe that humans are made up of three elements—blood, spirit, and soul. The blood they receive from the mother; the spirit (which I take in this sense to mean "essence") is from the father; and the soul is from God. This is the God-bit that is tied to morality, and hence the person who lives unworthily is said not to be "human" (61). A variation of this concept is found among the Yorùbá, who point to the "oracle of the heart" as the guiding principle of humans.[43] Among the Gãs of Ghana, the human being, *gbomo adesa*, is a composite of three parts: the *susuma*, corresponding to soul (an approximate word since there is no real English equivalent to the original meaning), the *kla*, which corresponds to the concept of the self, and the *gbomotso* (literally, the "human tree"), which is the frame of the person (the body, corpus). The first two constitute the immaterial aspect of the human being. It is believed that the *susuma* is able to leave the body in dreams and is often, not always conscious even in waking moments. Thus one can hear people say that they do not know what their *susuma* wants.[44]

How does one think about morality, human agency, and destiny in this context? The Akan of Ghana account for the inexplicable cases of good people coming to bad ends through a mixture of ill fortune and character

42. This attitude is, in a sense, a contrast to that found in other cultures in which anthropocentrism fosters a humanistic philosophy that eschews religion because reality is areligious (or irreligious). The demographics of irreligion by country provide a telling statement of the distinction between African anthropocentrism and that of secular humanists. See "Irreligion," at https://en.wikipedia.org/wiki/Irreligion.

43. Idowu, *Olódùmarè*, 154, cited in Dickson, *Theology in Africa*, 61.

44. I take this to refer, possibly, to a way of noting and accounting for restlessness in a person's behavior and personality, tied to indecisiveness at the low end and recklessness at the high end, without any known reason for the state or action.

flaws by elaborating on how the individual receives the *kra* (soul). There is a complex of events entailed in the creating and sending forth of humans from an earlier spiritual existence. According to the tradition, this complex involves God, the gods, and ancestors, all of whom play a part in predetermining what each individual would become in the universe.[45] Consequently, all moral questions involve God, the gods, the ancestors, and human beings.

What, then, of the idea of wrongdoing, or sin? First, there is the basic question of whether African culture has a concept of sin against God, since one usually encounters concepts of sin in social relationships in the form of taboos, many of which revolve around sex and sexual relations between men and women—emphasizing the importance of communal living. They regulate social structures to ensure that harmony is maintained, on which the blessings of the gods and the ancestors depend (65). In this respect, these taboos are not unlike those encountered in the Ancient Near East and exemplified in the relationships and ritual commands of the Old Testament.[46]

This emphasis on sin as taboo and as a rupturing of social relations, with concomitant curses on the whole community, does not indicate that sin is not also conceived of as an individual missing the mark of his or her true humanity. Neither does it preclude the notion that the individual has consciousness of sin as guilt, nor concept of sin against God.[47] As I have

45. See Eva L. R. Meyerowitz, "Concepts of the Soul among the Akan of the Gold Coast," *Africa* 21 (1951): 24–31, esp. 24–25, for further elaborations on this belief.

46. Here one can recall some of the ritual laws in Leviticus. Coupled with this is the notion of the attendant curses that follow infractions, not just for the culprit and immediate family, but sometimes for whole clans, especially concerning taboos that have direct bearing on relationship with Yahweh (Josh. 7:1–12, 19–26).

47. Much has been written, especially in anthropological and cross-cultural studies, about shame and guilt cultures and whether collectivistic culture, such as the African culture, may be more a shame-based culture, indicating that individual consciousness of sin and associated guilt—an intrapsychic phenomenon—may be absent or less prevalent than shame—and interpsychic emotion that stems from communal ethos. Such differentiations are, however, embedded in Western cultural ideas and practices and may stem from the past stratification of cultures as developed or developing. The stratification also includes the assumption that guilt cultures are more morally advanced, when in fact they could be a mark of an individualistic culture. See a recent work by Anna Wierzbicka, *Emotions across Languages and Cultures: Diversity and Universals* (Cambridge, UK: Cambridge University Press, 1999), for an anthropological, psychological, and linguistic treatment using a cross-cultural perspective that debunks some of these traditional stereotypes.

noted earlier in the discussion on the relationship between God and the gods, the role of some of the lesser divinities as *abrafoɔ*—executioners who bring punishment and blessings from *Nyame* for bad or good behavior, respectively—gestures toward the understanding of sin as infringement ultimately against God, even if it is couched in language that is embedded in a social/familial matrix. This insight finds support in the work of Nigerian theologian J. O. Awolalu:

> Although sin can be and is punished by either the divinities or the ancestors, we must realize that Africans believe that such sins are still regarded as offenses against God who is creator and Sustainer of the universe and its inhabitants, who expects His creatures to maintain good relationship with one another and with the super-sensible world and on whose behalf the divinities and ancestors punish immoral deeds.[48]

The infringement of taboos causes evil, whether it is believed to be directly or consciously a sin against God or just against the gods and ancestors.[49] It is assumed that evil ruptures the fabric of relationships (natural and supernatural), and elicits retribution in one form or the other. When inexplicable natural disasters occur, the Akan are known to lay blame on the avenging gods and, ultimately, *Nyame*, as the prime cause. Individual calamities that are inexplicable, however, have a more complicated causality, with other spirit beings, including ancestors and God, often being thought responsible. The Akan say, "When God gives you a disease, he also gives you a cure" to acknowledge that God is not only a source of cure but a cause of the ailment. But there is also a widespread belief that diseases, other inexplicable misfortunes, and death are caused largely by other malevolent

---

48. J. O. Awulalo, "Sin and Its Removal in African Traditional Religion," *Journal of the American Academy of Religion* 44, no. 2 (1976): 275–87, cited by Dickson, *Theology in Africa*, 67. Dickson also points to evidence from Tanzania and Uganda, and further adds that this African concept of sin is not that different from an attitude widely held in the past regarding a certain stratum of the concept of sin in the OT as being "a defective sense of sin." This is because sins tied to custom were not usually regarded as an infringement against Yahweh, an attitude and idea that have changed with the acknowledgement that such a sin, while not a breaking of a moral code, was still violation of a command of Yahweh.

49. I should point out that Dickson assumes that the truth lies between the possibilities presented, especially since, in ritual practice, he refers more explicitly to the gods and ancestors from whom forgiveness is sought, and to and through whom restitution is made (*Theology in Africa*, 67).

spirit beings, especially witches. These witches—humans with supernatural powers—are claimed to have animal familiars that they turn into at night, engage in cannibalistic rituals, and are believed to be responsible for a host of calamities people find inexplicable: diseases associated with the wasting away of the body for no apparent reason; the failure of infants to thrive; premature deaths; losses in business and sudden loss of wealth, and so forth. But there is also the belief that some witches are good, and these are the ones who work against the evil witches and the malevolent activities they engage in against individuals and communities (63).[50]

Evil, then, is seen as arising out of various otherworldly causes: God, the gods, ancestors, and the evil spiritual powers, usually in the form of witches. The current pervasiveness of belief and accretion of causes to these evil spiritual powers and their capricious acts that terrorize humans, even Christian believers, is absent from Dickson's analysis of evil, and it is not immediately obvious why Dickson does not include these issues. For it is unquestionable that no theology will be viable for the African context today if it ignores the central place of—and pervading influence of—belief in witchcraft (whether for good or ill) in most African cultures, and, for that matter, such beliefs among practicing members of Africa's Christian churches. It is common, for example, for people in African Christian churches to attest the powers of demons and spirits in their lives, and this shows up in pastoral practice.[51]

The account of humanity in African thought described by Dickson gives evidence for the following: the first point is that the Old Testament offers an idea of both the continuities and discontinuities between African and Hebraic thought and opens the way for a genuine encounter between the two; the second flows from it, though somewhat dialogically—that is, that African religiocultural realities can make a contribution to Christian theology.

In light of this, let me turn to explore African religiocultural realities vis-à-vis the cross—the center of Christian belief—as a gateway for African

50. These ideas about witches are corroborated by C. R. Gaba's extensive research among the Anlo Ewe of Ghana. See the latter's "Anlo Traditional Religion: A Study of the Anlo Traditional Believer's Conception of and Communion with the 'Holy'" (PhD diss., University of London, 1965).

51. The complexities of belief in and attitude toward demons as they relate to the African culture and religious worldview, I will give further attention to later in this chapter, esp. as Dickson's ideas regarding the inherent continuity of African religiocultural reality coincide with the biblical world picture.

Christian theology. The goal is to try to forge a theology that resonates with African worldviews and can contribute to the health of the church and its future growth within and beyond the continent.[52]

The Cross in African Cultural Perspective

Dickson situates his discussion of this most significant symbol of Christian belief with respect to the role that African culture can play in redefining and reframing it for African Christian theology. He points to the cultural moorings inherent in all interpretations and significations of the cross in different historical contexts and times. Noting the variations of emphasis from the New Testament (especially the Pauline passages that deal with the cross and the resurrection[53]) through the early church up to the patristic periods, Dickson suggests that the language and meaning of the cross has always worn the garb of the sociocultural concerns and has allowed hearers to interpret the meaning of the cross for their day (185–86).[54] What is being attested here is that even the meaning of the central symbol of Christianity, the cross, has always been refracted through cultural lenses.

Dickson observes that this meaning-making dates back to the treatment of the cross in the New Testament itself. When Paul interprets the cross in sacrificial language, he is choosing a language out of the religio-cultural context of Passover sacrifices to Yahweh. Christ is the new Passover lamb offered to God to atone for human sin and procure forgiveness

52. See Philip Jenkins, *The Next Christendom: The Coming of Global Christianity* (Oxford: Oxford University Press, 2011).

53. Dickson notes that the choice of Paul is not intended to be restrictive but rather expansive because Paul provides the most comprehensive and detailed expression and interpretation of the cross and resurrection in the NT.

54. He notes, for example, that the ransom theory, which proposes that a ransom was to be paid to the devil to free humanity from his clutches, was appropriate for the patristic age, which was filled with social unrest, pillaging, brigandage, and the capturing and ransoming of captives. This was later displaced by the satisfaction theory, proposed by Anselm of Canterbury in the twelfth century, in which the death of Christ was seen as sacrifice to satisfy the honor of God, which had been defiled by human sin and affront, a theory consonant with the prevailing sensibilities of honor and chivalry in the medieval period. Then there is the substitution theory of the atonement, which accompanied the post-Reformation period, which was dominated by law and jurisprudence, and in which Christ's death becomes one on behalf of humanity, taking the punishment for guilt meted out from God the Judge.

and cleansing so as to accomplish our salvation. In other words, Paul comes to this language and understanding of the cross and the death of Jesus within the Jewish tradition into which he was acculturated. But Paul does not fudge with the language of the cross in demonstrating its power to save and secure pardon when he witnesses to Gentiles. Neither the possibility of its being a "stumbling block to Jews or foolishness to Gentiles" minimizes the importance of the cross and Jesus as the sacrificial victim. In Paul's thought, the cross is the power for procuring salvation for Jew and Gentile alike (1 Cor. 1:18).

But the centrality of the cross is tied to the event of the resurrection in Paul's thought. A two-pronged cross-conscious and resurrection-conscious emphasis is what one witnesses in Paul's treatment of the grand theme of the Christ event. For Dickson, the double foci in Paul's treatment do not in any sense suggest that Paul views the two events as a seamless narrative. His treatment indicates that he distinguishes between the two: the cross as the event in which our salvation is worked out, and the resurrection as the pivotal instrument in which what has been worked out on our behalf is affirmed. These are appropriated when we are brought into new life with God through Christ (190).

How are we, then, to interpret the cross in the African context, a world that Dickson narrates as teeming with such physico-spiritual reality? How do we do that in light of the assertion that the cross has always been interpreted in a way that is apt for the context in which it encounters and is encountered by people? In the context of the African world and church, how does the cross confront the belief in evil spiritual powers and demonic forces that threaten the people in all aspects of their lives with the terror of death?[55] For Dickson, the answer lies in emphasizing both cross and resurrection and using them in tandem to reframe and appropriate interpretation for the African context. The cross is not a "transition station" on the way to the resurrection; rather, death with resurrection is what brings the power unto salvation. Taking the death/cross seriously is essential to understanding and living into the resurrection. And the African soil has an expansive understanding of death and life that speaks to the kind of double-pronged approach to death and resurrection that the New Testament enjoins.

55. African Christologies that emphasize the role of Jesus, especially as charismatic leader and healer, attend to this question more effectively, and I will return to some of their answers below.

In much African thought, death and life are intertwined, and, as with life, death is never a private affair but a communal event. And here Dickson contrasts death in the African context with that of the Western context, where death is becoming more and more an individual, private affair and the community can continue to function without noticing death. The African celebration of death is marked by certain pertinent beliefs, which in many settings dictate mortuary, burial, and funeral rites and depict the African understanding of the integration of life and earth, and the overlapping of the spiritual and physical worlds in broad relief. In the first place, death is always assumed to be caused by evil, which comes to the human being through the spirit world, a world that is not separate from the physical. Even if the immediate cause is known and recognized—a sickness, an accident, old age, and so on—the underlying cause is always attributed to other than the physical causes. "The religious beliefs of the people are used to offer the explanation, and Africans turn to their relationship with God, fellow members of the community, ancestors and spirits."[56] There is, therefore, an inherent spiritual or perhaps theological accounting not only for the cause of death but also for coping resources. Thus while the loss is mourned, there is the strong belief that death has not ended the life of the departed since it is in reality a transition of the departed from the physical to the spiritual plane where he will continue a physical existence, sometimes as a revered ancestor. Rituals performed to sever ties with the departed may seem to indicate the finality of death, but they are in reality an attempt to prevent the departed person, who is assumed to be very much alive, from continuing ties with the living (193).[57] And because the departed still live, these rituals also ensure that they are properly situated on the other side, where they continue to provide care and especially moral guidance for those on earth.

But the dead, now on their way to living in the spiritual realm, offer opportunities for the living to have messages transported to the former dead relatives in the spirit world so that resources for a fecund life might be attained by those still on earth. For death becomes an occasion to affirm life and to celebrate the departed. The whole community, not just the be-

56. J. N. Kanyua Mugambi and Nicodemus Kirima, *The African Religious Heritage* (Nairobi: Oxford University Press, 1976), 94; cited in Dickson, *Theology in Africa*, 193.

57. Dickson cites cultural widowhood rites as an example of this belief; the rituals then allow for reintegration into the community as a single woman and for remarriage.

reaved, is invited to join in moving life forward, in eating and singing and dancing (all things associated with bodily movements), creating a convivial atmosphere, not just in spite of the death but because of the death.[58]

What are the significations of these markers of death in African thought for framing a theology of the cross and thus a Christian theology for Africa? Dickson points to how readily some of the aforementioned African concepts, attitudes, and practices surrounding death can be recalled when one reads the teaching on the significance of the cross in the New Testament. The African belief that death draws people together, "revitalizing the living and underscoring their sense of community," is displayed in Paul's language about the death of Christ and its significance memorialized in the great thanksgiving meal (1 Cor. 10:16–18).[59] When Paul explains the Lord's Supper as our participation in the death of Christ, indeed the blood of Christ, and the bread we partake of as "our communion with the Lord and with one another," he has in mind the communal meal of Israel after the peace offering, when kinsmen partake of the flesh of the animal, thereby uniting the community with God and strengthening the kinship bond at the same time (197).[60] The similarity of this ritual to an African communal meal following death is evident to the reader of the Old Testament and the observer of an African death scene. In Christian parlance, Jesus is now the sacrificial lamb, the lamb without blemish, on whose death the communal meal is still eaten with kinsmen and the church, which is the new Israel of God.

58. Dickson notes the confusing sentiments of Thomas Birch Freeman, Methodist missionary to Ghana, in his report (dated 30 July 1838) who once witnessed the dancing of women and children the same day on which a loved one dies. While the Ghanaians danced, Freeman grieved, not so much for the dead but for what was obviously to him the anomaly of dancing women and children.

59. On this score, Dickson shares the views of most African theologians and their understanding of Jesus as one who participates in the human community, fostering a unity that is essential for existence in African thinking. The church becomes the community that surpasses the old clan boundaries. One should perhaps also note the connection between this idea and the ecclesiological expression of the church as the new Israel of God, a move from one kinship group to another. See Harry Sawyerr, *Creative Evangelism: Towards a New Christian Encounter with Africa* (London: Lutterworth, 1968), esp. 73–79, in which he argues for the continuity of this concept with the Bible.

60. Note Dickson's comment on this Israelite practice and the distinction he makes between what pertains in the ritual associated with the peace offerings and what is being described as analogous in the African context, because it is clear that in the latter God is not thought to partake of the meal with the community.

The second similarity between some African concepts of death and what is depicted in Paul's language regards the notion of the need for a sacrificial animal without blemish. Here it is Christ himself, the spotless Lamb of God, who in an African context is a prime candidate for being an ancestor par excellence.[61] Unlike other ancestors, Jesus would forever be recalled as one of the living-dead since there will always be people who "knew" him in existence (I take this to mean encounters through conversion that will continue as long as the gospel is preached). The cross of Christ, then, occupies a symbolic place of significance within African Christian thought equal to other ancestral and royal insignia that Africans keep in memory of the departed, and in this case of the ever-living presence of Christ.

A final noteworthy point of intersection Dickson calls attention to is the one between African celebrations of death and the Christian understanding of the significance of the cross. Rather than the cross being viewed as an event that obscures the self that encounters it, it instead reifies the identity of the one who is confronted by it. It makes such people, as it were, more "themselves," finding their identity within their own original ethnicity and more able to fully express the gospel.[62] While he notes the inherent limitations in this idea, however, even with Paul's own witness, he is doubtless also calling attention to the need for African Christians, especially those in the mainline churches with whom he served and with which he is familiar, not to become anglicized in their attempt to witness to the gospel. This is a major point that ties in with his whole project concerning African theology: the need for an authentic African expression of the gospel that can be embraced by African Christian believers in their full identity as Africans, whose culture is affirmed as such by the God who calls people everywhere to Godself; and for them to be able to answer back in their identity as Africans and as creatures of this one God, who is their Creator.

---

61. African theologians who favor the adaptionist approach to method in African biblical hermeneutics have often favored the view of Jesus as ancestor and see it as the most fitting conception of Jesus and the one that Africans can easily understand and embrace, rather than other Christological titles imported into African contexts, which hardly fit. See Kwame Bediako, *Jesus and the Gospel in Africa: History and Experience* (Maryknoll, NY: Orbis, 2004), esp. chap. 2, as well as articulations of a similar concept in Sawyerr's treatment of Jesus as the firstborn of creation in *Creative Evangelism*, 72–79.

62. Dickson cites Paul's conversion experience and his insistence on his identity as a Jew as becoming the pivot for his powerful witness to the gospel not only to Jews but to Gentiles.

Dickson's Implicit Critique of Bultmann: An Assessment

Whatever the weaknesses of Dickson's approach, his search for a biblical hermeneutics that makes sense of the world imagined and evoked by Hebrew Scripture points out one important implication for theological hermeneutics: Dickson's approach brings him into conflict with the prevailing views of Rudolf Bultmann, whose notion of demythologizing demands that the world of Scripture be separated from or even abandoned by those living in a modern world. Moreover, Dickson's assertion of the importance of the Hebrew worldview for African theology indirectly exposes a fundamental weakness of Bultmann's program. In the following, I will seek to show how.

Bultmann in Retrospect and Perspective

Rudolf Bultmann's proposal for attending to the mythology of the New Testament is the most comprehensive approach to the task and problem of demythologizing to date, and his work on the issue spans two decades of writing. Bultmann's primary thesis is that there exists an enormous gap between the modern worldview and the biblical worldview, and the leap of faith it requires to read and believe the testimony of Scripture is inaccessible to modern human beings—with their scientific worldview. Thus the mythical component of Scripture becomes its bane in attempting to reach modern humans, Bultmann argues, and since the purpose of Scripture is that it may be believed and faith may work redemption in the hearer, it is only right that the elements that hinder this hearing and believing be removed so that the kernel of the message—the salvific work of its central figure—be accessed without the myth that bogs it down. The intent of Scripture to bring all peoples to faith and to recognize the lordship of Christ will thus be fulfilled in this way.

> Demythologizing seeks to bring out the real intention of myth, namely, its intention to talk about human existence as grounded in and limited by transcendent, unworldly power, which is not visible to objectifying thinking. Thus negatively, demythologizing is a criticism of the mythical world picture insofar as it conceals the real intention of myth. Positively, demythologizing is

existentialist interpretation, in that it seeks to make clear the intention of myth to talk about human existence.[63]

Bultmann's approach to understanding the biblical language of demons and miracles and principalities and powers, especially when one explores the philosophical basis and connection between his thinking and demythologizing, is based on the assumption that texts are bound by sociotemporal parameters. Therefore, every author can only think and write through the thought forms of his or her time and culture.[64] The biblical language of the powers, for Bultmann, belongs to a historical epoch where thought forms had not yet been formed by scientific thinking. The worldview of the biblical writers is "mythical," and their language of the powers is best situated within ancient Jewish apocalyptic and Gnostic redemption myths.[65] For Bultmann, the advances of science and technology have rendered the biblical world picture obsolete, and no one in the modern era can take seriously nor comprehend the mythological biblical world picture.

Bultmann views mythology as a certain mode of thinking, which is the opposite of scientific thinking. Mythical thinking proceeds from the assumption that the world is an "open" system—that is, occurrences in the world and in the personal lives of humans can be influenced by the intervention of otherworldly powers. Scientific thinking, on the other hand, views the world and its occurrences as a "closed" continuum of causes and effects; the forces that govern natural processes are embedded within them, and this causal continuum of the world process cannot be disrupted by supernatural powers.[66] Scientific thinking posits that all effects have natural and rational causes, and that the world is not open to the intervention of transcendent spiritual powers.[67]

---

63. Rudolf Bultmann, *New Testament and Mythology and Other Basic Writings* (Philadelphia: Fortress, 1984), 99.

64. See Bultmann, *New Testament and Mythology*; see also Rudolf Bultmann, *Theology of the New Testament*, 2 vols. (New York: Charles Scribner's Sons, 1951), 1:257–58.

65. Rudolf Bultmann: "Myth is the report of an occurrence or an event in which supernatural, superhuman forces or persons are at work" ("On the Problem," in *New Testament and Mythology*, 95).

66. Bultmann, "On the Problem," in *New Testament and Mythology*, 155.

67. Bultmann, "On the Problem," in *New Testament and Mythology*, 96.

The Promise of Bultmann

Bultmann's singular efforts in this enterprise to make Christianity believable again, as it were, and thus capable of engendering faith, is to be lauded. As a New Testament scholar, his interest was both historical and existential. Historical because he was interested in what Scripture meant for the original recipients in their context; but his existential bent also required that he probe how modern persons are able to *live* by the words of Scripture as it is also addressed to them in their day. On this latter score alone, Bultmann is to be commended, because his project is in line with the purposes of Scripture and the Christian religion: that it engender belief and that people find guidance for their lives. For this purpose it is essential to de-husk the fruit and reach the kernel. It is the task of Christian witness, therefore, to escape the attempt to expect people to believe in the gospel in the garb in which it was presented in the first century, with its mythic world picture as equally relevant. Not only would it be pointless to do so; it would be utterly impossible, Bultmann observes. At the same time, he knows that "it is entirely possible that in a past mythical world picture truths may be rediscovered that were lost during a period of enlightenment; and theology has every reason to ask whether this may be possible in the case of the world picture of the New Testament." Surprisingly, he answers his own question, however, suggesting that since it is impossible to "repristinate" the mythic world picture when we know better, and since we cannot "unknow" what we now have come to know about the mechanics of the world, to force modern people to believe as first-century Christians did would be to coerce them into committing intellectual dishonesty and even, in Bultmann's judgment, suicide![68] It is a reasonable suggestion Bultmann makes after all, except that it does not reckon the majority of Christians within his own North Atlantic region who believe, *with* the earliest churches and the many more across the globe, especially in the places where Christianity is seemingly exploding, who live at technologically advanced levels, as do their North Atlantic counterparts, and yet hold to a world where such belief perdures. It seems that ultimately Bultmann reckons without faith that is not born out of the will of the believer but engendered from without by the object of faith regardless of sociotemporal parameters or strictures.[69] And further, as David Augsburger notes,

68. Bultmann, *New Testament and Mythology*, 3.
69. One may raise the question whether there are any alternative positions be-

"there's a benefit to a three-tiered universe for psychological and spiritual health, and we lose a lot in discarding horned creatures."[70]

The Challenge to Existentialism

Bultmann has not escaped criticism of his ideas, especially his seminal essay "The New Testament and Mythology" (published in 1942). I do not intend to rehearse all those criticisms here, because my aim is to chart a way forward to a viable engagement with his ideas and by so doing to provide an alternative to demythologizing that serves the interpretive and ecclesial needs of the global church. Moreover, Bultmann himself preempted and offered a response to critics a decade later in his essay entitled "On the Problem of Demythologizing," in which he addresses a number of issues and provides a relatively concise summary of his basic position regarding myth in the New Testament and the need for demythologizing. I enumerate some of these ideas in the comments below.

The Point of Myth and of Demythologizing

For Bultmann, mythological thinking is thinking that pertains to supernatural or divine forces because it assumes the world and occurrences to be "open" to intervention from otherworldly powers. This mythic worldview, with its talk of transcendent powers and of demonic forces "on which we know ourselves to be dependent," or at least influenced by, as the case may be, assumes that the world in which we "live is full of enigmas and mysteries" and that humans are not lords over the world—or even their own lives.[71] This is false, says Bultmann, for the mythic approach is in-

---

tween these two as in, say, a faith derived from the object of faith as mediated through sociotemporal parameters. As long as faith is considered a gift to the believer, as well as something created between the believer and the object of faith, such a third alternative is possible. What I argue against here is the position in which the sociotemporal is bracketed as inconsequential and not relevant to "faithing," which is how we come to believe, including the psychosocial dynamics entailed.

70. David Augsburger, *Pastoral Counseling across Cultures* (Philadelphia: Westminster, 1985), 274.

71. Bultmann, "On the Problem of Demythologizing," in *New Testament and Mythology*, 98, 161.

adequate to speak of transcendence since it portrays the transcendent as spatially distant (heaven above, hell below, earth in between) and equates transcendent powers with immanent powers superior to the latter only "in force and unpredictability"—a caution worth noting.[72] Myth thus gives expression and meaning to a certain understanding of human existence, and is anthropocentric rather than theocentric.

On the other hand, scientific thinking reckons with a closed continuum of cause and effect and presupposes a unitary world that operates without any intervention from otherworldly beings. From the viewpoint of scientific thinking, then, mythic thinking is full of gaps in its attempt to make sense of the inexplicable by adducing otherworldly beings. Of course, Bultmann admits that scientific thinking today differs from that of the eighteenth and nineteenth centuries. But for him, the decisive thing is not the results of science but science's *method*. And this scientific approach is what demythologizing does in interpreting myth in terms of existentialism. This is not a process of abstraction (i.e., abstracting timeless pieces from a mythical framework) but a hermeneutical method, essential if the New Testament narrative is to be believable.

According to Bultmann, the real deal-breaker, the problem with the New Testament is that it is couched in mythic language and has to be interpreted in our day to modern humans. His premise is, however, not peculiar since it tallies with the general ethos of and in continuity with classical liberal theology, which favors an existential approach to interpreting what seems like the breaking in of the otherworldly in time and space and thus sees all biblical miracles as reducible to the existential significance of their message.[73] Without such an existential interpretation, the kerygma is ghettoized and separated from the real, tangible, historical world.

Bultmann further holds that such demythologizing is already in existence within the very Scripture passages of the New Testament—in its hermeneutics and understanding—for instance, in its reconceptualization

72. Bultmann, "On the Problem of Demythologizing," in *New Testament and Mythology*, 98, 161. This is a caution worth noting, especially in views that align with belief in personal evil spiritual beings.

73. Theologians such as Adolf von Harnack, Albrecht Ritschl, and perhaps even Schleiermacher to some extent, are good examples of classical liberalism that attempted to reduce Christianity to its ethical core—its true "essence"—which would be protected from philosophical and scientific prying eyes. To protect the traditional teachings of Scripture, including Christ and his divinity, the cornerstone of Christianity, they reinterpreted them nonmetaphysically—opting for an existential reinterpretation.

of the Fall and its aftermath in death, as explained in Pauline theology,[74] and in his understanding of the "spirit" not just as a supernatural mysterious force outside of the human that breaks in upon the human, but ultimately the "Spirit" and gifts as for the edification of the whole body and as "the possibility in fact of the new life that is disclosed in faith."[75] Furthermore, Bultmann sees that the fruit of the Spirit portrayed in Galatians makes his claim to demythologizing more solid because, in opening ourselves to the Spirit, we become exocentric rather than egocentric, and thus we are freed from the cares attendant to egocentricity. This way, "the Christian understanding of being has been interpreted non-mythically, in existential terms."[76] Bultmann here is making reference to Paul's instructions concerning worship in the new believing community in Corinth (1 Cor. 15:44–58); but it is doubtful whether he reads Paul's intention accurately and whether Paul was already indeed demythologizing what seems to amount to the Jesus legend, in Bultmann's analysis.[77]

In addition, claims Bultmann, many interpreters engage in a form of demythologizing unawares. Such is the case, for example, when people draw out the symbolic meanings of texts in interpretation, as with the Psalms. The facility with which this is done should, in his estimation, minimize anxiety about demythologizing; and any existing angst we might feel is because we assume in part "that there is an either/or between mythology and science"; that is, we are always speaking either mythologically or scientifically. But that is not the case at all. Into what category, for example, do we place phrases such as "I love you" and "pardon me"? Science or myth?[78] Clearly neither category, and yet we know and understand their referent.

Why, then, is there a need for existentialist interpretation? We go to Scripture, a historical document, to learn something about human existence that we might apply to our lives: "[T]he proclamation of the church

---

74. Bultmann, "New Testament and Mythology," 16.

75. Bultmann, "New Testament and Mythology," 20.

76. Bultmann, "New Testament and Mythology," 20–21.

77. See, for example, Marva Dawn's critique of Wink's misreading of Paul and Wink's tendency toward reductionism in his analysis of the language in Ephesians, in Dawn, *Powers, Weakness, and the Tabernacling of God* (Grand Rapids: Eerdmans, 2001), esp. 15–17; and more recently, Robert Moses, *Practices of Power: Revisiting the Principalities and Powers in the Pauline Letters* (Minneapolis: Augsburg Fortress, 2014), esp. chap. 2.

78. Bultmann, "On the Problem of Demythologizing," in *New Testament and Mythology*, 101. Hereafter, page references to this work appear in parentheses within the text.

refers me to scripture as the place where I may hear something decisive about my existence" (106). Demythologizing as existentialist interpretation thus seeks to make clear the character of Scripture "as personal address as kerygma" (114). It is the only context (meaning-seeking moments) in which we hear the word of God addressed to us as individuals in our situations in the now. Of course, that is a purpose of Scripture: to address the individual as an individual and to return us to God's address at creation, "Where art thou?" and to attempt to fashion as honest an answer as possible about where we are located in the grander scheme of things—existential. The only problem is that Scripture is not only history and, secondly, that personal address in terms of the existential dimension is not the primary purpose or direction of Scripture—or even of the address. The address is not to remediate an individual and his or her situation within the existentialist dimension. It is rather that we are confronted with God as the Creator to whom we owe allegiance, honor, and obedience—first and foremost.

Bultmann, however, would disagree; in fact, in an anticipated response to such a charge, he says:

> [E]xistentialist interpretation does not produce the existential relation of Scripture to the reader; it only discloses this relation. It does not justify the truth of Scripture but points to this truth and teaches us to understand it. Similarly, existentialist interpretation of Scripture does not justify proclamation, although it does provide proclamation with the right conceptuality. (104)

Demythologizing does not seek to make faith "rational" or to offer any proof of God. Faith remains a leap. "Demythologizing as existentialist interpretation seeks to make clear and understandable the real mystery of God in its authentic incomprehensibility" (104). For Bultmann, understanding is quite different from rationally explaining something. Moreover, there is no real need to couch kerygma in mythological language, as if the historical epoch in which the salvific event took place is essential to its being believed. The validity of the effects of the event can be recognized anytime.[79] That may well be, except that in Christian faith the event is irrevocably tied to the one believed to be God incarnate, and the invitation is not to know and adhere to a set of axioms but to the one believed in as

---

79. Bultmann, *New Testament and Mythology*, 13.

God. Bultmann seems to jettison the Bible's own internal logic, meaning, and import of the events within the history portrayed in favor of his own meaning of the events, possibly in favor of the philosophical mores of his day and the essential existentialist agenda, as if Scripture were primarily about human beings. As Klein observes, "Bultmann rightly has been criticized because he places so much emphasis on the existential dimension that for him it matters little if any objective or historical events recorded in the New Testament even occurred. This is a serious flaw, because, though Christ's death or resurrection may be inspiring 'mythical events,' if they did not actually occur in history, how can they provide objective atonement or assure the Christian's own resurrection?"[80] His brand of form criticism went as far as putting at risk the historical bases of the Gospels insofar as he assumed the historical aspects of the narrative unnecessary to belief and Christian life.

Demythologizing and Philosophy of Existence

Bultmann deflects the charge that he is too dependent on philosophy by pointing to the purpose of Scripture itself and why modern humans, removed from its initial contexts, read it at all. According to Bultmann, we only approach a text in the first place because we have questions that we are seeking to answer. So we begin with the question. He assumes his question to be as good as any. "The appropriate question with respect to the Bible—at least within the church—is the question about human existence. . . . This is a question that finally motivates questioning and interpreting historical documents generally" (106–7).

How are humans to understand and interpret themselves? Bultmann asks. Is it not true that

> [w]e do not understand ourselves to be so divided as the New
> Testament presents us, so that alien powers can intervene in our
> inner life[?] We ascribe to ourselves an inner unity of states and
> actions, and we call any person who imagines this unity to be split
> by the intervention of divine or demonic powers schizophrenic.[81]

80. William W. Klein et al., *Introduction to Biblical Interpretation* (Dallas: Word, 1993), 105.
81. Bultmann, *New Testament and Mythology*, 5.

In one swoop Bultmann does away with any possibility not only of being influenced by demonic or other evil spiritual forces in the spiritual realm, but also of God and the Holy Spirit intervening in and transforming human life! Regardless of whether we are "nature" or "spirit"—or both simultaneously—we "understand ourselves as unified beings who ascribe their feelings, their thinking, and their willing to themselves."[82] Again, one can agree with Bultmann to a certain extent, especially in terms of ascribing our sins and foibles to ourselves and not defaulting to "the devil made me do it" mode, as is sometimes the case with strong belief in personalized accounts of evil. At the same time, we wonder, then, how to read other accounts of sin as the evil that impinges on us from without or the deliverance from sin and temptation that occurs by prayer and the intervention of the divine, which is so basic to Scripture. For Bultmann, any such talk of the "spirit" and the efficacy of the sacraments ought to be eschewed as unintelligible and thus inappropriate to address modern human beings.[83] How can we or should we talk about the divine? Again, Bultmann anticipates such a question and provides a fairly adequate response in this regard.

How to Talk about the Act of God

Bultmann disavows any charge that demythologizing precludes the possibility that God actually acts. For him, we cannot speak about whether or not God acts without also necessarily speaking about our own existence.

> To talk about God's act means to talk at the same time about my own existence. Because human life is a life in space and time, God's encounter with us can only be an event in the particular here and now. This event of being addressed, questioned, judged, and blessed by God here and now is what is meant by talk about the act of God. (162)

Further still, "being affected by God's act can be talked about only as an existential event that cannot be established or proved objectively" (162). It therefore becomes a confessional statement of faith and not a general

82. Bultmann, *New Testament and Mythology*, 5.
83. Bultmann, *New Testament and Mythology*, 6.

truth. God acts more according to me rather than that God acts. This, according to Bultmann, is a confession of faith. But it seems to me that here Bultmann equates or conflates faith with hope—and perhaps providence. To read my life providentially, which in some extreme cases can slip into fatalism, is not the same as what Scripture describes as faith, that living faith which believes God acts because it knows and has seen that God acts and can thus believe and wait for God to act again (Heb. 11; Rom. 8:28; 2 Cor. 5:7).

Again, Bultmann also declares that to make statements about God's action is to speak first analogically and at once paradoxically. Any other way of framing or thinking about God's act reduces God's act to a process within the world rather than a process of "a God who stands beyond the world," and thus objectifies God (162). In other words, we can only speak existentially with respect to ourselves and God's act; otherwise, we slip into mythic thinking, which we should escape. In mythic thinking, divine action implies that God intervenes in the world continuum, that God acts between other natural events. On the contrary, Bultmann contends that "the idea that divine action is unworldly or transcendent is preserved only if such action is represented not as something taking place *between* occurrences in the world but as something that takes place *in* them, in such a way that the closed continuum of worldly occurrence that presents itself to an objectifying view is left intact" (162). Moreover, it seems that Bultmann is saying that faith needs no evidence for believing. "Radical demythologizing is the parallel to the Pauline-Lutheran doctrine of justification through faith alone—without works of the law. Or, rather, it is the constant application of this doctrine to the field of knowledge. Like the doctrine of justification, it destroys every false security . . ." (162). In short, what we, in objectifying faith, note as miracle is no breaking in of the otherworldly into our world in a way that derails the ordered natural laws of its operation or, in Bultmann's words, "perforate[s] by supernatural powers."[84]

When we consider Bultmann on myth, demythologizing, and the history of the central figure of Christianity—Jesus and the Christ event itself (incarnation, life, death, and resurrection) bracketing ascension—we are left with a fascinating tale that seems to bear little resemblance to the reports of eyewitnesses (martyrs, those who die for their testimony),

---

84. Rudolf Bultmann, *Jesus Christ and Mythology* (New York: Charles Scribner's Sons, 1957), 61.

and thus we have Christian theological words without the Christian meaning.

According to Bultmann, we may believe in the life of Christ without the account of his life as presented in the gospel as historical fact, simply because we cannot believe some passages to be historical fact.

> That God has acted in Jesus Christ is not a historical fact that can be established objectively. . . . On the contrary, the very fact that in the New Testament the person and work of Christ are described in a mythological conceptuality shows that they cannot be understood in the context of world history if they are to be understood as a divine act of salvation.[85]

In other words, we may believe in the teachings of Christ as attested by world history and can be proved or disproved from an objective perspective. But it is pointless to include in such belief other portions of the same Scripture passages that speak about the virgin birth or ascribe deity to Christ, since we cannot prove that objectively, and this latter we leave in the realm of myth, which we can elide in our Christian teaching.

Myth entrenches the gospel and its actors in a particular context and era, and demythologizing is the only way to give it wings and to avoid its being petrified, and so Bultmann believes that demythologizing is essential to faith itself, regardless of one's world picture:

> If the task of demythologizing was originally called for by the conflict between the mythological world picture of the Bible and the world picture formed by scientific thinking, it soon became evident that demythologizing is a demand of faith itself. For faith insists on being freed from bondage to every world picture projected by objectifying thinking, whether it is the thinking of myth or the thinking of science.[86]

Thus does demythologizing call faith back to its original essence: demythologizing is a gift, ultimately, to faith and thus to the kerygma.

---

85. Bultmann, *Jesus Christ and Mythology*, 119–20.
86. Bultmann, *Jesus Christ and Mythology*, 121.

Summary and Critique of Bultmann

In an attempt to make the gospel palatable to modern people—on the face of it, a reasonable idea—Bultmann makes nonsense of the message by first implying that the Gospel writers used the wrong approach to frame their experiences and thus made it impenetrable. This is how Bultmann sees it: what happened to the disciples was what might be called the kind of scales falling off eyes that happens when a crisis moment tips us over the edge and when we see clearly what truly matters. At the crucifixion the disciples, who had been in despair, suddenly woke up out of the stupor of unbelief and understood what Jesus was all about and found new verve for living and rushed out to tell the wonderful news of life after despair. When they proclaimed that Jesus was alive, they did not intend for modern people to think that meant physically alive—but that his story moves onward. Their choice of words and expression was mythological and merely germane to their culture.

The glaring problem with this kind of explanation is that it bypasses the disciples' own claim to confusion and cowering fear after the crucifixion (John 20:1–10, 19) and makes no sense of the enduring, unshakable insistence on a physical resurrection in spite of persecutions and death (see Acts 7–9, which contains the first martyrdom as well as the conversion of the chief persecutor, Paul). Moreover, how could the people of the first century, with their knowledge of metaphorical language, miss the fact that the disciples were just speaking about an experience of new understanding and not an actuality, and how can modern humanity arrive at that particular insight when they are distantiated from the events?

Bultmann's demythologizing, which is steeped in existentialist philosophy, with its very Kantian mechanical direction that assumes a structural reasoning behind religious language, is problematic. This understanding of language and reason leaves us with a language of faith, which assumes that that is what is produced by the believer and is peculiar to the believer without the corporate body. The church, as an offshoot of Israel, exists with a communal identity within a collectivistic culture and ethos, and would find private individual devotion and interpretation an anomaly. Moreover, the same understanding of language assumes that there is something hidden behind the religious language and its expression that the religious believer is not fully aware of. This opacity of language can be addressed only by those outside it who look under and around the language to arrive at what is actually intended in those expressions. Whether the language is spoken in creeds or ritualized in sacraments, what is meant is not really known to the religious believer or, for our purposes, the worshiping body. What Bultmann says could apply to a study of the phenomenology of religion, but as theology it is bankrupt, for it almost comes off as ethnography—and bad ethnography at that. One cannot be outside, or even a participating observer, and claim to know what a religious experience and expression mean for a particular believing body. For in religious believing we do not just *learn* something, but we know experientially; and in the case of Christianity, what we know is not merely something, but someone—a certain someone who inscribes his very life, through his death, indelibly on his followers, enabling them to take up his life and to live it as their own—and yet as his.

Bultmann also assumes that the faith of the believer, the faith that is engendered when the gospel confronts human beings, is itself already inherent in them and is not given to them from outside. The assumed freedom to believe, and thus to decide what one would believe, is itself a false premise. From a Christian theological perspective, while faith does come by hearing, the object of faith is the one who engenders faith in the hearers. The faith of hearers, then, is not something under their own manipulation; it is always still what is given and received. The assumed freedom that is adduced by existentialist philosophy is spurious at best, because it is always circumscribed by the object of faith. Granted that language is not adequate to describe religious experience (not even feeling language can quite capture epiphanies and theophanies). Nevertheless, noetic knowing exists unshakably and has to be expressed in one form or another. To say that language is inadequate to express the experience is one thing; to assume that the experience is not real because of the inadequacy of the language to express it is quite another.[87]

I believe that Wittgenstein can help us here. In his explication of epistemological language, he says that there is nothing hidden behind the language; the language expresses adequately what is; if the religious believer, therefore, uses the expression, for instance, of what God has done or said, then that is it. Moreover, if one belongs to the same language group, that is, if one resides in the language, then one is automatically

---

87. Consider baby talk, e.g., or the basic steps one uses for acquisition of language and to test reading readiness. Equally, as in a game, the rules governing the game are what is important, and their test is whether the game is allowed to be played or not.

included in this declaration. Ronald Thiemann phrases it well when he says that Christian theology is a language, and you either speak it or you don't.[88]

At the same time, there are tensions within Bultmann's primary argument and approach, which, even though I cannot resolve them within the pages of this book, bear noting for further inquiry, because it is likely that his work is more centered than it appears, and the detractors of his seminal approach might be his own inner tensions between his faith and his burgeoning philosophical approach to exegesis. He seems, at best, to be speaking out of both sides of his mouth. No wonder Clark Pinnock describes Bultmann as a polarizing figure in theology today: he wants to hold on to the centrality of Christ for the Christian faith without buying completely into the claims of the first eyewitnesses to the Christ event. That is, the one whom the disciples witness to is both Lord and God, as confirmed in his miracles (Matt. 14:13–21); and his authority over the elements, including death (Luke 8:22–25; John 11:1–44); and his bodily resurrection and ascension (Matt. 28 and parallels). In the final analysis, then, Bultmann is the epitome of one who is too liberal for the evangelicals and too conservative for the liberals. In this he fails Christianity and, even more, himself, because he invites all who would dare be theologians and preachers to be authentic in what and how they believe. He warns both theologians and preachers to desist from picking and choosing what they can believe and disbelieve in the mythical presentations of the gospel, and to be sure of what they are saying if they present the gospel—that the choices are complete acceptance or complete rejection of the mythical world picture.[89] It seems as though Bultmann is inviting us to see Scripture as myth, when the biblical witnesses themselves have stated categorically that what they present is not myth (Paul, Peter, John) and, as Pinnock rightly notes, "one can demyth" myth, but one cannot unevent an event. He underscores the fact that the truth question cannot be dodged or fudged.[90]

88. Ronald F. Thiemann and William C. Placher, *Why Are We Here? Everyday Questions and the Christian Life* (Harrisburg, PA: Trinity Press International, 1998); Thomas Torrance, *The Ground and Grammar of Theology: Consonance between Theology and Science* (Edinburgh: T&T Clark, 1980).

89. Bultmann, *New Testament and Mythology*, 9.

90. Clark H. Pinnock, "Theology and Myth: An Evangelical Response to Demythologizing," *Bibliotheca Sacra* 128, no. 11 (July 1971): 221.

Conclusion

If we have followed the Bultmannian demythologizing route, we have to declare that not only are the devil and the demons nonpersonal spirit beings, but that in reality they do not exist. Jesus did not really cast out demons, since the only world we have and know and in which we operate is that of tangible reality. In the final analysis, what we may glean from Bultmann is that the gospel is better served by jettisoning concepts such as the Fall, Satan, demons, miracles, resurrection, eschatology in the biblical sense—in short, the whole realm of otherworldly beings. In doing so, we also deny the Hebrew worldview that gave context and meaning to the proclamation of the gospel. For Dickson and others like them, that is not a viable prospect.

Embracing the Spirit?

The New Testament gives the Christian world its most comprehensive understanding of spiritual forces and the place and influence of spirits in human affairs. To this end, I will return to our investigations of New Testament sources in the later chapters. Now it is necessary to acknowledge that even the Gospels, the primary sources from which many derive their language and understanding of the principalities and powers, do not contain a univocal portrayal of the place, function, and understanding of the presence of these powers in humans' affairs in general, and in Christians' affairs in particular.

Graham Twelftree's extensive work on exorcism in the first century yields very important findings for our discussion because it provides a glimpse of what could be considered traditional/orthodox Christian pictures of the unseen world painted in Scripture, which we usually find under the rubric "principalities and powers," based on ideas about exorcism. Twelftree notes that patristic writings of the first century amplify for modern readers what they can easily miss about the significance of the presence of these powers and belief in them in New Testament documents, especially the Gospels.[1] Rather than focus on the Gospels exclusively, Twelftree starts with the Pauline Epistles because they are the earliest writings. His explorations of these texts, and the emphasis on Paul's language of the powers, led him to conclude that Paul was aware of Jesus as an exorcist and miracle-worker. Additionally, he points out that within Paul's own context, the demonic is extended to include the supernatural operat-

---

1. Graham Twelftree, *In the Name of Jesus: Exorcism among Early Christians* (Grand Rapids: Baker Academic, 2007), 31–32.

67

ing powers behind world systems and organizations, as evidenced by his usage of "principalities and powers" (Eph. 1:19b–23; 6:10–13). While there is seemingly scant attention devoted to exorcism in Paul's own ministry in Acts and in the several Epistles to the churches, there nevertheless exists sufficient evidence to indicate that Paul was familiar with Jesus's engagement with demonic spirit beings, and that he had followed this example in his own ministry. For how else are we to understand the following biblical texts and Paul's allusions to "signs and wonders" and the proclamation of the good news in "word and deed"?[2] Furthermore, Paul's own involvement with exorcism is portrayed in Acts 16:16–18, as well as in 19:11–20, which involves Paul's clothing and the story of the sons of Sceva and their encounter with the demonic. The point of the story is to underscore the power of Paul as an exorcist of such spiritual power that even healing was transmitted, unbeknownst to him, through his clothing to sufferers, as the demonized and the evil spirits came out of them.[3]

Treatments of the Powers in the Gospels

The Gospels give us by far the most comprehensive architecture of exorcism in the New Testament, though it is by no means a univocal picture, as I have already noted. In the synoptic Gospels, for example, we observe Mark's depiction of Jesus as a miracle worker who confronts the devil and his cohorts via various exorcisms; and the language of the demonic attends almost all of Jesus's healings that Mark records.[4] Matthew's healing sto-

---

2. See Rom. 15:18–19; 1 Cor. 4:20, which is found in the synoptic Gospels (Matt. 12:28; Luke 11:20), indicating the possibility of Paul's knowledge of the miracles of Jesus. For elaboration, see Twelftree, *In the Name of Jesus*, 62–63.

3. There are NT scholars who argue for a discontinuity in thought between Paul and his portrayal of Jesus's ministry and early Judaism and rabbinic literature (cf. Hendrik Berkhof). This is an important issue, and I will take it up later, when I will deal with the various approaches to understanding the powers in modern NT scholarship and argue for a continuity within discontinuity as the proper stance to assume toward the Pauline position on the powers.

4. Twelftree, *In the Name of Jesus*, 118. Twelftree argues persuasively that it is as possible to read in Mark's accounts of exorcism a complete lack of sociopolitical connections despite the Roman occupation of Judea, as some have suggested. Citing examples of Matthew's references to legions of angels, he demonstrates adequately, I think, why a sociopolitical reading should not be favored over the theological reading. See details of the argument in chapter 5.

ries carry the same profile (Matt. 4:23–24; cf. Luke 8:32–33). The disciples themselves are taught and given authority to cast out demons in the name of Jesus; in fact, exorcism is seen as the disciples' major task during the time they await *parousia*.

The Lukan account follows a similar pattern, listing the casting out of evil spirits as among Jesus's miracles and as evidence of his divinity (Luke 7:20). It depicts him, in his healing of Peter's mother-in-law, in the pose of a traditional exorcist of the first century, "standing over her" and "rebuking" the fever.[5] Not only are the twelve sent out to teach and heal and cast out demons in the name of Jesus, but also the seventy, and all other followers, are to cast out demons in the name of Jesus. They are seen as workers in the kingdom even if they are not part of the identified band of followers (Luke 10).

The Gospel of John, however, pays little to no attention to the language of the demonic attached to miracles as such. Among the various explanations for the silence, the most plausible explanation is not that John was unaware of Jesus's role as an exorcist; rather, it was that he "was aware of the traditions reflected in the synoptics and intended to correct and surpass them."[6] Rather than dwelling on healings and exorcisms of a few people, John shows Jesus himself as being accused of demon possession. In his responses to those who so charge him, Jesus confronts the powers behind this questioning of his credibility as one who derives from God. In this way, the battle between Jesus and Satan is fought in the arena of the unbelief of the Jews (especially the Jewish authorities)—and a far more important zone than in the lives of individual broken persons (John 8:44).[7] Altogether, the Gospels portray a world in which evil spiritual beings were believed to be the cause of several ailments and diseases, and Jesus, who went about doing good, was depicted as one who overcame these evil spiritual forces by the word of command and rebuke in the manner of

5. Twelftree, *In the Name of Jesus*, 132.

6. Twelftree, *In the Name of Jesus*, 188. Here Twelftree examines arguments from several textual criticisms and draws the conclusion that a growing number of NT scholars find this explanation most adequate for understanding the evangelist John's silence about exorcisms as well as miraculous healings. Regarding assumed silence about exorcism: rather than seeing the absence of exorcisms as silence on the subject in this more theological of the Gospels, the intensification of the importance of the demonic to John is highlighted in the way in which the Son of man, not humans, is the one who is accused of being demon-possessed.

7. Twelftree, *In the Name of Jesus*, 205.

the exorcists of his day, bringing freedom to all who sought his help. The Gospels thus portray Jesus as operating *within* his religiocultural context, not transcending it.

Since the Epistles—and later the Gospels—are a window into the life of the earliest churches, and further because these churches gave us the Gospels, what we understand from them tells us what the first Christians believed about the spirit world and our proper attitude toward it. From our descriptions so far, we can conclude that the earliest Christians believed in a personal evil that inhabited and controlled individuals—and also sometimes controlled social entities, such as political structures.[8]

Christians are given authority to rebuke and exorcise and free those bound by evil spiritual powers—not by some textual formulas, but in the name of Jesus—based on a relationship with Jesus that confers authority for such a task on the part of the believer. In addition, demons and other evil spiritual beings are personalized rather than depersonalized in the various Gospel accounts.

The Patristic Period and the Powers

There is an obvious continuity in the patristic literature, with the biblical views on the spirit world due to the early church's proximity to the events recorded in the New Testament. As with the New Testament, we find no uniformity in thought regarding belief in the spirit world and its influence on earthly existence. The church fathers I have surveyed all held strong beliefs and conveyed them in ways unique to their purpose and aim, often alongside other doctrinal teachings and especially concerning the celebration of the sacraments. Even though some of the theological ideas in the texts will become relevant later in this discussion—as I forge a theology of the spirit world for pastoral practice in the concluding chapter—in this section I will include a selective overview and relevant quotes.

8. It is possible to raise the question of a transpersonal or suprapersonal evil as well, considering the analysis of the powers and their influence at the individual and sociopolitical levels, but that would be beyond the scope of this project. What exactly transpersonal evil and/or suprapersonal evil might portend—and whether it affects the ascription of a person to these powers in any way—is perhaps irrelevant in the long run. We can only surmise any such possibilities, at best, and their presence or absence adds nothing to and detracts nothing from what we are offered in Scripture about sources and causes of evil.

Justin Martyr

In Justin Martyr's' *First and Second Apologies*, especially in the first, we are offered glimpses of his belief in the influence of the demonic in the lives of ordinary people.[9] In the *First Apology*, as part of his refutation of anti-Christian slanders, Justin suggests that his accusers are acting irrationally under the influence of demons.

> In our case [i.e., that of the Christians], who pledge ourselves to do nothing wicked, not to hold these godless opinions, you do not investigate the charges made against us; but, giving in to unreasoning passion, and the instigation of evil demons, you punish us without trial or consideration. For the truth shall be told; since of old these evil demons manifested themselves, both defiled women and corrupted boys, and showed terrifying sights to people, that those who did not use their reason in judging the acts that were done, were filled with terror; and being taken captive by fear, and not knowing that these were demons, they called them gods, and gave to each the name the demon had chosen for himself. And when Socrates tried, by true reasoning and definite evidence, to bring these things to light, and deliver people from the demons, then the demons themselves, by means of people who rejoiced in wickedness, compassed his death, as an atheist and impious person, on the charge of introducing new divinities; and in our case they show a similar activity.[10]

The figure of Socrates stands as the counterexample: clear-thinking, virtuous, and similarly accused. If among the Greeks the divine Logos revealed itself through Socrates, among the Gentiles the Logos actually took shape and became the man Jesus Christ. Provocatively, Justin does not hesitate to say that the pagan gods are actually demons in disguise.[11]

9. Justin Martyr, *The First and Second Apologies*, trans. Leslie William Barnard (Mahwah, NJ: Newman Press, 1997).

10. Justin Martyr, 1 Apology, 5: 29–33, in Justin Martyr, *The First and Second Apologies*, 25–26.

11. Justin Martyr, *The First and Second Apologies*, 27. Included in this treatise are the translator's helpful sketches of the main features of second-century belief in demons, which was widespread and influential, particularly among the Stoics (note esp. 30 and 108).

Athanasius

The single most influential patristic source of information on demonic activities and spiritual warfare is Athanasius's *Life of Antony*.[12] By providing such a persuasive and appealing portrait of Antony's ascent to holiness, Athanasius's work ignited a fire of interest in monasticism throughout the Mediterranean world. Of course, it would be possible to elaborate or occasionally disagree with the material found in these pages, but Athanasius's account unquestionably provides the template with which subsequent writers (e.g., Cassian) would take up the themes related to Christian asceticism and the quest for holiness. The context and content of that work is the treatment of demonic activity and the monk's proper attitude and response to it, which appears primarily in the course of a long address given by Antony to the monks who had followed him out into the Egyptian desert (paras. 21–33, pp. 107–33). The passage needs to be read carefully in its entirety, but some general observations are in order.

1. Throughout *The Life*, Antony's example and words give the impression that following God through prayer, poverty, and so on, is a freeing and joyful thing, not an onerous or depressing way of life, and even Antony's great physical suffering at the hands of the demons does not substantially alter this picture (para. 8.2–3, p. 79).[13] In at least one place, this "easy yoke" of Antony's discipleship is described in terms of the virtues.[14]

12. Athanasius of Alexandria, *The Life of Antony: The Coptic and the Greek Life*, trans. Tim Vivian and Apostolos N. Athanassakis (Kalamazoo, MI: Cistercian, 2003). (Hereafter, paragraph and page references to this work appear in parentheses within the text.) It may be of interest to some readers that this translation is from a critical text developed by G. J. M. Bartelink for the French patristic series Sources Chrétiennes, and is thus an improvement over older translations dependent upon Migne. Most of the quotes below have been taken from the Greek version of *The Life* and are noted thus: *The Life of Antony* (Greek).

13. See, e.g., para. 59, pp. 183–85; para. 61, p. 189; and para. 63, p. 191. In a way, this is surprising, given the great number of pictures showing Antony pulled and pummeled by demons. (An engraving on this theme, produced by Martin Schongauer, served as the basis for Michelangelo's first-known painting.)

14. We need not ascribe these virtues purely to the sanctifying work of the Holy Spirit, for as note 140 points out, "the influences here are stoic, platonic, and origenist" (Athanasius, "The Nature of Virtue" in *The Life of Antony* [Greek], para. 20, p. 105). Antony: "Do not be afraid to hear about virtue and do not be surprised at the term. For

2. The basic framework of a contest waged against invisible powers is found in what the apostle Paul established in Scripture.[15] So he requires the monks to understand the nature and extent of the demons' deceptions: forewarned is forearmed (para. 21, p.109). Yet more than mere knowledge is required here. Prayer and ascetic discipline have value insofar as they lead to the proper use of the gift of discernment of spirits (para. 21, pp. 111, 135).[16] Wrestling with demons is, of course, not the purpose, but a by-product of the monk's calling.

3. Antony regards the demons as sinful, shape-shifting spirits. When defeated, he notes, they may quickly return in another guise. Ultimately, however, the demons are powerless, and Christians have nothing to fear from them (para. 21, pp. 115, 117, 123, 125). Some powers the demons appear to possess, like foretelling the future, are in fact illusory (pp. 129–35). And we can add that some gifts in operation today may be more mediumistic gifts than charismatic gifts from the Spirit.[17]

The proper Christian attitude, therefore, combines contempt for the devil with total confidence in God. The following quote expresses the typical brio Antony brings to the subject: "Let us be even more courageous and let us always rejoice because we are being saved. Let us reflect in our souls that the Lord is with us: he has routed the demons and rendered them impotent. Let us be mindful of this and always remember that when the Lord is with us, our enemies can do nothing to us. . . . If they find us rejoicing in the Lord and thinking thoughts about the good things to come, keeping our hearts set on the Lord and his works and reflecting on the fact that everything is in the Lord's hands, that a demon has not power against a Christian and has absolutely no authority

---

virtue is not far from us, nor does it stand outside us; it works within us, and the task is easy if only we want it to be" (*Life of Antony* [Greek], para. 20.2–3, p. 105).

15. *Life of Antony* (Greek), para. 21, p. 109 (cf. Eph. 6:12–17).

16. Cf. 1 Cor. 12:7, 10. "Their villainies are numerous, as are the disturbances caused by their connivances, but the blessed Apostle and his companions knew about such things: 'We are not ignorant of his thoughts'" (para. 22.4, p. 111 [cf. 2 Cor. 2:11]).

17. Certain modern-day "prophetic utterances" from self-styled men of God that attempt to predict the future of individuals with details of their life in the more charismatic/Pentecostal congregations are a good example of what I mean here.

over anyone, then seeing the soul made secure with thoughts of this kind, they turn away, ashamed" (para. 42.3–7, p. 149).

4. Christians have many weapons they can use in spiritual battle:

    a. First and foremost is a deep knowledge of Scripture. Athanasius emphasizes how Antony learned via attentive listening and obedient action (para. 42.3, pp. 57, 59). "Indeed, he paid such close attention to the reading of Scripture that nothing in it was wasted. He remembered everything, with the result that for him memory took the place of books" (para. 3.7, p. 63).

    b. The psalms, in particular, are useful for warding off demons (para. 3.7, p. 91).

    c. Other weapons include living an upright life and keeping faith in God. For the monk of the desert, such a life took concrete form in solitude and self-denial: "Without a doubt, demons are afraid of ascetic practices: fasting, keeping vigils, prayers, gentleness, tranquility, poverty, moderation, humility, love of the poor, almsgiving, the absence of anger and, above all, devotion to Christ" (para. 30.2, p. 127).

    d. Ignoring the demons and making the sign of the cross are also recommended (para. 30.2, p. 135).

John Cassian

John Cassian, in exhorting monks to be watchful and vigilant, cautions them about hidden temptations to vice, some of which could come from the devil.[18] The antidote to being tripped up is to subject all temptations to discernment, as a moneychanger would, weeding out the counterfeit by careful weighing and inspecting, for even seemingly good forms of piety can be harboring the seeds of evil. In other words, there was the belief in a personal devil who could tempt believers who were not watchful, and this concept has allusions to the temptation of Jesus portrayed in the Gospels (Matt. 4 and parallels). But, in *The Seventh Conference*, "On the Changeable-

18. John Cassian, *The Conferences*, trans. Boniface Ramsey, OP (Mahwah, NJ: Newman Press, 1997). Hereafter, page references to this work appear in parentheses within the text.

ness of the Soul and Evil Spirits," in which he establishes what we might term the locus classicus on spiritual warfare, Cassian notes that human beings preserve their *freedom* in the encounter with demons. We should not be quick to blame the devil for wandering thoughts: "It is in our power to set up in our hearts either ascents, which are thoughts that touch God, or descents, which sink down to earthly and carnal things" (250).[19] Also, on the nature of demons, and citing Abba Serenus, he notes that "they can only incite us to wickedness but do not force us" (255), and that though they may take up residence, so to speak, in the body—they, also, are embodied creatures, though in a spiritual fashion—but not in the soul, for only God is truly incorporeal (255; cf. 277n.7.13). From this it follows that demons cannot read our thoughts; rather, they carefully observe us and from our words and gestures deduce what areas of weakness we may offer (257); "thus they have subtle knowledge of who is given to what vice" (258), and herein lies the reason many fall rather than withstand temptations.

From the *Eighth Conference*, "On Principalities and Powers," which is made up mainly of Abba Serenus's thoughts on the nature and activity of demons, we gather that he envisions the air between earth and heaven to be populated thickly by demons, who are made invisible to us by the gracious ordination of God, for our benefit and safety (298). God has graciously ordained that these dread creatures be normally invisible. The scriptural names and titles have much to teach us about the nature of demons; for example, "dominations" seek to dominate and rule over different peoples (300–301). Moving beyond Scripture, "the clear visions and the experiences of holy persons also have much to teach us" (301).[20] As used by Serenus, experience functions in the mode of corroboration; it is not an independent authority to be weighed against the witness of Scripture. Cassian is not interested in what someone—anyone—has experienced, but only in what the holiest saints have to teach from their spiritual battling. This is an important point for reflection, and I will raise it in the following chapters as I consider present-day understanding of the

19. I will return to this later, when I deal with the issues affecting the Christian in the everydayness of life and the cost of the call to discipleship, which includes wrestling with "principalities and powers."

20. Later I will explore experience and what that means for affirming belief in a cogent way that does not turn into what Harvey Cox terms a cult of experience, becoming nothing more than expressing "touchy feeling"; see Harvey Cox, *Fire from Heaven: The Rise of Pentecostal Spirituality and the Reshaping of Religion in the Twenty-first Century* (Reading, MA: Addison-Wesley, 1995), 300.

principalities and powers among those for whom belief in evil spiritual beings characterizes common life.

Numerous other examples could be drawn from the writings of the church fathers on the nature of demons and the influence of spirit beings on earthly life, and how this undergirds belief and acceptance of such occurrences among the faithful.[21]

What we have in this treatise and the previous insights from the fathers is a clear indication that the church functioned with this literal belief about personal evil, following the example recorded in Scripture about numerous encounters with the demonic and other spirit beings; further, that such thinking and understanding, in light of what we observe in more primal cultures, endured until the modern, especially post-Enlightenment, period, as we see in some Puritan (and even Reformed) interpretations (which I will explore in chapter 5).

The distinctive component of these texts is the emphasis on the holiness and the tendency toward asceticism of the personalities we encounter.[22] It is likely that this growth toward holiness—ascent, movement to *theosis*—is the magnet to demonic attack and subsequent engagement in spiritual warfare.[23] This characteristic mimics the example of Jesus as portrayed in the Gospels, for in his presence the demons and evil spirits became agitated and revealed themselves (cf. Mark and parallels). Could it be that a lack of "holy living" and what the saints have described as "striving in prayer, vigils, fastings," and so on (the ancient spiritual practices that help to sanctify Christians and move them toward more godliness—*Theosis*—is what may be obscuring and even eradicating what was

21. For instance, there are indispensable catechetical materials such as those by Cyril of Jerusalem. See *The Works of Saint Cyril of Jerusalem*, vol. 1, trans. Leo P. McCauley, SJ, and Anthony A. Stephenson (Washington, DC: The Catholic University of America Press, 1969), esp. Catechesis II, "On Repentance, the Remission of Sin, and the Adversary."

22. These texts are usually referred to as the Hagiography of the Saints. See, e.g., John F. Haldon, *A Tale of Two Saints: The Martyrdoms and Miracles of Saints Theodore 'The Recruit' and 'The General'* (Liverpool, UK: Liverpool University Press, 2016); and David Williams, *Saints Alive: Word, Image, and Enactment in the Lives of the Saints* (Montreal: McGill-Queen's University Press, 2010).

23. We might perhaps ponder the link between apparent absence of demonic experiences in the West and a dormant church life with possible pointers to lack of conscious growth toward holiness among church membership. It is good enough to define holiness as meaning "set apart" for God, and to say that the saints are those called of God, but surely that which is holy should not preclude purity.

normal Christian life and experience of the apostles and earlier saints of the faith? Could it be that in the West the presence of the demonic is muted not because demons have ceased to exist or never were, but for the precise reason that no one fights against nothing? Perhaps, as long as lukewarm faith exists, perhaps the demons need not be troubled nor trouble themselves.[24] While the purpose of the Christian life is not to irritate demons and incur their wrath through spiritual attacks, a quasi Christianity that is washed out and bears little resemblance to what is epitomized in the Acts of the Apostles and the Epistles and demonstrated in the account of Jesus in the Gospels is also bankrupt in holiness and power. It is probable that the lack of knowledge and experience of the presence of the demonic in modern times—through to our current times—has made it easy to turn Christianity into a primarily cerebral, morality-infusing code for civilizing humanity, rather than the life-transforming, Satan-crushing, God-glorifying powerful religion or lifestyle that was intended. But the obverse is also possible: that the cerebral tenor of the message and messengers have robbed the gospel of its power. We seem to have exegeted (almost exorcised) the power out of the *Logos* and propped it up with philosophy.[25] In the final chapters, where I address the problem of the bifurcation in understanding of and belief in spiritual powers, I shall return to this issue and suggest a viable hermeneutical lens for a faithful reading of these pertinent texts.

Treatments of the Powers in Modernity

The question that continues to plague even Christians today with regard to issues of the demonic and other spirit beings is whether a modern scien-

24. We might say that even today, in the places where belief in the demonic characterizes common life and where exorcisms seemingly abound, Christians do not follow the scriptural pattern and have turned themselves into what could be termed "demon whisperers." But Scripture is clear that Jesus and the disciples were not demon-whisperers, but ones whose presence disturbed and threatened the forces of darkness.

25. This is not an indictment against philosophy, because I value its contribution to theological insights. But when the Bible is used in courses under the rubric of biblical studies and only peripherally, if at all, in other areas of theology, it gives pause for reflection. My experience in twelve years of theological education allows the conclusion that it is possible to study theology formally and grapple with weighty theological concepts for many years in a seminary without reference to the Bible. To be biblicist seems to be the worst error a theologian can commit.

tific worldview can accommodate, with any degree of credibility, the world encountered in the pages of Scripture. Modernity assumes a cosmos that is ordered and explainable by scientific means. The tangible reality that is presented is assumed to be the *reality* of existence. Reading the Bible through the lenses of modernity seems strange at best, and often passages that speak of a world teeming with demons and other spirit beings—a world in which the encroachment of the sphere outside human knowability and control constantly impinges on one's existence and whose favor we are to cull by various propitiations, and whose wrath we dread—are often dismissed as primitive and prescientific approaches to understanding the cosmos. For modern humanity, the cosmos is the tangible sphere under human control, governed by inviolable physical laws of nature. To believe in a biblical world, with its three-tiered cosmology—heaven above, earth in the middle, and an underworld of evil spiritual beings below—is unwarranted. With our scientific understanding of the universe has come the impetus to demythologize the language of Scripture in order to make it accessible to modern human beings.

There are many, however, who read Scripture in the present day with the understanding and lenses much closer to biblical times. In effect, their reading is in conformity with the earliest people of faith, and many of these readers still live in cultures where belief in a spirit world that impinges on the natural world is prevalent. If Christians are called to a living faith as one body, they are called not just to believe but are called to believe *with* the apostles and fathers of the faith. But how do present-day Christians live this faith in ways that are intelligible and at the same time remain faithful to the kernel of Scripture that grounds faith? Both of these components are essential for accomplishing the *telos* of Scripture: that all would believe in the one whom God has sent, and in believing have eternal life.[26] If we are called to believe not just with the saints of old but with the saints of today, and if, further, as Ray Anderson argues, our normative interpretive lenses should come from the future and not the first-century church,[27] what would reading Scripture today with, say, Christians from the global South look like? What lenses for interpretation and understanding should one wear?

26. Ellen Charry, *By the Renewing of Your Minds: The Pastoral Function of Christian Doctrine* (New York: Oxford University Press, 1999), explores at length the salutary purpose of Scripture.

27. Ray Anderson, *The Shape of Practical Theology: Empowering Ministry with Theological Praxis* (Downers Grove, IL: InterVarsity Press, 2001).

The above question becomes more pertinent because the largest numbers and fastest growth rates of the Christian church are in the two-thirds world, among those people who hold to the powerful myths of Scripture. If the momentum of theology, its study, its written legacy for the church, has always found its greatest expression where the church exists in its vitality (see examples across the church's various epochs from Jerusalem to Alexandria), it is imperative that we pay attention with ecclesial and academic seriousness to the theology that is evidenced by the life of the church in these regions, especially in Africa.[28] Reading Scripture with such people in mind might not only open up possibilities of growth for the church in the West, but also offer possibilities for dialogic encounters that seek to bridge the gap in interpretation and understanding of Scripture and offer both the Western and the Southern church the foundation for living into their common identity as those who declare about themselves that they are of "One Lord, One Faith, and One Baptism," awaiting "One Hope."

Wink and Our Times

Perhaps no other writer in our time has given breadth and depth to our knowledge and understanding of the powers and tried to offer the appropriate language with which to think and talk about them as has Walter Wink. In his trilogy,[29] which is based on critical analysis of the language of powers in several pertinent texts, he concludes that the powers are "the visible and invisible aspects of real social, structural, and material entities in the world."[30] More so—and here he follows Henry Corbin's archetypal psychology—these powers are, or have, "immaterial materiality" com-

---

28. As Andrew Walls observes, "What happens within the African Churches in the next generation will determine the whole shape of church history for centuries to come; what sort of theology is most characteristic of the Christianity of the twenty-first century may well depend on what has happened in the minds of African Christians in the interim" (Andrew Walls, "Towards Understanding Africa's Place in Christian History," in *Religion in a Pluralistic Society*, ed. John S. Pobee [Leiden: Brill, 1976], 183; for a fuller account, see 180–89).

29. Walter Wink, *Naming the Powers: The Language of Power in the New Testament* (Philadelphia: Fortress, 1984); *Unmasking the Powers: The Invisible Forces That Determine Human Existence* (Philadelphia: Fortress, 1986); *Engaging the Powers: Discernment and Resistance in a World of Domination* (Minneapolis: Fortress, 1992).

30. Wink, *Naming the Powers*, 118.

pared to the sensible world, since they possess corporeality and spatiality without substance.[31] The powers, then, seem to be almost real—but not quite.

I have elsewhere engaged Wink's trilogy on the powers, and here I shall extend that argument as I focus on him as a representative voice of a structural approach to the powers in a postmodern vein.[32] I draw attention especially to his insights on prayer as engagement of the powers, or what in today's parlance is known widely as "spiritual warfare." But first, let me briefly delineate his understanding of the powers—their origin and function.

The Powers: Inner Realities of Outer Structures

Postmodern approaches to the understanding of the spiritual world are nebulous at best, especially as Wink uses them in his work. He allows for the presence of the spiritual and even uses scriptural words to describe the spiritual world; but the words are shorn of their scriptural connotations, becoming quasi-psychodynamic in his use of them. The understanding of "spirit" here is the *essence* that drives individuals or corporations, rather than a corporeal autonomous being. It seems as though Wink is saying that these spirits are good spirits, but that improper use of them turns them into the demonic (giving the impression, again, of an essence rather than a superhuman being).[33] At the same time, there seem to be spirits that resist corruption, such as the angels, and it is unclear whether these also are spirits born of human goodness and preserved by human goodness or not. So here we have spirits that are tainted by human evil (never mind accounting for whence the evil comes), but spirits who have managed to evade the clutches of human evil, and who, in the final analysis, seem to be real entities and not some nebulous spirits or essence. Picture it, Wink invites us:

> The understanding of powers we're working with, then, is something like a circle with something—something hard to see—inside

31. Wink, *Naming the Powers*, 144.

32. See Esther Acolatse, *For Freedom or Bondage? A Critique of African Pastoral Practices* (Grand Rapids: Eerdmans, 2014).

33. This conclusion seems to be the main thrust of Wink's argument throughout his analysis and interpretation of the language of the powers in the New Testament.

of it. The circle is the outer form of the systems and structures: the bureaucrats, the buildings. . . and the territory that it has as its area of concern, its market. Those outer elements of the principalities and powers, which are visible, also provide a way into the spirituality of that corporation or institution or nation or church. By looking at the outer forms, we can infer the spirituality to some degree. Then there are other ways—prayer, meditation, intuitive sensing—of trying to discern the interiority of that institution or structure or system. That requires a new way of thinking.[34]

The obvious problem with Wink's attempt to explicate what the New Testament, as well as intertestamental literature and language, means by the powers is the inconsistency in his own language. While he does give us psychosocial approaches to reading the New Testament narratives and Pauline theological anthropology, his assumptions about what the words point to are a reaction to the tendency to overspiritualize evil—especially systemic evil. In using the same terminology, but with different meanings, Wink further contributes to the confusion of how to understand these powers and how they operate. For Wink, the signified and the process of signification are mediated by the signifier, and thus can change according to the viewpoint of the signifier. The signified is constantly shifting and thus not fully apprehended or appropriately named as such.

When it comes to the direct relationship to our project, how can we speak not only about the otherworldly powers, but how can we engage and put on the whole armor of God and its attendant prayer in the fight against evil spiritual powers, as Scripture enjoins? Wink's insights on prayer and what is at stake will be a focus.

Wink and the Powers That Be

Walter Wink's comprehensive studies on the language of power in the New Testament offer us a new avenue for considering the meaning of the powers in general and how to engage them in particular. His own point of departure, as he notes, is from the work of William Stringfellow, whose bold foray into a nonclassical individualistic account of the powers piqued

---

34. Walter Wink, "Principalities and Powers: A Different Worldview," *Church and Society* 85, no. 5 (1995): 18–28.

Wink's interest.[35] Cognizant of the inherent difficulties one can encounter while reading the New Testament and its descriptions of the demonic, especially its language of the powers and what it means to don battle gear and prepare for warfare, as it were, he attempts to provide meaning and traction for the word "power" in its overall usage in Scripture. In particular, how can we understand Satan and the demonic—their character and their function vis-à-vis the created order? The difficulty with pinpointing exactly what these powers are lies largely in the fluid way that word is used throughout Scripture. Drawing synthetically on usage throughout the New Testament, he identifies certain characteristics of power. His conclusion is that power has both physical and spiritual dimensions, and that in any given situation both dimensions may be operative.

In the first place, though the language of "power" pervades the New Testament, the word occurs in several forms with different nuances of meaning. In several places we encounter the pair "principalities and powers." We also see "authority and power" (Luke 4:36); "power and name" (Acts 4:7); "kings and rulers" (*archontes*, Acts 4:26); and "those in authority" (*hoi exousiazontes*, Luke 22:25). "Not only do expressions for power tend to be paired, they also attract each other into series or strings, as if power were so diffuse and impalpable a phenomenon that words must be heaped up in clusters in order to catch a sense of its complexity."[36] Take, for example, this passage from Romans 8:38–39, with its enumeration of various powerful structures and its references to powers that impinge on human affairs:

> For I am convinced that neither death, nor life, nor angels, nor rulers, nor things present, nor things to come, nor powers, nor height, nor depth, nor anything else in all creation, will be able to separate us from the love of God in Christ Jesus our Lord. (Rom. 8:28–29)

The things enumerated above, the string of representative powers are what confirm for Wink the possibility of the powers also being earthly governments, political and/or oppressive social systems of any kind. This fact,

---

35. See Wink's review essay on the work of William Stringfellow: "William Stringfellow: Theologian of the Next Millennium," *CrossCurrents* 45, no. 2 (1995): 205–16.

36. Wink, *Naming the Powers*, 8. Hereafter, page references to this work appear in parentheses in the text.

he notes, is by no means an avenue to demythologizing them into categories of modern sociology, depth psychology, and general systems theory. There are "inner spiritual aspects of these outer realities" and hence the need to attend to their composite dimensions. These inner aspects are the "the spirituality of institutions," the innards, as it were, of the containers or outward structures of power. These inner aspects constitute the "spirit or driving force that animates, legitimates, and regulates its physical manifestation in the world." So, whatever the institution, secular or sacred, whatever the position of power it wields, there is an inner dimension at work in the visible system at play that must not be discounted in our reckoning with them, for these inner dimensions are what determine the life of the institutions and structures. Wink says that, if any power "places itself above God's purposes for the good of the whole, then that Power becomes demonic" (5). Articulated thus, the demonic is not an inherent quality in things so much as the result of "thingingness" gone awry: a thing that has lost its proper moorings with respect to the Creator and the creative purpose, and that, in the end, will be rehabilitated in time to the glory of Christ. While some of this concept is on point and in agreement with Scripture—in that, for example, rulers and authorities can be brought under subjection to God and thus be transformed—it seems spurious to be speaking of rehabilitating death.

To illustrate, Wink offers us what we might term the metamorphoses of "the Satan" and his demonic hosts. In the Old Testament we find three appearances of the Satan, and every aspect of those appearances points to Satan as God's servant, one who comes to human beings as an ally of God to refine, sift, and extract the dross from humans so that they might, as it were, conform to the *imago Dei*. In fact, there was no real differentiation between God and the Satan: good and evil alike were attributed to Yahweh; it was only gradually that a differentiation began to develop, as Israel sought to make sense of both the dark and light side of God. The obvious splitting (like an infant splitting the good and bad mother in psychodynamic understanding) is what creates good angels as opposed to Satan and bad demons. Somehow we have a fragmented Godhead to accommodate Israel's moral dilemma, but there does not seem to be an adequate explanation for how we get Satan and demons, as opposed to God and the angels, in Wink's scheme.[37]

37. We need to note that stories of Satan's origin are not clearly spelled out in Scripture, that what we have is shrouded in paradox, and that the ambiguity of the re-

Satan's first appearance on the world scene points to exactly this primary characteristic. In Job, when he tests primordial man, Satan is God's collaborator, and the narrative indicates that he is a member of God's court, perhaps God's prosecuting attorney. He is in every sense God's servant, until he oversteps his bounds and his prosecuting turns into entrapment (Job 1:6–12); this is quickly followed by his instigating people into sin, such as his appearance in the census, which causes David's falling out with God (1 Chron. 21:1); and on to being an accuser and judge when he dares to trample a weak vessel of the Most High, the high priest of Israel, Joshua (Zech. 3:1–5). In these three episodes we see the demise of a servant of Yahweh, one who falls from grace because he oversteps the bounds of his office—as happens to all earthly powers when they use their office out of line with the Creator's intentions. The powers are thus not evil in themselves; it is their intent that produces evil. It is almost as though they are victims of the evil that they themselves produce. What is unclear is how Wink accounts for the genesis of this evil at all; he never addresses such an important part of his work, and that absence gives one pause.

In the New Testament, Satan is again depicted by Wink as playing the role of God's ally in certain key passages. One such passage describes an exchange between Jesus and Peter, who is intent on persuading Jesus not to go to Jerusalem and his impending death. Jesus sounds the warning cry to Peter, when he refers to the latter, point blank, as Satan and commands him to retreat. In his admonishment and encouragement of Peter, Jesus speaks of an attempt on Satan's part to sift the band of disciples; but the prayer of Jesus would strengthen Peter, who would, in turn, offer such strength to the rest of the disciples (Luke 22:31–34). For Wink, this was no more than the artful work of refinement that they needed for their faith to mature.

> Satan is God's sifter, the left hand of God, whose task is to strain out the impurities in the disciples' commitment to God. . . . Satan has made a legitimate request; they deserve to be put to the test. Jesus has to grant Satan's request. He does not pray that they will be delivered from the test but only that their faith will not fail through it. Satan is depicted here as able to accomplish something that Jesus had himself been unable to achieve during his ministry.[38]

---

ality of both Satan and other evil spiritual beings, such as demons, is part of the mystery we encounter in the narratives concerning evil that we are certain of.

38. Walter Wink, "The World Systems Model," in *Understanding Spiritual Warfare:*

Thus, according to Wink, Jesus seemingly conscripts Satan into his disciple-forming agenda. Not only is Satan an ally in this project of forming disciples for the kingdom, which would overthrow Satan's kingdom in a sense (never mind that Jesus has already been asked this question and has answered it with the illustration of what happens to a house divided against itself). Wink even sees the temptation of Jesus depicted in the synoptic Gospels in the same light. It is only because Satan is a sifter that he first asks to sift the disciples like wheat, and that the Holy Spirit delivers Jesus into the hands of Satan to be tempted after the Spirit had descended on Jesus. It would not make sense for Jesus to be delivered into the hands of Satan if the latter were truly evil personified.

"What kind of collusion is this?" asks Wink, because the Holy Spirit could easily have purified Jesus for his impending task (54)! Wink goes on to elaborate the plot for such "sifting" one temptation after the other in detail over three pages of text. In his defense for seemingly coming off as belaboring the point in defense of humanity's straitjacketing of Satan, Wink says he would do so even more to "rectify two millennia in which Satan has been so persistently maligned" (56). While Wink posits that "Satan is not a fixed, unnuanced figure" and should not be reduced to rigid doctrinal categories (as many are wont to do), it seems that he has his own biased agenda: to redeem Satan—or at least rehabilitate him—as one of the powers (Rom. 8:38).

I agree with Wink that "[t]he tendency of some Christians to regard Satan as unambiguously evil breeds a paranoid view of reality" (33), which one can see depicted in large portions of the global South. But to speak of rehabilitating Satan—or even of redeeming him—comes dangerously close to blurring the lines between good and evil and to leaning toward a monistic view of Christianity. It turns Satan into a neutral lucky-dip game, where what comes up depends on who dipped in. For the weight of the scriptural evidence supports the claim of a personal evil being an enemy of God and his creation intent on destruction and havoc and not to be underestimated. Jesus himself draws a firm line between himself and Satan: he dissociates himself from Satan and his works, and in fact says that he has come in order to expose Satan's death-dealing ways and to destroy them and him (1 John 3:8).[39]

Four Views, ed. James K. Beilby and Paul R. Eddy (Grand Rapids: Baker Academic, 2012), 52. Hereafter, page references to this work appear in parentheses in the text.

39. See also Matt. 9:34; 12:26–28 and parallels, on a house divided against itself

Generally speaking—as I have argued previously—Wink's insights about Satan and the powers have scriptural backing.[40] For instance, both Old and New Testaments suggest that God establishes governments, kingdoms, and authorities—and jettisons them at his will. God sets them up to fulfill God's purposes in time and space, as readings in both the Major and Minor Prophets demonstrate. A New Testament example is the Epistle to the Romans, in which Paul exhorts Christians everywhere to subject themselves to governing authorities: they are to be viewed as entities set up and deposed by God (Rom. 13:1; regarding Christian authorities, see Heb. 13:17). The language of Satan asking to sift the disciples recalls the primordial scene of the Satan asking to test Job (Job 1:1–12).

In addition, Wink refers to the powers, the interiority of earthly structures that are variously termed the angels as established by God, who even in their fallenness (not depravity or evil) would be redeemed by God in Christ, through whom and for whom all things were created and would thus be reconciled by the cross (Col. 1:15–20).

The understanding of powers that we are working with, then, is something like a circle with something—something difficult to see—inside it. The circle is the outer form of the systems and structures: the bureaucrats, the buildings, the trucks, the fax machines, and the territory in which it has its market as its area of concern. Those outer elements of the principalities and powers that are visible also provide a way into the spirituality of that corporation or institution or nation or church. By looking at the outer forms, we can infer the spirituality to some degree. There are other ways—prayer, meditation, intuitive sensing—of trying to discern the interiority of that institution or structure or system. It requires a new way of thinking.[41] This new way of thinking includes, among other things, not demonizing these powers but thinking of them in the same way that we think of all creation: as fallen and on their way to being redeemed in the reconciling work of the cross.

But there is a picture of spiritual powers that is more complex than Wink portrays in his trilogy and other writings—and in his own equivocation in several places in his discussion.[42] For his characterization of

---

and casting out demons by Beelzebub; on binding the strong man, see Mark 3:27, which depicts the distinction and opposition between Jesus and Satan.

40. Acolatse, *For Freedom or Bondage?*

41. Wink, "Principalities and Powers," 23.

42. Consider, e.g., his reflection on the key text of his statement about the rehabilitation of the powers. He says: "More recently, liberation theology has introduced

the powers suggests that he is perhaps aware of these spirits as personal beings, but could it be that a certain need for "respectability" prevents clear articulation of such a position? At best, his analysis seeks to minimize the possibility of the powers as personally autonomous beings and thereby the scriptural witness and account of evil. Scriptural testimony envisions these powers as spiritual beings that are inherently evil rather than as earthly structures or benign neutral inner spirits of outer poles that become demonic through bad behavior or choice, and that thus the cross is also raised up to destroy and triumph over (John 12:31; Col. 2:15; 1 Cor. 15:24; Eph. 4:8). The actions and attitude noted in these verses are indicative of what is done to one's enemies following their defeat in a war. To suggest otherwise turns all Scripture on its head and makes nonsense of the Christ event, for that would become no more than an internal schism—civil war at best. But Scripture is also clear on the fact that there are two kingdoms, even if one is an upstart.

What is even more confusing is the kind of posture Wink assumes with the powers concerning spiritual warfare. His conclusions about the spiritual aspects of these "principalities and powers" are different from what we would assume, especially as he turns to the role of prayer in light of systemic evil. Here I follow his discussion that is in dialogue and tension with two other leading voices in the spiritual warfare movement, as he summarizes in his contribution to the subject, which engages other viewpoints on a spectrum of understanding spiritual warfare.[43] For if Satan

---

the idea that these principalities and powers might be institutions and systems and structures. That's a lot closer to what I suspect to be the truth, but something is left out there, and that is the spiritual dimension of these powers. The New Testament talks about these powers as both visible and invisible, both earthly and heavenly" (Wink, "Principalities and Powers," 19). We might ask how these powers are visible and yet not personal beings, especially if, as Wink says, they are not merely the structures.

43. James K. Beilby and Paul R. Eddy, eds., *Understanding Spiritual Warfare: Four Views* (Grand Rapids: Baker Academic, 2012). The "spiritual warfare" camp—if that is an appropriate term—is split along certain notable lines across the church spectrum: the classical model, while holding the view that demons are personal spiritual beings, gives little attention to spiritual warfare as a separate category of Christian life and sees it as part of discipleship and commitment to godly living; the world-systems model, which sees demonic powers as nonpersonal, understands warfare as engagement with structural powers—and Wink would be in this camp; the model in which personalization of the demonic is both too individualistic and runs the risk of inattention to human culpability in accounting for evil is reflected in African spirit cosmology. But we can also observe this phenomenon in some pockets of Western ecclesial spaces.

were not so much "a person, a being, a metaphysical entity," but rather "a function in the divine economy," what would be the need for engaging in spiritual warfare against the powers as inner entities of outer structures, and what form would this take (40)?

Wink on Spiritual Warfare

Drawing on the great prayer scene in Revelation 8:1–5, Wink calls for attention to what happens when saints intercede for a broken world. "The unexpected suddenly becomes possible, and the cries of the intercessors have been heard. . . . The message is clear: history belongs to the intercessors who believe the future into being."[44] The world systems and structures are about to be shifted in light of prayers, changing woes to hope (Rev. 8:7–13) because, for Wink, what John is referring to in this revelation regarding the kingdom of the world refers not to "geographical or planetary" but to "the alienated and alienating reality that seduces humanity into idolatry: the worship of the political powers as divine" (63). What tips the scales in the warfare is the prayers of people who look to a future that is not closed, but more importantly, to a God who hears prayer and ironically in Bultmannian terms "changes the world because it changes what is possible to God" (59). Here we are no doubt in the unscientific realm of an open rather than a closed system, a position he seeks to demythologize, it seems. At the same time, while Satan is envisioned as "an archetypal image of the universal human experience of evil and is capable of an infinite variety of representations" (58), and beliefs about this entity continue to be a matter of debate, "the experience of Satan is a brute and terrifying fact" (59). With concessions like the above statement, especially when it is followed by a report of a horrific encounter with evil, we have even more pause to wonder. In this narrative, a man on the brink of suicide reported hearing an audible voice encouraging him to jump to his death. The voice, with what can only be termed destructive evil goading him on, became adamant and was screaming at him to jump the more he resisted the invitation and the urge to destroy himself. This ordeal lasted for about two hours; it happened to someone known to Wink.

---

44. Wink, "The World Systems," 62. (Hereafter, page references to this work appear in parentheses in the text.) One may be right in wondering whether Wink's view of God and possibility is necessary for an open system or only one option for such a system.

Wink's interpretation of the incident avoids naming the evil as personal, and it concludes that, whether Satan was actually inside or outside, what is real is that the incident undoubtedly occurred, and "what this man experienced as 'Satan' was an actual force of evil, however it be conceived, craving his annihilation." Wink goes on to add that such occurrences are more frequent "in human experience than most people are aware" (59). Missionaries have been reporting such incidents over the years, and no doubt Wink's own work in South America has brought many such encounters to his attention. It is likely that these encounters have tempered his outright rejection of the depersonalization of evil; and yet he cannot completely escape the long arm of demythologizing in his theorizing—in that he speaks with a bifurcated tongue and detracts from any concrete contribution to how we may understand the powers in our day vis-à-vis the biblical world picture.

I will seek to demonstrate this in a critique I make of his structural approach below. However, he does pull an overly personalized account of evil from the brink of a narrow conceptualization that leaves no room for systemic evil and from the need to address the "structuring structures" that contribute to human languishing and destruction.[45]

Further Critique of Wink and the Structural Approach

While Walter Wink helps us probe the language of power in the biblical narratives and suggests alternative understandings, his interpretation leans more toward reductionism: that is, he sees demons and evil spiritual powers as sociopolitical structures rather than as inherently evil spiritual beings. The Bible does present us with both types of evil, but the Gospel narratives seem to indicate that the weight of interpretation should fall on the spiritual side. And it is also clear that, at least in the New Testament, Satan is not a neutral force but an enemy of God and God's people. Wink's

---

45. Here Wink uses the term in the way that Pierre Bourdieu talks about both functionalist and structuralist traditions in the study of culture: the former being too fixed—what he calls "structured structures" of tradition based on primitive societies; and the latter reifying traditions as "structuring structures" and imposing ideology on others by the dominant class. His corrective is to move toward a structure that is both structured (thus open to objectification) and structuring (thus able to produce both thinking and action). See Pierre Bourdieu, *The Logic of Practice* (Stanford, CA: Stanford University Press, 1990).

concept of the demonic and evil as inner personal demons or the interiority of sociopolitical structures has too Jungian a leaning—with its concept of collective possession.[46]

When he speaks of the demonic spirit latent within the secularity of a crowd, he does that with the firsthand knowledge of one who has witnessed what most in the West have not encountered. But when he speaks of that encounter, for instance, of prayer as "the interior battlefield where the decisive victory is won before any engagement in the outer world is even possible," we hear warfare prayer as explicated in Ephesians 6.[47] Wink thus uses the language of Scripture but allows the modern scientific parlance to rule his articulation and lead us into what Clinton Arnold rightly calls an anachronistic interpretation of the language of the powers. This is because Wink imposes a twenty-first-century sociopolitical Jungian depth-psychological reading of the passages on to people who lived in a culture rife with magic and belief in otherworldly powers, powers that Wink sometimes covertly—and sometimes not quite so covertly—uncovers in his own writing. Think, for example, of his astute point about and caution to people on the ability of the demonic to falsify and confuse. Doesn't this point to some ambivalence in his own thinking, and doesn't it favor Scripture and suggest that he accords some independent ontology to the demonic?[48] Furthermore, he comes dangerously close to the heretical when he notes the effect of prayer on God.

Prayer is rattling God's cage and waking God up and setting God free and giving this famished God water and this starved God food and cutting the ropes off this God's hands and the manacles off God's feet and washing the caked sweat from God's eyes—and then watching God swell with life and vitality and energy, and following God wherever God goes.[49]

Such a statement goes against established Christian thinking and teaching about God and doubts the very essence and reality of God, almost collapsing the Creator/creation boundaries.[50] It is a theological perspective grounded in process theology, which is aligned with Whiteheadian approaches to the concurring God. It is questionable whether his insights are at all consonant with Hebraic anthropology and its implications con-

46. Wink, *Unmasking the Powers*, 51.
47. Wink, *The Powers That Be: Theology for a New Millennium* (New York: Doubleday, 1999), 181.
48. See a similar comment made about Satan in Wink, *Unmasking the Powers*, 40.
49. Wink, *Unmasking the Powers*, 186.
50. On this point, see Wink, *Engaging the Powers*, 327, and *Unmasking the Powers*, 124.

cerning God in relationship with the cosmos, a stance that differs from that of most mainline Christian thinking.[51]

Though Wink's hermeneutical aim was to offer a viable language to help modern people access the language of powers and how they were understood and used in the first century, as in the case of Bultmann, the twenty-first-century need for comprehension so influenced his reading of the first-century understanding that what he is left with is a twenty-first-century understanding of the language of the powers rather than a first-century meaning and understanding of these principalities and powers, a culture in which belief in otherworldly spirit beings and magic characterized common life.

I need to point out that, while members of the universal Christian church might live in the twenty-first century, many are nevertheless centered in the kind of dualistic worldview that reared its head in the first-century church and was rejected by Christian orthodoxy.[52] While Wink makes a strong case for noting both the interiority and spiritual basis of the powers and the need for attending to their allowed public manifestation in social institutions and political structures, as I have argued previously, his hermeneutical analysis does not line up with the understanding of the first recipients, and one may ask whether in that sense it can line up with the need for belief in the Christian faith of the contemporary church. For Christians are not just people who believe certain truths and tenets, but they are those called to believe alongside and *in fellowship with* the apostles and the first eyewitnesses, carrying on a tradition of belief and practices handed down over centuries of faithful living. Is it possible to use the words without summoning the images they were intended to conjure? For at the end it seems as though Wink's position is a minor variation on the theme of demythologizing signaled by Bultmann's project.

51. William S. Kurtz, "Naming the Powers: The Language of Power in the New Testament," *The Catholic Biblical Quarterly* 48, n. 1 (1986): 151–52.

52. While there was dualistic theology (for example, Marcionism and Manichaeism) in the early church, this view was ultimately rejected by Christian orthodoxy because it implied two separate and equally ultimate first causes (two Gods).

Evangelical Perspectives and Personal Evil Beings

Of the more evangelical voices, such as John Stott[53] and Clinton Arnold,[54] Gregory Boyd's invitation to think seriously about inexplicable large-scale natural disasters when we try to account for evil is credibly persuasive. To speak of the devil in personal terms and to name the evil that springs from him and other evil spiritual beings is taken for granted in works such as Boyd's. Many of these seek to redirect us from the tendency to either valorize the devil by drawing attention to evil, or ignoring him altogether by not factoring him into inexplicable evil. If a name is a signifier, then to even mention Satan or the devil is, in the first place, to claim in some sense the personalization of evil, the presence of a personal evil being. This is the primary and necessary component of the New Testament's multivalent explanation of evil. When the New Testament speaks of evil, it means that it is real and supernatural (that is to say, personalized) evil. As Boyd points out, the scale of evil in the cosmos is only explainable—philosophically and theologically—by the idea of a (semi-)autonomous devil: any conception lacking Satan (an actual personalized being, a more fully developed being than the one found in Job) will be intellectually unconvincing and pastorally unsatisfying.[55]

It is ironic that in the places in which what can be termed structural evil is so prevalent in the form of despotic governments and untold poverty, and so forth (mainly the global South), the tendency is to focus on the powers as personal spiritual beings intent on the destruction of individuals—a situation that is often approached in pastoral practice with the one-shot prayers of deliverance through spiritual warfare, one person at a time.[56] On the other hand, in the places where social structures are seemingly geared toward the welfare of individuals, who nevertheless face struggles that psychological and psychiatric interventions alone are unable to adequately meet (mainly the global West) and thus needing other explanations to human ills, such as a concept of personal, evil spiritual

---

53. John R. W. Stott, *God's New Society: The Message of Ephesians* (Downers Grove, IL: InterVarsity, 1979).

54. Clinton Arnold, *Powers of Darkness: Principalities and Powers in Paul's Letters* (Downers Grove, IL: InterVarsity, 1992); Clinton Arnold, *Power and Magic: The Concept of Power in Ephesians* (Eugene, OR: Wipf and Stock: 2001).

55. Gregory Boyd, *Satan and the Problem of Evil: Constructing a Trinitarian Warfare Theodicy* (Downers Grove, IL: InterVarsity, 2001).

56. See Acolatse, *For Freedom or Bondage?*

beings, the approach to the powers is to view them in mainly structural terms. It is fair to say that in both scenarios the powers are not encountered and properly named, unmasked, and engaged in a contextually believable way, and that the powers continue to blind people to their character and nefarious activities by using camouflages, which are aided by the blinders of the worldviews through which we insist on viewing and understanding them.[57] It is perhaps not coincidental, but intentional that modern Western rationalism discredits the existence of spirits. We do not much see what Scripture and others term "demonic," for they use culture to deceive us. Pastorally, then, the question we face in our attempts to rightly name and testify against the powers is one of how to move between New Testament texts and their host culture and our own cultural assumptions and world.

After this general survey of the representative approaches to an understanding of the powers in the New Testament, it is safe to say that each approach is incomplete in capturing the multidimensional nature of the numerous satanic schemes and the much larger demonic forces at work in our world. An approach that overvalues the powers and views them solely as personal demonic forces that use people as tools to carry out their devices is too narrowly simplistic and undercuts human volition, the very essence of being; and any approach that totally dismisses the reality of spiritual forces at work in the church's battle with the powers will not be true to the scriptural witness nor suffice for the task of liberating people from the snares of Satan and his minions.

It is important to note that it is only in the West that the tendency to marginalize the New Testament's principalities and powers, as personal spiritual beings, both in ecclesial settings and in theological scholarship, exists to the extent it does. Yet, if the West's shortcoming is its obsession with the material world (and currently the major place in the world where the reality of spiritual forces is overwhelmingly denied), the obverse is true of contexts that accept the existence of spiritual forces. In the places where belief in the spiritual and other otherworldly existence characterizes common life, people tend to valorize the pervasive nature of the powers and to overspiritualize every issue, seeing demons every-

57. According to this view, it is critical to further note not only that the spiritual world contains personalized forces of evil, but that these take on human-cultural forms and use human-cultural guises. See C. S. Lewis's portrayal of the workings of this aspect of the spiritual forces vis-à-vis the culture in his *Screwtape Letters* (Uhrichsville, OH : Barbour, 1990).

where.[58] What is needed is a critical balance in which churches in the West and in other contexts can be in meaningful dialogue with each other about the powers. In this regard the unity of the church is at stake, and its future as "a provisional demonstration of the kingdom of God" in power and transformation of individuals and peoples begs for a reclaiming of the all-encompassing mission of Jesus: to destroy the works of Satan. And to that end, the New Testament conception of the notion of principalities and powers is of vital importance.

The current situation in the global church, with its dichotomous understanding of and attitude toward the powers, such that each has a framework for approaching diagnoses and care in pastoral situations, which in the long run do not adequately meet the multifaceted underpinnings of presenting problems, I surmise, stems largely from differing attitudes toward myth in general and the mythic content of their one common Scripture reference. In the following chapter, I propose a new and more nuanced understanding of myth that has the potential to challenge, inform, and perhaps even transform the way both sides conceptualize myth in an attempt to reclaim it for theology and pastoral practice for the global church.[59] In this regard, a postmodern agenda provides fertile soil for the kinds of growth needed to both overcome modernity's disdain and the premodern overvalorization of myth, while simultaneously correcting for the postmodern penchant for interpretative plurality that often lacks clarity and concreteness, especially in pastoral practice.

---

58. In the West, works like the series by Neil T. Andersen, as well as those in popular culture, such as Mark Bubeck's *The Adversary* and *Overcoming the Adversary*, are classic examples. In the global South, the writings coming out of the Pentecostal-charismatic movements that portray this tendency are well documented. See Acolatse, *For Freedom Or Bondage?*; J. Kwabena Asamoah-Gyadu, "Pulling Down Strongholds: Evangelism, Principalities and Powers, and the African Pentecostal Imagination," *International Review of Mission* 96 (2007): 306–17; Nimi Wariboko, *Nigerian Pentecostalism* (Rochester, NY: University of Rochester Press, 2014).

59. I have used the term "global church" throughout this chapter, while the emphasis has been on the African and Western churches for reasons that may not be readily obvious. The two churches under survey have been partners in sending and receiving mission fields from the founding of intentional missionary movements/societies at the turn of the twentieth century to the present, and continuing ongoing dialogues at ecumenical levels demand that core hermeneutical issues and what it means to do theology and be church in a postmodern/postcolonial global context engage these two spaces.

Western *Episteme* in Theological Perspectives

There seems to be a shift in attitude toward the spirit world in the North Atlantic social imaginary and in its theology, a movement from belief in the reality of such a world and even of evil spiritual powers as personal beings, to what we see today—a disbelief in and jettisoning of myth. I have suggested that in theology this trend is due largely to Bultmann's existentialist approach, which sought to demythologize the concept of principalities and powers in the New Testament for our day. But as my analysis above demonstrates, the culture itself, even with its postmodernist or Enlightenment ethos, continues to display mythic sensibilities. Rather than a demythologized existence, with the assumption that we have left behind the naiveté and credulous attitude of less sophisticated minds/cultures, we seem to have only blindly replaced one myth with another. For that is the characteristic of living myth—"that it is unavoidable and elusive."[60]

But the fact that the structural approach has a large following in New Testament scholarship, as well as in some psychological interpretations, and has found its way into pastoral practices is clear in a wide variety of theological literature.[61] The effect of this way of interpreting the principalities and powers allows for the use of terminology among several strands of Christianity with double, and sometimes treble, meanings—none of which speak to each other. The social gospel of the 1970s and 1980s has given way to slogans of "speaking truth to power" in order to dislocate the

60. Colin Grant, *Myths We Live By* (Ottawa: University of Ottawa Press, 1998), ix. Grant posits that the problem is the general misunderstanding of myth as something related to the past stories of gods and argues for a reclaiming of myth as the perspectives and positions that we take for granted. I note here the analogy between his concept of myth and worldview. Furthermore, rather than seeing one as emanating from the other, we are instead to see the necessity of myth as the foundation for all existence and even disciplines including science. He warns of the false resolution usually arrived at between the fields of religion and science and suggests that both disciplines have their respective underlying myths. On this point, see his chapter entitled "A Science Myth," 19–36.

61. See, e.g., Charles Campbell, *The Word before the Powers: An Ethic of Preaching* (Louisville: Westminster John Knox, 2002); Archie Smith Jr., "Alien Gods in Black Experience," *Process Studies* 18.4 (1989): 294–305; Gerd Theissen, *Psychological Aspects of Pauline Theology* (Philadelphia: Fortress, 1987); see also, Reinhold Niebuhr, *Moral Man and Immoral Society: A Study in Ethics and Politics* (New York: Scribner, 1960). The reflections could be augmented and extended in light of interpretations of Rom. 1:18–32. Neil Elliott, *Liberating Paul: The Justice of God and the Politics of the Apostle* (Maryknoll, NY: Orbis, 1994), esp. 114–24, is also of interest.

structures of political and economic oppression and free the oppressed and marginalized. In such understanding, the principalities and powers wear the face of demagogues in the political corridors of power. In popular culture, we hear people use the phrase "demonizing" someone or other without a hint of the underlying biblical/spiritual undertones; that is, that demons are real personal beings capable of influencing and even inhabiting humans and institutions. As I have tried to argue, our approach to understanding the powers, and how we define and interpret the language of the New Testament regarding them, needs to be carefully nuanced and balanced. The valorization of the powers solely as personal demonic forces who inhabit and direct humans is too narrowly simplistic. It also undercuts other aspects of theological self-understanding: the issue of human volition and of God the Creator and the one who ultimately guides all things. Any approach that totally dismisses the reality of spiritual forces at work in the church's battle with the powers and ignores the embattled Christian will not be true to the scriptural witness nor suffice for the task of liberating people from the snares of Satan and of forming people for life with God. The question of what to do with "myth" as such remains before us.

Reclaiming "Myth"

CHAPTER 3

After Bultmann

When most people use the word "myth," they probably assume that it means what the Oxford English Dictionary (OED) defines it as: "a purely fictitious narrative usually involving supernatural persons, actions or events, and embodying some popular idea concerning natural or historical phenomena."[1] In everyday parlance, to speak of myth is to think in terms of fable: that is, untrue or unrealistic accounts of the origin of the gods and humans and other created entities, which may nonetheless be important for understanding one's purpose on earth, and may help in meaning-making. But it is also possible to think of myth in another way.

Myths are a part of every culture and are in reality the undergirding structures of human life across cultures and epochs; they allow us to make meaning of our lives, and they endure from generation to generation. Myths show how human history progresses and how people in the present find themselves in the past and chart their future. The ancients wove myths into everything to explain what actually occurred and what was inexplicable; their religious life and ideas were especially carried through ritual and myth. Evolutionary treatments of religion in the history of religions have followed the trajectory of gradually diminishing myths that were relegated to the period when religion was intuited and acted out, to current times, when religion is more thought out, that is, as the rational act of sentient beings. Little attention was paid in the past—nor is paid now—to the hidden properties of myth, the function of myth in reasoning about reality that reasoning alone is unable to cover, because sometimes

---

1. See entry under "myth" in the *Oxford English Dictionary* (Oxford: Oxford University Press, 1989).

the apprehension of the world of reality—and the inexplicable occurrences we experience—requires more than our five senses to understand. This is the realm of the ineffable, of Rudolf Otto's *Tremendum*; it is the state that Pascal sees that we apprehend when the heart has reasons that reason knows nothing about. In a sense, we are talking here about the limits of rationality and the expansiveness of myth to meet the requirements of understanding in the everydayness of life. An expansiveness that is inherent in myth and accounts for its enduring character, compared to the niggardliness, if you will, of rationality bound up with the Enlightenment philosophy displayed in secularism. As Raymond Lee and Susan Ackerman observe, while critiquing Habermas's take on the advance of secularism, the inward-looking posture of secularism

> . . . may in fact be fueling the search for religious meaning. In short, the self-limiting nature of secularization suggests its own paradox: the institutionalization of world mastery on a grand scale inadvertently problematized the quest for meaning and provided a source for the development of new religious movements.[2]

Later in this chapter I will take up this notion of the expansiveness of myth and the gift of secularization in myth's forward and sideways march even in our technologically bounded age; but it is important to flag it here, as we turn to tracing the contours of myth as an important meaning-making component of life.

A Brief History of Myth in Modernity

The focus of this chapter is on reclaiming myth and, in so many ways, the idea of enchantment, for the life of the religious believer. I will seek to demonstrate how uncovering its meaning-making function—in particular in tandem with the imagination—aids in apprehending the *Real*. However, my focus follows the wisdom of Evans-Pritchard in turning away from the pursuit of the origins and history of myths as unhelpful due to the lack of scientific basis of its methodology and the meager sources of its claims, and concerns itself mainly with the nature and definitions of

---

2. Raymond Lee and Susan Ackerman, *The Challenge of Religion after Modernity: Beyond Disenchantment* (Aldershot, UK: Ashgate, 2002), 6.

myth, probing the reason for myth's rejection as a viable and valid mode of transmission of Scripture, and especially its portrayal of the other-worldly realm for today.[3] At the same time, I shall remain mindful of the pitfalls of reflecting on myth without attention to mythopoeic systems and the cosmological ontologies upon which myths are grounded. Thus I will draw a history of myth without giving in to the idea of its being linked to a primitive age of reasoning from which it is gradually being rescued by rationalism; it will be a way of talking about myth beyond primitivization and exoticization.

In the preceding chapters I explored the spirit world in the African context across the epochs of Western Christianity, eras starting from the first century through the premodern to the modern epochs, especially the period of Enlightenment to the postmodern era, and also as representative of the perspective from the global South. I especially drew attention to the African belief in spiritual powers as rife because even a worldview that is cognizant of the advance in technological know-how did not diminish belief in an open world in which otherworldly spirits traversed between the physical and spiritual realms. There is no dichotomy between the two worlds as such, and nowhere better than in a belief in the presence of the principalities and powers (not to mention belief in witches and other dy-namistic powers even among Christians) is this fact demonstrated, since Satan and especially demons are seen as personal beings. African perspectives on such beliefs, as shown via Kwesi Dickson's analysis of African religiocultural lenses, offer not only a vantage point for viewing such beliefs, but also necessary correctives for beliefs gone awry—that is, beliefs that have become toxifying rather than vivifying.[4]

In the West, we observe the obverse of what pertains in the global South in large part, and we have discovered that our modern and post-modern approaches to the question of determining the powers are inadequate. The modern rejects the presence of the powers or any external spiritual reality; psychologically, it explains the demonic mainly in psychodynamic terms and views it as what is occurring in the psychology of the religious believer. Thus, all experiences are explained in the ter-

3. E. E. Evans-Pritchard, *Theories of Primitive Religion* (Oxford: Clarendon Press, 1965), 73, 111.

4. See Esther E. Acolatse, *For Freedom or Bondage? A Critique of African Pastoral Practices* (Grand Rapids: Eerdmans, 2014), esp. chap. 1, for elaborations on what is meant by spirituality gone awry and becoming toxifying rather than vivifying.

minology of psychic phenomena, and ultimately even the main object of religious belief is dismissed as such.[5]

Nature and Definitions of Myth

Understandings of the spirit world correlate with conceptions of myth and mythology, and this alone poses several problems of definition today. From the Enlightenment until the twentieth century, myth was assumed to be a primitive mode of thinking that nevertheless aided primitive human beings account for certain phenomena. And yet "myth" is a word that is often in currency in the present day because human life is always bound up in myth in one form or another, and our constant attempt to be dismissive of it continues its inescapable hold. The attempts by rationalism and its collaborator, secularism, to eradicate mythic thinking in favor of what is assumed to be scientific objectivity is not tenable. This is due largely to the fact that that theory and the arguments for it have been debunked by philosophers of science; in fact, many scientists married their faith (what might be dismissed as mythic thinking) to great scientific discoveries.[6] Furthermore, some of these discoveries and theories derived from following hunches and "gut feelings" and were not always based on abstract thinking and precise objective approaches. In fact, we might say that the myth of the objective subject has been exploded on just that account.[7] Paul

5. A good example would be the writings of Sigmund Freud on religion's affect and its origins. See his *The Future of an Illusion* (New York: Norton, 1961) and *Totem and Taboo* (Greentop, MO: Greentop Academic Press, 2011).

6. Michael Polanyi, *Personal Knowledge: Towards a Post-Critical Philosophy* (New York: Harper and Row, 1964) and *The Tacit Dimension* (Gloucester, MA: Peter Smith, 1983). At the same time, we are acutely aware of the validity of William J. Abraham's caution against using what I would call "outliers" in an attempt to overcome the obvious and well-deserved critiques of subjectivity in our arguments by latching on to figures that point to the inner subjectivity within science. For Abraham, this is only a stopgap measure that should not become the default for how we navigate the tensions within the epistemological quagmire, a ready temptation. A hermeneutical turn is what he proposes as the proper stance. See Abraham, *Crossing the Threshold of Divine Revelation* (Grand Rapids: Eerdmans, 2006), 24.

7. See Christine Charyton, ed., *Creativity and Innovation among Science and Art: A Discussion of the Two Cultures* (London: Springer, 2015), for a multidisciplinary discussion of this idea. In addition, today we are not even certain that the scientific observations of Darwin were noted purely objectively, but depended on what we call hunches or gut feelings. And in our day, the discoveries in science continue to bear

Avis's point about myth being the "greatest casualty of our contemporary suspicion of figurative language and imagistic thinking" is well taken.[8] In everyday parlance, to speak of myth is to think in terms of fable: untrue or unrealistic accounts of the origin of gods and humans and other created entities, which may nonetheless be important for understanding one's purpose on earth and may help in meaning-making. Thus, if what is expressed in myth contains a grain of truth, it must necessarily be recast in what we assume to be a rational and scientific language. At the same time, modern/postmodern human beings cannot escape the long reach of myth. The penchant for myth as frivolous entertainment and relaxation belies a subconscious need and necessity of myth for full human functioning.

In scholarly circles and literature, myth takes on a more nuanced meaning and significance, though at the same time eluding definition. However, current studies in fields such as depth psychology and the history of religions, as well as language and narrative studies (of particularly the French school[9]), have rehabilitated the image of myth and given it an almost respectable place as a legitimate mode of knowing and even thinking. Myth has been defined variously by different schools of thought over time, and while we need not be unduly fussy about definitions, the various definitions need to be probed and clarified. As I indicated earlier, when people hear the word "myth," the Oxford English definition is what comes to mind most promptly, not only in popular culture but also in academic settings, where a certain perspective of science and philosophy has set the tone for what is credible, and where all other subjects must pass the bar of the strict standard of credibility not to be associated with the OED definition of myth. William Abraham points out that the fault lies in the fact that theology has ceded ground to philosophy: based on a certain commitment to

---

out the need for the imagination, creativity, and hunches in arriving at findings. See the recent breakthrough in gravitational waves based on earlier theories by Einstein: Geoff Brumfiel, "Einstein, a Hunch, and Decades of Work: How Scientists Found Gravitational Waves," National Public Radio, February 12, 2016, http://www.npr.org/sections/thetwo-way/2016/02/12/466559439/einstein-a-hunch-and-decades-of-work-how-scientists-found-gravitational-waves.

8. Paul Avis, *God and the Creative Imagination: Metaphor, Symbol, and Myth in Religion and Theology* (London: Routledge, 1999), 114.

9. For example, philology offers helpful insights into how to parse myth, a concept I will explore with the help of Ernst Cassirer on language in this chapter.

evidentialism, theology has formulated an account of its engagement with philosophy.[10]

A helpful way to address how myth has been conceived of over time is offered in a short article by J. W. Rogerson. Starting from two views of myth: as "a way of knowing that it is different from science" and as a largely naïve and prescientific thinking that "must retreat as science advances," Rogerson helps us see why there remains a controversy about myth and why the two ways of thinking remain in conflict with each other.[11] Theories about myths go as far back as 4 BCE, when Euhemerus, a Sicilian, advanced the first theory of myth (what became known as Euhemerism): he posited that the gods were former humans who were later deified; and since his definition, myths have been with us to stay.[12] However, such thinking about the gods—and about myths in general— was vehemently opposed by Christian writers. They were simultaneously interpreting parts of the Old Testament allegorically and making every effort to distance themselves from what they thought was the false and mythic thinking of the other nations surrounding Israel. The early writers saw those nations as morally bankrupt and perceived their religious ideas to be nothing compared with the Christian religion; they conceived of the latter as superior, while they saw the other nations as propounding myths. The Christian apologists passed such judgment on the so-called pagan religions even while the former were allegorizing about what can be easily observed as the mythic content of Scripture and its anthropomorphic deity.[13] The Renaissance—and especially the Enlightenment—saw a renewed interest and rediscovery of myth in many parts of the world, including North America. Thus myth was not only bound up with the

10. William J. Abraham, "Turning Philosophical Water into Theological Wine," *Journal of Analytic Theology* 1, no. 1 (2013): 3. While his comments issue from an assessment and response to one such theologian, Van A. Harvey, whose essay "The Alienated Theologian," sparked his interest and comments, what Abraham bemoans here may apply to many such theologians disenchanted with their craft.

11. J. W. Rogerson, "Slippery Words v. Myth," *The Expository Times* 90 (1978): 10.

12. Rogerson, "Slippery Words," 10. It is worth noting that this concept is not different from the myth of the gods in African thought, and perhaps in other ancient cultures where ancestral veneration/worship is important.

13. Rogerson, "Slippery Words," 10. On this point, I suggest that the larger problem of demythologizing that Christian theology is left with today, and its repudiation of the mythic content of Scripture, stems from this earlier distance placed between itself and the rest of what it sees as the myth, construed as fable, which occupied the so-called pagan religions of the Greco-Roman world.

Norse and "Nordic mythology of the Eddas, first made widely known to European scholars as late as 1755," but was recognized as a phenomenon among humankind, thus sparking a desire to unearth its genesis.[14] Enlightenment thinkers claimed that the genesis of myth lay in the thinking of primitive human beings everywhere; however, their premise for such a conclusion was wrong, for as Rogerson points out, "the simple equation 'ancient man equals primitive man' concealed a whole mare's nest of questions, many of which are still live issues in social anthropology." The bigger question he poses is whether we can even determine such "a thing as primitive mentality" in the history of human progress, and whether "primitive" always meant untutored and uncultured and, furthermore, whether there is any "relation between being technologically undeveloped and being artistically and philosophically underdeveloped." Rogerson's point is that modern human beings are still unclear about how humans evolve and assume that they evolve along similar lines of progress and make comparisons among them even without giving thought to the geographical extent of their separation in time. Because of these anomalies surrounding the understanding of myth, says Rogerson, "to restrict the question of myth to its meaning in relation to the Bible is to court disaster." And this is an appropriate caution as he goes on to show, because

> time and again, myth (however understood) has been taken into biblical studies from other disciplines, and it is only by appreciating the wider study of myth that we shall avoid the "slipperiness" of the word, and the confusion that this inevitably brings.[15]

Indeed, the demythologizing project that is still bound up with all biblical—and especially New Testament—studies indicates that Rogerson is right in his surmising, for it is the concept of myth as fable, as linked to primitive humans, as something to be outgrown by modern human beings that feeds the charge to rid the kerygma of the embarrassing encumbrances of myth.

I propose a good working definition that I think shifts the boundaries of current binary thinking on the subject but also delimits the epistemo-

---

14. B. Feldman and R. D. Richardson, *The Rise of Modern Mythology, 1680–1860* (Bloomington: Indiana University Press, 1972), 200. Cited in Rogerson, "Slippery Words v. Myth," 10.

15. Rogerson, "Slippery Words," 10.

logical skepticism that attends views of religion and myth and whether we can apprehend and speak intelligibly about the Real *an sich*. In particular, it shifts to another mode and binary opposition in the proof/ disproof norm of thinking about what can be believed. In this way of thinking, disproof equals not believable, and thus the believer, in this instance the Christian, has to scrounge around to find propositions that are provable to support belief. Transcending the false dichotomy of binary oppositions that currently rules how we conceive of myths, I believe, offers us a way for conversation that allows theology not to be the handmaiden of the other disciplines, which set the agenda and parameters for credibility, forcing theology to make the move to appeal to its own internal grammar as the basis of its judgment, meaning that it can thus be dismissed and marginalized in the conversation about what is real.[16] By being thus marginalized, theology is rendered mute in our secular world, and especially in the sphere where it is most needed, the public square, where human lives are on the chopping block or—to use modern imagery—being sold in store windows for a pittance. Thus theology's life-giving utterance becomes mere opinion.

In the social sciences, myth is conceived of as the narrative of supernatural entities interwoven into the stories of human beings and other living things, and the influence of these stories on interrelationships and functioning in the social space occupied by humankind and other created beings. Theories of myth are further divided into psychological, functionalist, structuralist, and political,[17] and since the political is only tangentially related to our current project, this analysis will bracket that aspect in the ensuing discussion of myth.

Myth is, by its very nature, evocative and ambivalent, with multiple layers of meaning that continue to expand the horizons of understanding that a particular myth seeks to uncover. It is not so much a way of stating a truth, which itself could be multifaceted, requiring multiple viewings by many, to arrive at meaning and understanding (hence the importance of communal discerning) rather than a unitary viewing point. Charac-

16. Christian theologians have insisted on the grammar of theology germane to itself that cannot be conflated with any other, such as science, with which it is usually placed in tension in epistemological conversations. See, for example, arguments by Thomas F. Torrance in *The Ground and Grammar of Theology: Consonance between Theology and Science* (Edinburgh: T & T Clark, 1980).

17. Chris Shore, "Myth," in *The Blackwell Dictionary of Modern Social Thought*, ed. William Outhwaite (Malden, MA: Blackwell Publishing, 2002).

teristically, Scripture necessarily invites this approach of arriving at the kerygma because Scripture comes from God, a communion of three beings, to a people called and fashioned into first a nation with a collectivist ethos, and then a church (*ecclesia*), a gathered people with the same communion-seeking and -forming characteristics. For even when a prophet receives an inspired message or an apostle writes an Epistle, it is not a private moment, because the whole community is always present with and in the individual. Thus even in what might seem a private moment, a communion-seeking God helps give birth to Scripture in community with the prophet, and in the power of the Spirit (more communion), it is transmitted to community and learned and lived together in community. Furthermore, the media, through which theological truth is transmitted and ascertained as such, is as important as the truth attained. For myth serves more than an informative function; it is a symbolic system, a corollary to modern understandings of language—often with direct and surface meaning.

Recovering a credible working construction/definition of myth is especially important to understanding and articulating a spiritual realm that is designated by the words "principalities and powers." In doing so, a community traces the history and contours of myth in religious, theological, and psychosocial perspectives, returning to the mythic language of Scripture (with an emphasis on the appropriateness of the medium to the timeless and fluid, yet consistent, message of the Bible) with an eye to underscoring the relevance and necessity of myth for apprehending biblical truth. I intend to make a case for the place and necessity of myth in understanding Scripture and its relevance for the life of faith for the Christian believer. In doing so, I wish to make the Bible the focus and basis of an appropriate remythologizing venture that augers well for contemplating the spirit world in church and society and ultimately for incorporation into pastoral practice, especially in pastoral-care diagnoses and intervention. In turning to the scriptural appropriation of myth and the mythopoeia of biblical times, we will discover how the Bible is its own witness to the proper posture toward myth, and further makes the case for myth and remythologizing for contemporary ecclesial spaces and for pastoral ministry that transcends specific cultural bounds.

History and Theories of Myth

Nineteenth-century cultural anthropologists, in their bid to understand diverse cultures and how they evolved, studied the myriad myths of those different cultures and concluded that myths were no more than unscientific, inaccurate accounts of primitive ideas about events in history.[18] This modern understanding of myth has a long history, but for our purposes, this history is delimited by its use in modern and postmodern biblical scholarship. In modern biblical scholarship, the history of myth, understood in both its broad and narrow terms through the pioneering work of Christian Hartlich and Walter Sachs, is based on the theories of the classical philologist C. G. Heyne, who saw myth as a universal form of expression used by primitive humans to explain inexplicable events that they attributed to the intervention of the gods.[19] In this sense (following an evolutionary concept of myth), all cultures would operate with myths that function in similar ways. Those who dichotomize life into profane/secular and sacred/spiritual—and thus view myths as a form of sacred speech in which particular yet universal religious sensibilities are manifested (such as Friedrich Schleiermacher, who defined myth as a "historical representation of the supra-historical" divine)—have occupied a central place in religious discussions. Of note at this juncture is a study by Talad Asad that critiques such binary thinking and argues for the need to curtail the travesty of binary features today.[20] When we dichotomize and draw fast lines between sacred and profane (and this by inference includes myth, since religion is the other half of the sacred/profane scale) it allows for conceiving myth as attached to the traditional (often read religious) in the world. But this is a fallacy of modern thinking that assumes that the

18. We have in mind earlier exploratory endeavors by the European pioneers (who eschewed armchair anthropological and cultural findings) and the theorizations that emerged from these encounters with the non-European world. These explorations and observations of non-European cultures resulted in many of the labels and assumed universal categories of religion and nature and following from that, the more pejorative terminologies (pagan, primitive, nature folk, fetish, animism) we have inherited in much of ethnographic scholarship and particularly the primitivization of the other and the repudiation of myth as irrational and inferior.

19. Brevard S. Childs, *Myth and Reality in the Old Testament* (London: SCM, 1960), 13, citing Christian Hartlich and Walter Sachs, *Der Ursprung des Mythosbegriffes in der modernen Bibelwissenschaft* (Tübingen: J. C. B. Mohr, 1952).

20. Talal Asad, *Formations of the Secular: Christianity, Islam, Modernity* (Stanford, CA: Stanford University Press, 2003). See esp. the intro. and chap. 1, 1–66.

secular follows and grows out of the sacred/religious and is a progressive move from the irrational to the more rational mode of being. (I will elaborate on this point in later sections of this chapter.)

The move away from such evolutionary theories of myth and a rejection of myth as simplistic and ethnocentric, would give way to a foray into more psychological and sociological accounts in the works of proponents such as Sigmund Freud and Carl Gustav Jung.[21] Freud and Jung based their work on the inherent similarities among all myths because of noticeable universal tendencies across all cultures to form mythic symbols. Such an understanding about myth is still current in the psychodynamic literature, despite the influence of recent anthropological accounts to the contrary in the field.

Depth-Psychological Views of Myth

In general, the psychoanalytic perspective holds that the similarity of the contents of dreams, the wishes and anxieties that occupy the unconscious, are replayed in myths, folktales, legends, and so forth. Secondarily, these objects that occupy dreams, as well as populate myths, derive from primary-process thought (the preverbal, dreamlike, irrational state) and not from the reality principle (the rational thinking state bound up with the ego libido). A pioneer in the field, Freud believed that the seeming irrationality of myth arises from the same source as does the disconnectedness of dreams—and that both are symbolic reflections of unconscious and repressed fears and anxieties. Such fears and anxieties may be universal aspects of the human condition or particular to distinct societies. Freud saw themes of universal psychic repression among these various cultures, repressions linked to various taboos within the culture (such as incest, fratricide, sibling envy, the Oedipus complex, etc.), and concluded that the universal appeal to myth is based on these universal primordial childhood fears.

C. G. Jung, a depth psychologist, also posited a link between myth and dream content in the unconscious process; however, his insights are

21. One can think, e.g., of those like E. Burnett Tylor and his ideas in *Primitive Culture: Researches into the Development of Mythology, Philosophy, Religion, Language, Art, and Custom* (New York: Brentano's, 1924), or Andrew Lang, *The Secret of the Totem* (London: Longmans, 1905), or the better-known works of James Frazer, collected in *Man, God, and Immortality: Thoughts on Human Progress* (New York: Macmillan, 1927).

more favorable toward myth, myth-making, and the function of myth for psychic health and human flourishing. Through his various analyses of the collective complex, Jung underscores the importance of myth for meaning-making—and especially for religious life. While they viewed myth as something related to the nonrational ego, Jung and his followers did not relegate those nonrational aspects to childhood experiences, but argued that these myths (especially the hero myths) and myth-making were part of the maturation and individuation process of human becoming. In this regard, then, a relegating of myth to the abyss, as has been done in our post-Enlightenment culture, is seen as stymieing our universal storehouse of wisdom that the functioning psyche can tap into, a storehouse appropriately identified in the collective unconscious of Jung and other depth psychologists. Our current enchantment with myths and hero tales attests to this important aspect of the health of the ego, as Jung claims. So crucial is myth for growth and human functioning, that Jung understands myth—and all symbolic forms, for that matter—to always have positive connotations; he suggests that as sacred tale, it expands into the realm of the religious and transcendent. Of the Christian formulations of this "myth," so to speak, Jung has this to say:

> The dogmatically formulated truths of the Christian church express, almost perfectly, the nature of psychic experience. They are the repositories of the secrets of the soul, and this matchless knowledge is set forth in grand symbolic images. The unconscious thus possesses a natural affinity with the spiritual values of the church, particularly in their dogmatic form.[22]

22. C. G. Jung, *The Psychology of the Transference* (London: Ark, 1983), 29, cited in Avis, *God and the Creative Imagination*, 139. Of course, one must be wary of so much psychological reductionism that may attach to the insights afforded by Jung's analysis. See, e.g., E. Thurneyson's *A Theology of Pastoral Care* (Richmond, VA: John Knox, 1962); Edward F. Edinger's psychological interpretations of key biblical stories in *Ego and Archetype: Individuation and the Religious Function of the Psyche* (New York: G. P. Putnam's Sons, 1972); Daniel Price's "Karl Barth's Anthropology in Light of Modern Thought: The Dynamic Concept of the Person in Trinitarian Theology and Object Relations Psychology" (PhD diss., University of Aberdeen, Scotland, 1990); and Deborah van Deusen Hunsinger's well-articulated rebuttals on the issue of psychological reductionism in some post-Jungian psychodynamic theorizing. Of course, there are some myths and symbols with negative connotations that need to be watched, and Jung does rule out some of these, because they are fashioned sometimes within the dysfunction of familial matrices and stunt the growth of the psyche and block the work of the self toward

Status of Myth in Recent Times

Some studies of myth, however, have portrayed a departure from most of the aforementioned conceptions of myth (though their reevaluation for pastoral ministry is still pertinent) and have turned away from attempts to explain myth, based largely on similarities in content across social spaces, by calling attention to the different contexts in which myths occur. These studies reveal myths as functioning in a multiplicity of ways within any given culture, as well as differing in function from culture to culture. The anthropologists Bronislaw Malinowski[23] and A. R. Radcliffe-Brown,[24] for instance, considered the way in which myths validate established practices and institutions, thereby reiterating what is held as normative within the cultures. Their functionalist approach criticized the earlier psychoanalytic approaches to detaching myth from its social moorings and suggested instead, based on empirical studies of the Trobriand islanders, that "myth fulfills in primitive culture an indispensable function," that it is the product of a vital faith that aids to codify and reinforce group norms, safeguard rules and morality, and promote social cohesion.[25] The seminal work of Claude Levi-Strauss returned to the study of all myths, not by examining common motifs and elements of the stories, but by focusing on their formal properties.[26] He called attention to the recurrence of certain kinds of structures in widely different traditions of folk literature, and has reduced them to particular binary oppositions, such as nature/culture and self/other, contending that the human brain organizes all perceptions in terms of contrasts and concluding that certain oppositions are universal. He advocated the interpretation of myths as culturally specific transformations

---

wholeness (Deborah van Deusen Hunsinger, *Theology and Pastoral Counseling: A New Disciplinary Approach* [Grand Rapids: Eerdmans, 1995]).

23. Bronislaw Malinowski, *The Foundations of Faith and Morals: An Anthropological Analysis of Primitive Beliefs and Conduct with Special Reference to the Fundamental Problems of Religion and Ethics* (London: Oxford University Press, 1936).

24. A. R. Radcliffe-Brown, *Method in Social Anthropology: Selected Essays*, ed. M.N. Srinivas (Chicago: University of Chicago Press, 1958); see also A. R. Radcliffe-Brown and C. D. Forde, eds., *African Systems of Kinship and Marriage* (London: Oxford University Press, 1950).

25. Bronislaw Malinowski, *Myth in Primitive Psychology* (Westport, CT: Negro Universities Press, 1925), 79.

26. Several of Paul Ricoeur's essays in *The Conflict of Interpretations* (Evanston, IL: Northwestern University Press, 1974) explore Levi-Strauss's work and prompt hermeneutical considerations.

of these universal structures. It is these binary oppositions that, I assume, account for what now appears in our primitivizing of the other—particularly the Christian other from Africa or the global South. Mary Douglas's comment about the danger of being naïve about the beliefs of others is pertinent here. Of particular note is the point about the "comfortable assumption in the roots of our culture that foreigners know no true spiritual religion."[27] Moreover, she notes, based on the work of Robertson Smith, that parallels can be drawn between what is ascribed to the primitive other as magic and what is ascribed to nonprimitivized religions (in this case the Roman Catholic religion) as miracle. The same variables accompany both magic and miracle and in much the same way; as the early Christians expected miracles to erupt everywhere "in response to the virtuous needs or demands of justice," so it is with what is termed magic among those who are "primitive" today.[28]

Altogether, the basic theories and history of myth map out an uneven and unclear terrain. Assumptions behind ascriptions of myth as irrational/primitive seem questionable at best, especially since such labeling comes from the outsider based inside, the currently acclaimed Geertzian fieldwork, with its thick descriptive categories in cultural anthropology. Anthropology thus becomes a springboard for understanding and articulating myth. But the forms of life that articulate these theories (that is, technologically bounded ways of being), especially when "truly human" is ascribed by the excluder to him- or herself and "less human" to the excluded, need to acknowledge the primitive other (less technologically bounded ways of being).

Another important issue connected to the above is that Enlightenment thinking, and thus modernity/secularity, is assumed for the Westerner, and currently modern and secular necessarily bracket the religious. But as Asad points out, this dichotomy assumes the erroneous anthropological character of myth as "sacred discourse," and hence the easy temptation to stand over against it and use it as a "synonym for the irrational or non-rational, for attachment to tradition in a modern world."[29] This

27. Mary Douglas, *Purity and Danger: An Analysis of Concepts of Pollution and Taboo* (New York: Praeger, 1966), 58. One must, at the same time, point out the same danger of naïveté about the religious beliefs of the Christian South because the experience on the ground often suggests a lack of attention to the Christian religion *qua* apostolic religion, regardless of the need for its acculturation to the various contexts.

28. Douglas, *Purity and Danger*, 59.

29. Asad, *Formations of the Secular*, 23.

understanding of myth, which is a throwback to nineteenth-century anthropological explorations and certainly a contributing factor to demythologizing (or de-demonologizing, perhaps, a point we will further analyze in later sections), assumes the kind of binary opposition expressed earlier: "*belief* and *knowledge, reason* and *imagination, history* and *fiction, symbol* and *allegory, natural* and *supernatural, sacred* and *profane.*"[30]

The history of the advent of these binary oppositions, often adduced in a polemical way in academic discourse, shows in the flawed assumptions and implementation of these concepts, especially in the history of western European history, which first propagated this idea. One such example is the overvalorizing of the secular (often read as modern/scientific) and its detachment from the religious (often read as primitive/irrational/mythical). The assumption, for instance, even in its positive use, that secular follows religious and is at best a mere break from the religious that preceded it, overlooks the fact that there is no linear cause-and-effect relationship or historical progress between the two, especially in the genesis of the latter. For the "secular is neither singular in origin nor stable in its historical identity, although it works through a series of particular oppositions."[31] The fact that myth is not merely a precursor to the secular but coexists with it confirms its inherent unavoidable nature and points rather to the wisdom in embracing and setting proper limits to its appropriation, rather than vilifying and distorting it.

Therefore, I am talking about myth in relationship to the secular, and the fact that myth is ubiquitous and unavoidable: myth and its relationship to wisdom is indispensable to a method in biblical interpretation and theology, has a great deal to offer theology, and is useful for the work of the church. I am inviting readers to consider what we have here: a way back to myth by means of the growing theories of myth that allow for a second look at its methodologies and uses, as well as its primary discursive spaces.

New Ways of Looking at Myth: Community, Ritual, and Practices

There are other understandings of myth that do not define it in the old anthropological way as "sacred discourse"—that is, by definition "irrational" or "nonrational"—and promise avenues to rescue myth from degra-

30. Asad, *Formations of the Secular*, 23 (italics in original).
31. Asad, *Formations of the Secular*, 25.

dation and make it possible for post-Enlightenment thinking to engage the world picture of Scripture without needing to first demythologize it. These new ways of refracting myth require looking at myth within the internal practices of communities and their religious rituals, practices that frequently manifest themselves beyond the realm of the internally private and inscrutable, becoming public and hence accessible to scrutiny, and thus offering a way to understand the myth by which a community lives. In this way the logic of myth is appropriately linked to life and the lived experiences of a community, and it derives from those experiences rather than from the philosophical props rooted in the binaries of the nineteenth century. It is an attempt to connect the truths of myth to tangible reality that is enacted in community, and it is imperative that we understand community in its diversity rather than as monolithic and viewed through a particular cultural perspective. In light of the pluriformity of cultures (including intra- and intercultural differences) and the inscribed invitation in the Bible for all cultures, tribes, nations to be addressed by Scripture, this book seeks, among other things, to help us cross the divide in our understandings of myth insofar as our ideas about myth affect interpretations of our common scriptures. Thus the global church gathers in conversation about its truth claims from the scriptures that are expressed—partly via myth—in ways that allow all voices to be heard.

Rethinking Myth in Modern Biblical and Theological Studies

The disdain for ritual—a legacy of the evangelical movement that emphasizes inward purity over outward formality—is what accounts for much of what E. Koskenniemi portrays as a general lack of interest by early German theologians in miracle.[32] This lack of interest continues to inform the direction of much theological discourse in the West today. For example, with respect to the theological interpretation of Scripture, the approach of the German theologians was guided by their understanding of Christianity as a largely syncretistic religion (an interpretation deeply influenced by Greco-Roman philosophy), and thus their work was based in great part on analyzing those influences. They may have taken their cue from the aloof attitude toward miracle-workers and miracles in rabbinic times, es-

---

32. Erkki Koskenniemi, *The Old Testament Miracle-Workers in Early Judaism* (Tübingen: Mohr Siebeck, 2005), 144.

pecially with the stoning of Honi, the circle drawer who was known for his miracles, especially having to do with rain, and who was martyred outside Jerusalem about a hundred years before the birth of Christ.[33] Yet the works of Hanina Ben Dosa (about 70 CE) were clearly conceded among his contemporaries, and he was acknowledged as a man of deeds,[34] a fact that was not lost on even those who took a taciturn stance, and thus should not have been ignored by the German scholars.[35] Be that as it may, the reality is that Scripture has come to us from a Semitic culture unlike that of most of the Western world, and thus the thought patterns and imagery that were a part of the everyday life of these people would populate the message of Scripture. Rather than conceive of these images and symbolic forms— such as the monsters and what they represent, and the anthropomorphic content of many of the descriptions of Yahweh in the Old Testament, and angels, demons, principalities, and powers in the New Testament—as constricting the transmission of the message of the Bible, the opposite might be true.[36] Instead, we might see the form in which the particular encounters with the *Real* are narrated as an invitation to transcend the strictures of our worldview, a posture that would broaden our perspective and enrich the meaning and significance of the message across cultures.[37]

The New Testament world is contingent on the Old Testament, and what we may learn of the spirit world from the Old Testament and from the intertestamental period offers additional clarity to our conceptualization of the Bible and the spirit world. The New Testament fleshes out this concept through the life of Jesus, depicted in the Gospels and in some Epistles, and offers practical ways to attend to this world, often through language, that poses problems to modern humans because it is framed in myth that is associated purely with fable. Philosophy of language and philology have sought to distinguish between myth and reason or logic and have posited that myth belongs to primitive man and that reason articulated via language postdates and transcends mythos. This connec-

33. The legend of Honi can be found in the Talmud, and a historical account of Honi the Circle Drawer is told by Josephus. See his *Antiquities*, 14.2.1 21, in *Josephus: The Complete Works*, trans. William Whiston (Nashville: Thomas Nelson, 1998), 576.

34. *Josephus*, trans. Whiston, 109.

35. Erkki Koskenniemi, *The Old Testament Miracle-Workers*, 144.

36. Leviathan, behemoth, unicorns, and the beasts in Daniel and Revelation, to name a few of the ways in which God's anger and wrath are depicted.

37. See John L. McKenzie, *Myths and Realities: Studies in Biblical Theology* (Milwaukee: Bruce, 1963).

tion between language and myth is further denoted as deriving from the misuse of the names ancient humans applied to objects that they did not fully understand, objects whose sheer presence called forth wonder and to which they attributed personality and divinity. Such divinities were on a lower plane than were those arriving later on the scene, and were based on a planned, ordered functioning of human life. Therefore, every kind of activity, especially occupations, had a representative deity, or what Hermann Usener calls a "functional god": they were limited to their spheres, but over time these functional deities became custodians of the general activities they represented. Since the name of a god was tied to the essence of the thing named, if linguistic phonetic changes occurred that corrupted the name, and the link between the name and the thing signified was lost, then the word would become a proper noun, a name, and have personality ascribed to it. Gradually, then, a personal god is born who then demands devotion of those who created it in the first place. This is how history portrays the coming into being of gods, according to the myths of the gods. Since myth, parsed as fable, is the way in which gods are believed to have appeared on the human scene, and since the God of the Bible is seen to be "wholly other" and unlike these gods fashioned by humans, then it stands to reason that what sounds mythic in how the Judeo-Christian God and the Judeo-Christian faith are described be shorn of myth. But the Old Testament itself offers the proper stance toward myth, and it is the strongest advocate for the use of myth in the life of faith.

The Old Testament and Myth

In *Myth and Reality in the Old Testament*, Brevard S. Childs describes myth as "a form by which the existing structure of reality is understood and maintained. It concerns itself with showing how an action of a deity, conceived of as occurring in the primal age, determines a phase of temporary world order. Existing world order is maintained through the actualization of the myth in the cult." [38] In contrast to this way of conceiving reality, Childs argues rather persuasively that the Old Testament understanding of reality is already a demythologizing enterprise because it stands in

---

38. Brevard S. Childs, *Myth and Reality in the Old Testament*, Studies in Biblical Theology 27 (Naperville, IL: A.R. Allenson, 1960). Hereafter, page references to this work appear in parentheses in the text.

stark opposition to the concept of reality within its cultural milieu. Citing several instances in the creation story in the Genesis 1–3 account, he points out through careful exegesis the manifold ways the redactors used the myths of their contemporary culture, jettisoning some and allowing others to remain in tension with the historic reality of their encounter with Yahweh. As Childs points out, the priestly redactor (P) "did not fully destroy the myth. Leaving the elements within the myth he could use, he reshaped the tradition to serve as witness to his understanding of reality. Genesis 1:1 testifies to the absolute sovereignty of God over his creation. The resistance of verse 2 to this affirmation does not stem from the inadequacy of the witness, but from the complexity within world reality itself" (42). The Priestly writer's use of myth in Genesis 1:1 thus offers a way to conceptualize myth vis-à-vis the Bible in our context. Myth is seen as stemming from but transcending the cultural milieu in which it germinates—simultaneously with it and over against it.

A similar argument is made from the J account of creation. We encounter the acknowledgment of sin as inconsistent with a good created order and we simultaneously reject the serpent, to whom the entrance of sin into the created order is attributed as independent and coexistent with God from the beginning (43). Thus Childs declares:

> In saga, in legend, the broken myth through these unhistorical vehicles as well as through the historical, Israel articulated her understanding of her existence. Since the new reality has taken concrete form in the life of Israel, reality is tied to every part of her total life, not just to the events possessing confirmed historicity. (102)

The broken myth is the way Childs identifies how intertextual factors aid in the interpretation of texts to arrive at meaning. The myth—and the way former images it portrays exist in the shadowy unreal—now leaps from what Anthony Thiselton describes as "dreamlike or unself-conscious or uncritical signification of myth" into "myth-consciously-used-as-symbol" form.[39]

Where myth has been left untouched, it has served as a pedagogical instrument either demonstrating Israel's infraction of and opposition to

---

39. For an expansion and use of this concept in hermeneutics, see Anthony C. Thiselton, *New Horizons in Hermeneutics: The Theory and Practice of Transforming Biblical Reading* (Grand Rapids: Zondervan, 1992), 41.

Yahweh's law, or, more importantly, a look forward to the eschatological era (71). In Israel's history, therefore, demythologizing was ongoing, with old forms negated and transcended when a new reality opposed them. Israel's success in overcoming the myth of its surrounding cultures is due largely to her understanding of a reality that opposed the mythical. This reality was Israel's new experience with God, a reality that in turn was expressed by the transformation of all its institutions. Since Israel struggled constantly to live into the new reality, "the Old Testament ends in dissidence" (97), and it remains unintelligible without being viewed in tandem with the New Testament, in which Christ and the Christ event become the new reality.

In terms of our current focus on the powers, understanding myth and mythical views will depend largely on our Christology, since Jesus of Nazareth is, in Christian theology, the image of the ultimate reality of Israel's experience, as well as the fulfillment of Israel's hopes to live into that reality. It is the concrete reality of Israel, not an abstraction or any *idea* of Israel, to which such reference is being made. While wary of the danger of understanding Israel's history as more than salvation history, and thus not to be assessed by modern historiographical standards, the attempt to divide that history up into objective and subjective aspects is troubled by the same dilemma as are the recent searches for the historical Jesus in New Testament scholarship. According to Childs, the problem with his contemporaries (and here one thinks of not only Bultmann but Pannenberg as well[40]) is the tendency to "relate biblical reality to existential history while at the same time seeking to retain the event character of biblical reality" (5). For Bultmann especially, this approach is his way of trying to free reality from the sphere of historiographical standards while preserving the event character of the encounter with reality. But, as Childs observes, following Oscar Cullmann, without historicity grounded in objective happenings of history—for the Old Testament history is shaped and given form by Israel's concrete experience, and one could see that the New Testament was given its historical form by the Christ event and the encounter of the church with the then world—there remains only an abstraction of history, and the concrete nature of biblical reality is diminished.[41]

40. Here I refer particularly to Wolfhart Pannenberg, *Anthropology in Theological Perspective* (Louisville: Westminster John Knox, 1985).

41. Oscar Cullmann, *Christ and Time: The Primitive Christian Conception of Time and History*, trans. Floyd V. Filson (Philadelphia: Westminster, 1950).

What we learn of Israel's history and how to understand it vis-à-vis myth, mythology, and demythologizing, which we claim gives us insight into the proper stance toward myth in the New Testament, is that Israel's own history, experience, and self-reflexive and critical approach to reality are such that they admit of no external historical criticism, for they are almost self-authenticating, like other claims to revelation. That is, no historical criticism outside of its experience is sufficient or capable of passing judgment on its reality or mode of presenting or apprehending that reality. This is not to say that Childs is ignorant of the significance of form criticism or declines its use in his interpretative work or in his insights on myth, for he does on both accounts, as the telling quote above suggests. He also makes distinctions among the forms in which Israel's history and apprehension of God are to be read—saga, legend, broken myth—as unhistorical construals but also as literary forms, an indication of his use of historical and form-critical modes of interpretation.

Furthermore, Childs's reflection on myth, in which he delineates broad and narrow, ascribes the narrow to the form-critical understandings of myth—which he disavowed because it defined myth restrictively, "as a literary product," instead of opening up an understanding of reality that he felt his own favored phenomenological approach accomplished. Therefore, myth is not a genus but a way of being in the world, what I mean by the irresistible and unavoidable character of myth. How this understanding of myth aids in the interpretation of Scripture is Childs's explicit agenda, in both *Myth and Reality in the Old Testament* and *Memory and Tradition in Israel*, because for him the words of Scripture—and more, their context and the form in which they are expressed—matter in interpretation.[42]

What we find in the biblical approach to myth, using Childs's insights as an example, is that reality and *the Real* can be apprehended in myth and mythic forms in Scripture, and that there are ways of knowing other than the form-critical methods that require "demything" to arrive at meaning. The same understanding of a different way of knowing that is offered by myth is also encountered in some present postmodern approaches to knowledge.

---

42. Brevard S. Childs, *Memory and Tradition in Israel* (London: SCM, 1962),

Myth between Modernism and Postmodernism

In her essay "From Pre- to Postmodernity in Latin America: The Case for Pentecostalism," Bernice Martin deals a telling blow to postmodernism's penchant for philosophical abstraction and for focusing on the *how* of human knowing rather than on the *what* of knowing.[43] She goes on to suggest that, far from being relegated to the margins as obsolete, "intellectually untenable and mere relativized preference rather than Universal Truth, empirically fragmented and declining" (as the French strand of postmodernism might assume), the state of Protestant Christianity—at least in Latin America and Africa—is burgeoning.[44] There is certainly much of postmodernism's view of culture that is concerned with philosophical abstraction, questioning incessantly what may pass for knowledge and destabilizing any claims to objectivity and universality that modernity espoused in all ranges of disciplines.[45] Martin is on the mark when she points out the often-ignored fact that many of these deconstructionist/postmodern thinkers (e.g., Lyotard, Baudrillard, and even Foucault, who has gained such a large following) project a fatalistic attitude toward the intentions of those in power and, by inference, structural powers—which include religion. They believe that those powers intentionally use discursive discourse to rope in individuals for exploitive purposes; and religion, if it can be labeled "fundamentalism," is further distinguished as obsolete.

Yet these theorists, Martin implies, are more dependent on what she refers to as "shattered fragments of Enlightenment reason," even while they seek revelation and emancipation through the essentially intellectual exercise of deconstructing "dominant discourse."[46] In short, willynilly, a certain adducing of metanarrative, a truth, a reality as framework for probing even the *how* of knowing is inescapable, even for postmodernism, which in the final analysis cannot completely escape the long reach of modernity. If what Martin implies is valid—and I believe it is—it means that much of what passes for postmodernity, with its assumption

43. Bernice Martin, "From Pre- to Postmodernity in Latin America: The Case for Pentecostalism," in *Religion, Modernity, and Postmodernity,* ed. Paul Heelas (Oxford: Blackwell Publishing, 1998), 103.

44. Martin, "From Pre- to Postmodernity," 102.

45. On this score, both the French School and the Frankfurt School, for example, reject the idea that rationality can only be found in abstract forms.

46. Martin, "From Pre- to Postmodernity in Latin America," 104.

of nonfoundationalism/postfoundationalism—which undercuts any attempts to faithfully argue for a possibility of truth and experiential knowledge as a basis for belief in the revealed mode and medium of the Bible—can be questioned. It also means that in many ways we are still dealing with the realm of modernity, with its insistence on secularity and scientific advancement, which is assumed to have overtaken and rendered obsolete the sacred and religious that it has replaced, and which then necessitates the demythologizing (de-demonologizing) of Scripture, to allow human beings caught in the light of modernity and postmodernity (rather than in the light of the Word) to see their way and function with some integrity.[47]

Having probed postmodernism's underside, however, Martin herself concedes that there are ways of viewing postmodernism that preserve their hold on philosophical realism and thus offer a peg on which to hang the possibility of a reality outside the subjective realm of the observer. Indeed, the postmodern recognition of the shifting and fluid positionality of the observer allows for the fact that the observer can take in new information in ways hitherto untried, and that the observer can adjust his or her position to the observable viewing field as needed to learn new lessons. Such insight, I believe, is the key to demonstrating the possibilities inherent in (to borrow Bultmann's words) using electricity and still believing in a three-tiered world. It is this second dimension of postmodernism, one that retains its hold on what we have described as philosophical realism, that is most appropriate to envisioning conversation about the spirit world, the world of principalities and powers, of angels and demons, a world constantly impinging on this natural world that is so artfully articulated in Richard Bell's work on the subject of evil spiritual beings, and to which we now turn.[48]

47. And yet postmodernism has promised more than it can deliver by way of integrity (wholeness) for rational human beings. And Willie Jennings is right in cautioning us against the neutral playing fields it seems to offer for hermeneutics—and perhaps even a tolerant caring world—and insisting that we look at its invitation with skepticism and remain within the bounds of the revealed truth of Christian Scriptures and care, which I take to mean the growth toward wholeness (integrity) it offers. See Willie Jennings, "Baptizing a Social Reading: Theology, Hermeneutics, and Postmodernity," in *Disciplining Hermeneutics: Interpretation in Christian Perspective,* ed. Roger Lundin (Grand Rapids: Eerdmans, 1997), 117–27.

48. Richard H. Bell, *Deliver Us from Evil: Interpreting the Redemption from the Power of Satan in New Testament Theology* (Tübingen: Mohr Siebeck, 2007). Hereafter, page references to this work appear in parentheses in the text.

Breaking Bounds: Myth and Contemporary Life

Various writers, working within Kantian and neo-Kantian perspectives, have contributed valuable insights to our understanding—and perhaps to a reclaiming—of myth for contemporary life. Notable is Ernst Cassirer, who argues, from both a Kantian and neo-Kantian perspective, that at the least myth registers states of the soul and allows for expression of the inexplicable, providing meaning through what he terms the expressive function (*Ausdrucksfunktion*) of thought, concerned primarily with the affective components of knowing.[49] Such ways of knowing that underlie mythical consciousness, for Cassirer, effectively ignore the dichotomous distinction between appearance and reality. What things appear to be, how they present, are what they are *in se*, or at least all we can know about them, or what is capable of being apprehended by us, so that in many respects the frenzied scrutiny is absurd.[50] Furthermore, the fluid nature of the mythical world that opens up itself to those who indwell it in a way that allows for various points of viewing not in a stable and consistent "but rather in a fleeting complex of events bound together by their affective and emotional 'physiognomic' characters . . .exemplifies its own particular type of causality whereby each part literally contains the whole of which it is a part, and can thereby exert all the causal efficacy of the whole."[51] This statement can be extrapolated to bear on Scripture, which has come to us in its multifaceted form as history and saga, parable, poetry, and wise sayings, or couched in the rich mythic symbolic forms found in prophetic signs in the Old Testament and in the healing and deliverance accounts in the New Testament. Some thinkers who are under the influence of this reframed Kantian epistemology argue for the value of myth in the subjective order.[52] Bell has sought in his work to return us to a biblically based

---

49. Such is the case with the development of the Roman Pantheon and Greek gods, as well as the gods of the Ewe of Africa, for instance. See Jakob Spieth, *Die Religion der Eweer in Süd-Togo* (Leipzig: Dieterich'sche Verlagsbuchhandlung, 1911).

50. One recalls here the debates about the Godhead and the knowability of God that continue in much of Western theology. See Catherine LaCugna, *God for Us: The Trinity and Christian Life* (San Francisco: Harper, 1992).

51. Michael Friedman, "Ernst Cassirer," *The Stanford Encyclopedia of Philosophy*, Spring 2011 edition, ed. Edward N. Zalta, http://plato.stanford.edu/archives/spr2011/entries/cassirer/.

52. Even Aristotle, who bridged the gap between myth and logic, says Michael Fishbane, nevertheless notes the capacity of myth to be liberating. See Michael A.

understanding of the New Testament concept of deliverance from Satan (which I extrapolate to include other evil spiritual powers, since the latter are, so to speak, agents of Satan). Bell's contribution to the discussion on myth and mythology is germane to our project, and I will engage it at some length.

In his section on myth, Bell points to the characteristics of myth in the narrated world that obviously encompass the religious, and thus the theological, as fundamentally related to the text/narrative about the protagonist. In our discussion, therefore, myth would be about Christ/ Jesus. These myths are couched within what are assumed as mythic texts. Bell points to the fact that emphasis in this case is placed on the narrated, that is, the mythic world, and not the discussed world—the mythological world. Further, within this approach to narrative is what he notes as two levels: the isotopic level, dealing with the particular space and time of the narration, which is conceived as being on a different level from that of the hearer. With other types of narratives/narrations, the second level—the world of the narrator—is integrated into that of the narration. Such narration is distinct from the parable or the metaphor (35).

But myth can also be received in two specific ways that undercut the spatiotemporal dimension of narration and narrator, the narrated world and the narrator, as described above. The time of the narrator and the narrated world does not have to be diametrically coterminous. This is because myth can be received "either mythically" or can be received "mythologically"—that is, in a myth-critical way. A myth-critical way of receiving the narrative of Scripture (and for our purposes, the New Testament language of the supernatural), however, robs the New Testament of its power to transform, heal, and liberate, which is its *telos* (36). Furthermore, one has to indwell the mythic world it portrays in toto for its claims to be ultimately efficacious. The New Testament is not a textbook or rule book; rather, it is an invitation to a life-transforming existence in company with God, with no chance of returning to our former existence, as there is, say, in the brief suspension of disbelief that transports us into the aesthetic life (a drama or piece of literature in which we experience vicariously the world the actors portray onstage), from which we are returned, however, to our world to carry on life as usual when the play/narrative is over.

Bell bases his argument on a "Kantian-Schopenhauerian framework"

Fishbane, *Biblical Myth and Rabbinic Mythmaking* (Oxford: Oxford University Press, 2003), 2–3.

that is aligned with "transcendental idealism," which maintains the "distinction between the phenomenal world and the noumenal world" while "demoting" the role of "reason" (125–51).[53] This philosophical construct becomes the platform from which Bell makes his basic argument, which ties the whole book together: that the noumenal world may be impinged upon by the phenomenal world (158). In utilizing the subject-object orientation, he is able to argue, with scriptural examples, that Jesus's ministry affected the noumenal realm.

The biblical narrative attests Bell's assertion. The mythic content of the biblical narrative is *in toto genera* from the kind usually ascribed to myth as fable, for in these narratives, seemingly mythic figures—the devil, demons, and so forth—actually have an effect on humans in the physical world and in their encounters with Jesus and later the apostles (and similar claims of faithful followers today) via exorcisms, which effect physical healing in those suffering from myriad bodily diseases. In addition, they are, faith permitting, "transported into the reality of God" (184).[54] There was never any question about the physical manifestations of these exorcisms, even from Jesus's staunchest critics, the religious leaders of his day; their furor was about the source of his powers (Luke 11:14–20).

In addition, one of Bell's important observations and contributions is that the world can be apprehended in both noumenal and phenomenal terms: one can read the biblical narratives both mythically and mythologically without, in my view, doing harm to its significance. Thus, if one separates the two modes of reading (mythically and mythologically) and allows the appropriate mode of reading the text to address the appropriate form of the text as it presents itself in the biblical narrative, we find that Scripture will disclose a proper knowledge of God and salvation for all creation. To portray a concept/encounter through mythopoeic form is

53. Bell's argument flows from his dialogue with Kantian notions, despite the harsh criticism he levels against Kant, because Kant's work, as Bell and other philosophers suggest, pulls together the works of the classical philosophical schools of Plato and Aristotle.

54. Here Bell follows the insights of James Barr, who suggests that one of the characteristics of myth is the totalizing effect it has, in that it influences and is influenced by humans who appropriate it. Furthermore, myth is not a picture language with a mere figurative corresponding meaning in reality; it functioned for primitive humans in the way that, for example, scientific or logical language functions for modern humans. Instead, the correspondence is ontological. See James Barr, "The Meaning of Mythology in Relation to the Old Testament," *Vetus Testamentum* 9, no. 1 (1959): 1–10.

not to make the concept itself a myth—as in a tale. The revelation remains true despite the medium, and while the medium must be intelligible, it need not be so only noetically, since human perception and apperception involves sensing; bodily ways of knowing are essential to existence and survival. In revealing indirectly, God invites humans to partner in the revelatory performance, a seeing and being seen, and like the movements in a waltz—stepping forward and toward and moving apart and away—a movement that continues back and forth guided by the eternal music of God's existence and God's acts. Little wonder that R. Judah, son of R. Simon, says that myth "is another language of God's primordial acts, even one that goes deeper into the unknown and portrays the living drama of creation."[55] One is even tempted to regard R. Judah's teaching as an assertion that myth is itself exegesis, a mode of inspired imagination. More need not be said.

The Place of Myth in Current Theology and Ecclesial Practice

In the present, there are still many reasons for opting to leave in the shadows what continue to be troubling doctrinal issues regarding the spiritual world. At the least, we are confronted with Christological and Christopraxial issues, because the bulk of Jesus's ministry was devoted to "casting out demons" and healings that were performed by expelling evil spirits from the victims. The picture of the present church, at least in the West, is a far cry from what is presented in the Gospels and Epistles. It is largely differences in worldview that account for such differences: the premodern/primal vs. modern/postmodern. To an appreciable extent, these divisions need to be seen on a continuum, for there is observable reason to adduce that, for many in the Christian South (if the modern period is the dividing line), their backs are partially toward premodernity while they gesture toward modernity; for many in the Christian West, it is safe to say that they stand within modernity, while a few have their backs to modernity and lean into postmodernity with regard to myth.[56]

55. Fishbane, *Biblical Myth and Rabbinic Mythmaking*, 103.

56. Though this is purely speculative, it is interesting to wonder whether a move toward postmodernity and a subsequent turning away from it might bring an about-face into premodernity. I think here of Barth's critique of modernity and its epistemological foundations. In a comprehensive summary and analysis of Barth's critique, Graham Ward, in "Barth, Modernity, and Post Modernity," in *The Cambridge Companion*

The Case for Myth and Remythologizing

The importance of myth for religion and religious expression and for sheer existence is indisputable.[57] In fact, one needs to contend with the statement that myth must have a role in revelation, even of the Christian faith. As John Knox points out, it is impossible to have religion without adducing myth.[58] While myth and mythology have acquired a new respectability among cultural anthropologists, historians of religion, and even some theologians today, I fear that theology does not push the envelope far enough. The respectability accorded the assumed mythic content of Scripture narratives seems to be a thing left in its past, primarily with Jesus and the immediate disciples and apostles and, to some extent, the early church fathers and mothers.[59] Currently, it is almost accurate

---

to Karl Barth, ed. John Webster (Cambridge, UK: Cambridge University Press, 2000), notes what Barth sees as an anomaly. A case in point is the way in which "the how of knowing" is seen to precede "the what" or "the that" of knowing. What we have in the modern turn is the inversion of how knowledge should proceed; that is, the knowing subject takes charge of the object of knowledge and how that object should be known. In premodern times, however, the reality of the object determines how it is to be known by the perceiving subject. More important, as Ward notes, "postmodernism does not simply follow and succeed modernity, but precedes and underwrites it." In a sense, I see this in terms of light and shadow: the shadow of modernism and the light that precedes and even engenders modernity.

57. The human tendency to formulate myths, to adduce myth for explanations of the inexplicable, and to be formed and, willy-nilly, to live into myths all point to the irresistible nature of this phenomenon and underscore the tenets of this current work in various dimensions. See Colin Grant, *Myths We Live By* (Ottawa: University of Ottawa Press, 1998), who argues that we have not stepped out of mythic thinking or functioning; we just think we have. Grant notes, for instance, that even science, in essence, contains its own inherent myth, that of openness to a future of possibility of answers it cannot provide today. The anticipation of "a final unified theory must also bear the marks of mythic limitations" (44). See also Paul Avis, who, in *God and the Creative Imagination*, warns against jettisoning myth, since that is tantamount to a refusal to live within the Christian imagination—the basis of the faith we profess and the worship that propels it.

58. John Knox, *Myth and Truth: An Essay on the Language of Faith* (Charlottesville: University Press of Virginia, 1964), 28.

59. Several texts attest the credence given to and engagement with the principalities and powers by the church fathers and mothers (consider *The Life of Antony*), as well as belief in a personal devil by the Reformer Martin Luther, not only as he expressed it in the great hymn "A Mighty Fortress Is Our God," but also in the incident he reported in which he threw an inkwell at the devil.

to say that the credence given to myth and its significance are covered up by a thick cloak of dispensationalism. In my view, dispensationalism—and its current modified versions—covertly rejects the mythic content of Scripture by setting temporal and even spatial limits to the efficacy of the miracles, and thus to the source and causes of the bondage. Therefore, even among evangelicals/fundamentalists who may proclaim belief in the authority and revelation of Scripture, the spatiotemporal limits set for the basic elements in the Gospels (belief in exorcisms, healings, and so on) underscore the relevance and at the same time the necessity of Bultmann's demythologizing stance: the difficulty of modern humans to understand and accept true myth.

Other, more subtle forms in which our demythologizing takes place, even among impassioned believers, are seen in how words loaded with uncomfortable mythic import are subverted and disrobed. The gospel mandate to go and preach and teach and heal is well received, except that healing translates into "being Jesus's hands and feet" in the world, which then quickly translates to "acts of mercy and kindness" to the poor or references to various forms of healing that allow us to offer a panacea through medical science, adroitly bypassing the command to go and heal in and through Jesus's name, as he and the disciples had done. The call to cast out demons and to exorcise personal spirit beings quickly becomes a self-reflexive exercise aimed at avoidance of psychological projection, accompanied by a caution against demonizing others, including institutional structures of power. In this way, the language is used without granting it its original intended meaning and primary importance, resulting in a gradual erosion of its ultimate power to be efficacious and liberating. The danger is further heightened by the assumption that we have been obedient to Scripture. In short, we mask our unbelief about the possibility of such miraculous phenomena by reframing the words and then justifying such reading by what we legitimate as a modern/postmodern reading. What continues to be puzzling is the tendency to first alter the tenets of the faith by fudging its language and meaning, and then to make it a basis of creedal belief. It is as though we invite God to work within the limits of our belief, as if faith by its nature is not a prerequisite to Christian understanding and life. Indeed, while the Greeks (in this case, the enlightened Western world) seek wisdom, the Jews (in this case, the largely religiously premodern global South) ask for signs.

How can the one holy communion of the church be informed and formed around the issues at stake concerning belief in the spiritual world in a way that satisfies neither Greek nor Jew but offers a steppingstone for both to see into the richer glory of what Scripture offers for doctrine and full salvation with the promised abundant living in anticipation of eternal life? For at the core of all pastoral theology and practice should be this indisputable *telos*.

The discussion so far has raised, among other issues, the great concern with transcending the modern worldview in order to embrace the assumed mythic world of Scripture. I concede the problem involved in bridging the gap between the biblical world and our current world, with its technological and scientific advances that make belief in the mythical world of the Bible improbable; nevertheless, belief is not impossible given the dimension of faith (a necessary part of the equation of life in the religious realm), and thus it is unconscionable to ignore the mode of scriptural message and cast away the images and the mythic language through which revelation is given. Scientific and technology-savvy worshipers gather around the Eucharist most Sundays and other days and comfortably navigate the apparent tensions between the two worlds. Could it be that the real tensions exist between the theologians and the Western ministers of the Christian gospel who are called to the task of reclaiming truth within myth by appealing to the concept of the creative imagination that attends all epistemology and whose job is to help others do the same? Ultimately it requires working toward a comprehensive theology of the spirit world that grounds substantive belief, and especially pastoral practice, where the possibility of spiritual forces may collude to mitigate intervention and to ameliorate the situation.

Karl Barth in New Perspective CHAPTER 4

A *Theology of the Spirit and the Powers*

The place of culture in the translation and transmitting of the gospel has frequently been noted, even in Scripture itself, because since its inception the Christian message has worn the garb of the culture into which it is introduced.[1] Scripture lends itself to this form of transmission because of the nature of biblical understanding of authority and inerrancy (though there are varying dimensions and emphases across the theological, and sometimes denominational, spectrum) that does not hold rigidly to the vehicle of the transmission of the message.[2] Nevertheless, I note the necessary caveat that the worldview of the vehicle of transmission should not crowd out the message—nor be on equal footing with it. As I have shown in my exploration of the African Christian pastoral scene, there is an overemphasis on the worldview, both in terms of the African culture and the cultural elements, in the readings of Scripture related to the principalities and powers. There was noticeably little attention to the pastoral and theological practices in which these admonitions, consolations, and commandments were first articulated. There is the openness to the spirit world and thus an atmosphere that is primed for experiencing the powerful presence of God in the midst of the gathered people, among whom all

---

1. See Lesslie Newbigin, *The Gospel in a Pluralist Culture* (Grand Rapids: Eerdmans, 1989); see also Lamin Sanneh, *Translating the Message: The Missionary Impact on Culture* (Maryknoll, NY: Orbis, 1989) for further descriptions and articulations of the importance of translating the message in ways that are germane to the culture and also faithful to the essence of the gospel, but in a form recognizable to the whole catholic church.

2. For further elaboration on the uses and understanding of the authority of Scripture for theological and ecclesial practice, see David Kelsey, *Proving Doctrine: The Uses of Scripture in Modern Theology* (Harrisburg, PA: Trinity Press International, 1999).

are invited not only to experience and witness the workings of God in the present but also to participate in what ushers in the Spirit's presence. An ever-present Pentecostal sensibility of the Spirit's immanence and action is expected in African worship, but somehow it is delimited and contained by the leadership and shielded off from the congregation by a practice that mimics divination in traditional African practice. Discernment, a congregational and communal gift, is exercised by the pastoral leadership in a way that undercuts the full functioning of the church as the body of Christ in Paul's analogy (1 Cor. 12 and parallels). Since there are no appropriate theological grounding and direction for practice, the openness people have to the Spirit and the spiritual world seems to be working against the purpose of the very life-giving *charis*, which is grounded in openness to the Spirit. Instead of the presence of the Spirit, which is to "bring liberty to the captives" (Luke 4:17–19), the obverse—a constricting spirit that snuffs out fullness of life—becomes the experience.

Thus there is on the Western theological scene a certain disenchanted Christian ethos based inside a drastically demythologized biblical hermeneutics. Neither the extreme dualism of the global South's hermeneutics of the powers nor the monism of the West bodes well for refracting the language of the powers for pastoral theology and practice in a global church. Past attempts to reclaim the language of the powers have not been without their attendant difficulties.[3] Walter Wink, while his work is useful in providing a nuanced and variegated reading of the powers, equivocates and thus seems to deny the reality of evil spirit beings and the powers.

From an unlikely source comes a theologian who is not normally thought of with respect to the subject at hand, to provide a way of coming to terms with the difficulties noted in Wink and others. That theologian is Karl Barth. Not only does Barth's theology provide some clarity in addressing issues of the spiritual world and the place of worldview in biblical hermeneutics, but Barth's Christocentric theology also addresses the powers. The result is a practical theology for pastoral ministry for the church in its global expression.[4]

3. See, e.g., Walter Wink's trilogy on the powers: *Naming the Powers: The Language of Power in the New Testament* (Philadelphia: Fortress, 1984); *Unmasking the Powers: The Invisible Forces That Determine Human Existence* (Philadelphia: Fortress, 1986); and *Engaging the Powers: Discernment and Resistance in a World of Domination* (Minneapolis: Fortress, 1992).

4. See Esther Acolatse, *For Freedom or Bondage? A Critique of African Pastoral Practices* (Grand Rapids: Eerdmans, 2014), where I offer an earlier exploration of the usefulness and significance of Karl Barth as an exemplary practical theologian.

Barth offers substantial theological insights for thinking through the complexities of the language of the powers and the place of worldview in their interpretation. For our purposes, his teaching on demons, framed within his understanding of creation, is particularly useful. His approach derives from several sources: 1) a thorough exegesis of Genesis 1 and 2; 2) his idea of the "impossible possibility" of sin and its corrupting power; and 3) his understanding of evil as nothingness. When properly appropriated, Barth's view can help us think through the language and place of the principalities and powers and determine how we can better understand these realities with regard to how people live and must live, even in circumstances where people do not believe in otherworldly spiritual powers. In the following pages I will focus on his explorations of worldview and the properly Christian stance appropriate to it; but first I will offer a summary of the current prevailing situation in two contexts.

Theological and Ecclesial Context: South and West

A pervasive phenomenon all over Africa today is the presence of charismatic/healing and deliverance movements. These movements are not limited to the African Independent Churches (AIC) that were their original sphere, but are in the mainline denominations that were established through the missionary enterprise of the late nineteenth and early twentieth centuries.[5] Many of the phenomena have been documented in history of religions and mission literature.[6] The basic theological underpinnings of the faith and healing ministries include credence and openness to the spirit world and belief in the power of God, through the intervention of the Holy Spirit, to direct the minutest details of an individual's life—and influence cosmic affairs as well. It is a world that assumes spiritual reality as ultimate and conceives of the universe as being filled with spirits, that they are beings bent on harming humans and necessitating humans to be alert to the point of hypervigilance. It is a world in which a disciplined life focuses on spiritual warfare rather than on God and the enjoyment of God forever.

5. John S. Pobee, "African Instituted (Independent) Churches," in *Dictionary of the Ecumenical Movement*, ed. Nicolas Lossky, 2nd ed. (Geneva: World Council of Churches, 2002), 12–14.

6. See J. Kwabena Asamoah-Gyadu, "Pulling Down Strongholds: Evangelism, Principalities, and Powers and the African Pentecostal Imagination," *International Review of Mission* 96 (2007): 306–17.

An almost opposite phenomenon underlies pastoral theology and practice in the Western Christian scene, particularly in its mainline denominations. Presenting problems are addressed solely through sociocultural and psychotherapeutic modes. In fact, so prevalent is a psychotherapeutic approach to health and well-being that it is as much a norm to be in consultation with a psychotherapist or psychologist as it is the norm for the African to consult with a diviner or with a pastor who is a "seer." From debilitating addictions, fractured marriages, and emotionally crippled children suffering from the fallout of divorce—especially when such problems appear to have no tangible bases—to vicious killings and devastating disasters that destroy humans and beasts, gross personal evil, and "nature, red in the tooth and claw"—all are invariably attributed to some physically and scientifically explicable cause.

In the first chapter I explored the African religiocultural underpinnings of African theological anthropology and the way it affects biblical interpretation vis-à-vis the spirit world. Its overemphasis on evil spiritual beings intent on harming creation, and especially humans, pays undue attention to these spirit beings and thus detracts from the real purpose of Christian existence—the experiential knowledge and enjoyment of God on account of which all humans are expected to offer God lordship of their lives.[7] In the second chapter I expressed concern with the scientific worldviews and existential theological postures that pervade current Western theology, especially its pastoral practices, and the effects those worldviews and postures have on paying attention to the total well-being of counselees. I indicated that the disenchanted religious atmosphere in the church does not match the kind of enchanted reality prevalent in the society as depicted in the media, especially in film and literature. How can we bring African Christian theology, in general, and

7. The strictures of postcolonial living and the deep existentialist questions that attend extremes of poverty—ill health and joblessness on the one hand, the vulgar wealth and material flourishing on the other, especially when the latter group is made up of the Christian/spiritual leaders—produce the relentless yearning and hope, as well as frustration, that continue to drive many seekers to these externally vibrant places of worship. See Paul Gifford, *Ghana's New Pentecostalism: Pentecostalism in a Globalizing African Economy* (Bloomington: Indiana University Press, 2004); Philip Jenkins, *The Next Christendom: The Coming of Global Christianity* (Oxford: Oxford University Press, 2011); and Asamoah-Gyadu, "Pulling Down Strongholds," for further insights into these growing churches and trends and the promises and challenges entailed in thinking about church in the African context.

its anthropology more consistently into line with the gospel message of hope it seeks to expound without weighing it down by a cosmology that reinforces fear? How can we bring a more variegated theological approach that is able to effectively integrate a spirituality based in belief in the spirit world into the psychotherapeutic model of pastoral counseling in the West? For often the spiritually integrated models, helpful as they are in incorporating the spiritual perspectives of the counselees, do not give credence to the world of spiritual reality. Therefore, the understanding of and belief in raging conflicts between evil and good on a spiritual level to which care-seekers hold—which are in their "social imaginaries"—those implicit affective sensibilities that ground one's way of being in the world are given little to no consideration in the psychotherapeutic encounters.[8] A certain monism with regard to the spirit world, which believes in God but repudiates belief in other spirit beings as real, prevails.

Consequently, I turn to the theology of Karl Barth and the promise it holds for addressing both the global Southern and the Western churches on their belief and stance on the spirit world as it is refracted through the language of principalities and powers. Since such beliefs are part of a worldview that issues in certain religious sensibilities and practices, I turn first to Barth's explication of such a worldview and its place in understanding biblical reality; then I will explore his expositions on religion, especially on Christianity; finally, I will discuss his understanding and articulation of the biblical view of the demonic and evil as it relates to his concept of "nothingness," to which he accords no ontological reality. My aim is to begin to build a viable architecture of the spirit world as articulated and intended by Scripture for our traversing of this earthly existence as those in the world but not of the world (John 17:6).

Worldview and Biblical Hermeneutics

I need not rehash here the extensive debate and long correspondence between Barth and Bultmann on the place of philosophy and worldview in biblical hermeneutics, or on the development of Barth's thinking over the course of his life. Instead, I will limit our discussion to a few salient aspects

8. Charles Taylor, *Modern Social Imaginaries* (Durham, NC: Duke University Press, 2004), 23.

KARL BARTH IN NEW PERSPECTIVE

of Barth's thought. For Barth, faith is a gift of the Holy Spirit that enables belief from outside the believer and thus does not need shoring up by the justifications of philosophy nor accommodation to worldview, which was the way liberal theologians, before and during his time, were approaching biblical interpretation.[9] Since faith was a gift in which God chose to reveal Godself and invite humans to fall into the embrace of the unknown, any attempt to make it become a human achievement by setting up the props that clear the way to faith undercuts the very ground of faith. Faith as faith is groundless, because faith just is (Heb. 11:1).

Against Bultmann's insistence that it is impossible to speak only from the subject matter (citing the fact that Paul, whom Barth uses as exemplar, listened to other spirits), Barth could only point out the flaws in Bultmann's assertions, offering a rejoinder that the Spirit of Christ does not compete with other spirits in the scriptural narrative.[10] On the contrary, the other spirits are all brought under subjection to the "crisis of the Spirit of Christ."[11] Thus, while heterogeneity was acknowledged as present in the texts, how one was to understand these texts with respect to the real subject matter, Christ himself, was always to be directed by the example of Paul and the Gospel writers.

> We must be content if, despite other spirits we are not wholly bereft of the Spirit. . . content with a readiness to discern in a spiritual fashion what is spiritually intended; and satisfied also to recognize that the voice with which we proclaim what we have received is primarily nothing but the voice of those other spirits.[12]

9. Barth carried on a correspondence on worldview with Bultmann over a period of three years, as well as with his own teachers, Adolf von Harnack and Wilhelm Herrmann. For more on the debate and Barth's ideas, see Gary Dorrien, *The Barthian Revolt in Modern Theology: Theology without Weapons* (Louisville: Westminster John Knox, 2000). While the issues raised in these debates were shrouded in the understanding of philosophy as a foundational discipline in the 1930s and may no longer be viewed as such today, the tensions that called forth the debate continue in the theological psyche and, while often denied and or repressed, continue to show up in a fair amount of theological writing that concerns a theology of religions.

10. Rudolf Bultmann, "Karl Barth's Epistle to the Romans in Its Second Edition," 1922 review article reprinted in *The Beginnings of Dialectic Theology*, ed. James Robinson (Richmond, VA: John Knox, 1968), 117-20.

11. Bultmann, "Karl Barth's Epistle," 117-20.

12. Karl Barth, "Preface to the Third Edition," in *The Epistle to the Romans*, 6th ed., trans. Edwyn C. Hoskyns (Oxford: Oxford University Press, 1975 [1933]), 19.

The concluding phrase is the key to understanding Barth's sometimes convoluted thinking on the subject of the relationship between theology and worldview, especially philosophy. Barth understands that all language about God and the Word is fallible, tentative, and somewhat relative, coming as it does through cultural lenses. But it is by no means the proper posture of Christian theology to subordinate the Word to the lenses of modern biblical critical tools, reducing its primary reality, God, to a manageable aspect of the whole—so that modern humans may understand it. For Barth, the Word cannot be known fully (because there is hiddenness even in revelation) but can only be expounded "in weighty negations. . . and paradoxes." And one might argue for the salutary[13] nature of Scripture and posit that its purpose is not that it be understood, but that it transform all who come into contact with it, and that it has to be "apprehended as the negation of the starting point of every system which we are capable of conceiving."[14]

Barth goes on to develop a more extensive argument in the *Church Dogmatics*, declaring his stance against these systems, especially their bearing on the knowledge of humanity, the object of God's love, and the focus of pastoral practice.[15] Humans are in themselves a text,[16] a *poema* of God, and thus anthropological knowledge should stem from theology rather than philosophy or other scientific—especially social scientific—perspectives lest we miss the true human whom God addresses. It is clear that Barth eschews a reliance on philosophy and the social sciences, but makes allowance for acknowledging the inductive sciences as long as they do not set themselves up as possessing definitive insight about the "real" human and do not become dogmatic about such insights.[17] There is a real danger, he notes, that their knowledge and insights are set above those of theology, since such bodies of knowledge regarding humans stand in opposition to the Christian confession. We may make these bodies of knowl-

13. See Ellen Charry, *By the Renewing of Your Minds: The Pastoral Function of Christian Doctrine* (New York: Oxford University Press, 1999), for an extensive exploration of this point. Of course, one must also be careful not to deem this salutary aspect of Scripture as merely pragmatic.

14. Barth, *Epistle to the Romans*, 278.

15. Karl Barth, "Doctrine of Creation," in *Church Dogmatics*, III (Edinburgh: T. & T. Clark, 1960) (hereafter *CD*).

16. Charles Gerkin, *The Living Human Document: Re-visioning Pastoral Counseling in a Hermeneutical Mode* (Nashville: Abingdon Press, 1984).

17. Barth, *CD*, III/2, 12.

edge circumscribe what is theorized about the reality and limits of the world, the place of the humans in it, and what humans can legitimately believe—especially in modernity. In this case they influence religion as it is thought out and practiced by humans; that is, religion is thus at risk of being framed within the parameters not only of cosmology but also of a worldview that is akin to it.

Barth on Religion

Barth's understanding of and exposition on religion show that he saw religion as a stumbling block to knowing God.[18] His own views and writing style have evoked serious criticisms, some of which are warranted, but many of which have arisen from a misunderstanding of what has been shown to be a mistranslation of an important word in his work on religion. In this section I closely follow Garrett Green's work—which itself is close to Barth's—and begin by noting that in Green's introduction to Barth's *On Religion*, he points out that Barth has been misunderstood or mislabeled as "neo-orthodox" by certain groups, implying that Barth's theology is one that is purely reactionary. If anything, Barth should be considered postmodern in the sense that he became a thinker who believed that the subject matter at hand should dictate its proper approach, and that there is no reason to think that a certain secular canon of inquiry, approaches, reasoning, and presuppositions should be normative for one's writing, nor that such an approach is less biased than a committed one (e.g., that of a committed Christian who, like Barth, takes theological inquiry to be a "virtuous circle" of sorts).[19]

Green argues that Barth has been dismissed by those who focus on "the study of religion," first, because they erroneously believe that only "objective, neutral" viewpoints should be considered, yet these do not consistently apply their own postmodern, critical rhetoric; and second, because many people erroneously believe that Barth rejected "religion" outright. As to the first issue, Green contends that it can be helpful to read Barth in survey courses on the study of religion because he offers a fresh approach that invites interrogation, and such interrogation leads to self-

18. Barth, *Epistle to the Romans*, 98–99.
19. Karl Barth, *On Religion*, trans. and intro. Garrett Green (London: T. & T. Clark, 2006), 1. Hereafter, page references to this work appear in parentheses within the text.

awareness about prejudgments in even so-called objective approaches. As to the second point, Green blames it on the oversimplification of Barth's views on religion, an oversimplification that stems from a certain key German word in the text that was poorly rendered in the original translation. Whereas the original English translation of the German *Aufhebung* is "the abolition of religion," Green submits that "the sublimation of religion" is a better translation. We must not understand "sublimation" here in the Freudian sense; rather, Green means it to have both the negative meaning that "abolition" carries and the somewhat contradictory and paradoxically positive meaning of "making sublime."

The key to Green's position, and to the way he suggests that we interpret these three subsections of Barth's work, is a kind of Hegelian dialectic. That is, first Barth shows how revelation is religion—or rather, it appears in the world in this form. Then Barth argues vigorously in the second section that revelation smashes the many-headed idolatry, the works-righteousness that is religion; therefore, revelation is presented as religion's greatest threat and enemy. Then, in the third section, Barth brings the reader to a new point of synthesis, in which, after an absolute rejection of religion, it can be reaccepted in a qualified way. No religion "is" the true religion, but the Christian religion can "become" the true religion. By this, Barth seems to be pointing to the need to begin completely anew from the position of radical dependency and trust that the Christian can only have by God's gift of revelation. Then, from this standpoint, Christianity can be seen both as the demolishing and the sublimation of religion. In other words, because of its basis in revelation, Christianity has embedded in it the germ of antireligion that fights its own tendency to become a religion that is based in works-righteousness. This is a very important point as we consider the relationship of Christianity to African Tribal Religion and also African expressions of Christianity.

Barth's views on Christianity's place among the religions are complex. There is at times the treatment of Christianity as an exceptional case; at other times there is the suggestion that Christianity is no better than—and, in fact, not very different from—the rest (34–35). Christianity receives a privileged place when looked at from the standpoint of faith. By this, Barth does not assume that only believers can see that Christianity is best; rather, I think he also and more deeply means that Christianity is or becomes something different when approached from within the faith-world. For he strongly criticizes the early apologists who, in his view, seemed to take pride in arguing that their religion was better than that of the pagans; Barth believes that in so doing they were evaluating in the age-old human way and starting from a human standpoint rather than allowing everything to be radicalized by faith.

Barth is emphatic that revelation has priority (our thinking must be "Christological") over religion, so we cannot think about religion first and then fit revelation (that is, true Christianity, rightly understood and received as gift and confrontation) into the picture (51). Barth believes that certain Enlightenment thinkers and those who followed them made "religion" into a separate something to be studied in a very new (and problematic) way. Religion was no longer a sub-issue of Christian ethics (the virtue of religion, that is, proper worship due to God), but a generic term under which scholars grouped Christianity (in all of its aspects—its revelation, worldview, life-stance, and so on), along with all the other "religions" (now viewed as concrete, objectifiable things that we can look at as if from above or from the outside).[20]

This attitude toward the study and understanding of religion, I believe, is nowhere more problematic than in the sphere of the language of the principalities and powers, what is adduced to be mythology by the Enlightenment theorists. Their thinking still pervades the theological landscape and contributes no end to the assumptions of Christianity as a religion like any other religion without the caveat that Barth so artfully articulates. There is the need to sound the warning again, and perhaps even more loudly now in our postmodern era, with its penchant for relativizing truths and requiring of all disciplines, including theology, an objectivity that is nonexistent or unattainable.[21]

20. While the objection might be raised against Barth of being exclusivist in the worst possible way, it must also be pointed out that the Christian religion, according to its Scripture, presents itself in this way with respect to other religions. Further, the nuanced position of Barth's thinking on the relationship of Christian truth to that of other religions is often lost in the conversation on religious pluralism, especially in the West, where real religious pluralistic coexistence is in its embryonic stages. See Esther Acolatse, "All in the Family: Recasting Religious Pluralism through African Contextuality," in *Religion, Diversity, and Conflict*, ed. Edward Foley and Don S. Browning (Vienna: Lit, 2011), 261–71.

21. See current works in the field of theology and science, e.g., J. Wentzel Van Huyssteen, *The Shaping of Rationality: Toward Interdisciplinarity in Theology and Science* (Grand Rapids: Eerdmans, 1999); Michael Polanyi, *Personal Knowledge: Towards a Post-Critical Philosophy* (New York: Harper and Row, 1964) and *The Tacit Dimension* (Gloucester, MA: Peter Smith, 1983); as well as James E. Loder, *The Knight's Move: The Relational Logic of the Spirit in Theology and Science* (Colorado Springs, CO: Helmers and Howard, 1992).

Religion inevitably finds itself in self-contradictions and frustrating inner dialectics, but it is only exposed as faithlessness by revelation. "All religion is idolatry and works-righteousness, even at the allegedly higher stage where it seems to want to overcome idolatry and works-righteousness by its own powers and its own methods"; for it is "exposed on the one hand by *mysticism* and on the other by *atheism*," which pretend to be "alien forms" but are not (72). Religion, first of all, seeks satisfaction in the "representation of divinity and the fulfillment of the law" (72). Man wants "a truth *above* him and . . . a certainty *within* him, both of which he thinks he knows and . . . can produce for himself" (73). The starry heaven above and the moral law within him tell him these things exist and are attainable; so the need is not the absolute kind of need that can only be empty-handedness before God.

For Barth, "the divine judgment that religion is faithlessness" applies to everything human, including a judgment of Christians and Christianity. It is a judgment of revelation and thus not one that can be defended on any other grounds. In all respects, religion acts in a willful way, seeking to "grasp" God and truth. The externalization of this attitude is image-making (or philosophical conceptualization), which is no less problematic, whether of false gods/fetishes or attempting to "grasp" the true God. Barth seems to suggest that God, the Real, cannot be known, since we can only know something of the Real, with a slanted gaze at best. The opposite stance is faith, which can only be response. Faith in revelation is being receptive to "God's self-offering and self-presentation." And to this point, it is appropriate to add that the mode and medium of revelation be God-initiated and driven as well. (I will revisit the implications of this statement later in this chapter.)

Barth on Evil, Nothingness, and the Demonic

It is noteworthy that Barth situates his larger discourse on the demonic, what he terms the "lordless lords," in his treatise on the Christian life, where he deals primarily with the Lord's Prayer and offers an exposition on each of the petitions in turn. Barth sees the prayer and petition for the hallowing of God's name, as well as the prayer for the ushering in of the kingdom as intertwined with zeal, a zeal that is firstborn in our relationship with God, who is acknowledged and claimed as Father.[22] Further-

---

22. Karl Barth, *The Christian Life: Church Dogmatics IV, 4: Lecture Fragments* (Grand

more, for Barth, "zeal" rather than "desire" is the operative word because it necessarily coincides with suffering—suffering for the honor of the name of the Father that one petitions to be hallowed (113–14). This suffering, I take it to mean, anticipates the fellowship of the suffering with the Christ, who gives birth in the believer to the new life that is wrought on behalf of all humanity by the death of Christ on the cross. It is this sharing in the fellowship of his death that the Christian participates in, offering up his freedom for the very petition offered for the hallowing of God's name. On account of this, Christians are enjoined not only to pray for the establishment of the kingdom on earth as it is heaven, and are not only to be zealous for seeing that the kingdom is established, but they are to be actively engaged in revolt against the circumstances that mitigate the establishment of the kingdom on earth. "Christians are summoned by God's command not only to zeal for God's honor but also to a simultaneous and related revolt, and therefore to entry into a conflict" (206). Barth points out that the use of the word "revolt" (particularly its military connotation, which has an obvious reference to the Christian life as warfare) is intentionally placed in the New Testament so as to underscore what may not be so evident and might seem peripheral to some:

> Behind the idea of the *militia Christi* there obviously stands a general recollection of the story of Gethsemane [Mark 14:32–42 and par.], just as behind this there stands the story of Jacob-Israel, who wrestled with God (Gen. 32:24–32). In the New Testament, and especially the Epistles, the idea of conflict usually stands close to that of faith, to which it is related. It is a comprehensive term for the wrestling with inner and outer assaults on the existence and witness of the Christian—a wrestling that has to be militant and that carries with it effort, danger, and distress. (206)

Barth continues with an exploration of the dimensions of this warfare or conflict and incorporates other allusions to the Christian's engagement with such opponents by recalling Paul's injunction for how an athlete engages his craft in order to emerge a victor (cf. 1 Cor. 9:24–27; 2 Tim. 2:5) (206). As with the spiritual warfare, the athletic endeavor also entails suffering. Moreover, a defensive stance is required of the Christian engaged

---

Rapids: Eerdmans, 1981), para. 77, 112. Hereafter, page references to this work appear in parentheses in the text.

in this warfare, a stance that, while defensive, nevertheless proceeds out of the initial offensive tenor of the attack launched on the opponent through the preaching of the gospel, through righteous living, and through a manifestation of zeal for the kingdom of God on earth.

> But faith, in and for which we are to fight according to these sayings, is in itself and as such a spontaneous human action awakened by the Word of God. It does not exist for its own sake nor curve in upon itself but takes place in a movement of man out from and beyond himself, and therefore directly or indirectly in a challenge, in an attack on the dominion of unbelief. As this attack, it is itself attacked and has to maintain itself against the assault. Maintaining itself means standing in the attack that it has itself launched. It is on the defensive because it holds up its shield on the offensive. (206)

It is clear that Barth takes it for granted that Christians are, by virtue of their new location (*in* but not *of* the world), necessarily engaged in this conflict; and the fact that this discourse is placed in the section on *The Christian Life*, I believe, points to the normality with which he views the conflict that is inherent in Christian existence. The Christian's ability to be steadfast in this struggle and to endure to the end is dependent on being armed "with what is expressly described in Ephesians 6:11–17 as the *panoplia tou theou*" (206), descriptions of which shore up the point that this is an offensive/defensive battle requiring an offensive/defensive stance from the Christian. An additional element of this summons and response to stand in the battle is faith—faith that is engendered by the call of God through his word (206).[23] The target of this fight is the "wiles of the devil" and the unrighteous stance against God that issues forth in their own unrighteousness. In this stance that the Christian takes, there are the makings of revolt and rebellion—and not merely a rejection of the wiles of the devil or the encroachment of the world and cosmic forces. It is at once, then, a defensive stance into which an offensive stance is built, an active rather than a passive state. To pray the second petition of the Lord's Prayer is to be necessarily involved in its answering; it is the participation in this

---

23. It is important to note that, for Barth, while faith is a gift, it is not the private possession of the individual recipient. It is rather a calling forth of belief in the individual for encounter with God.

living and powerful event in the great hope of God's future, where the vitality and force of little hopes for the present of a person and of people will not be lacking: the free and responsible advocacy, actualized in little steps, of that which in the light of the act which God has commenced and will complete can be called human right, human freedom, and human peace, of that which very provisionally and incompletely can already be these things. (213)

The prayer, the daily act of communion with God the Father is to be thus also for the benefit of all humanity and the cosmos—in particular, that humans might live abundantly. Anything that lifts itself up against the possibilities and actualities of attaining such freedom is to be expunged by confrontation and rebellion. Praying and action are thus necessarily intertwined.

> Invocation of God in and with this prayer, obedient human action in this vertical direction, implies (as the same obedient human action) the horizontal of a corresponding human, and therefore provisional, attitude and mode of conduct in the sphere of the freedom which, as they pray for the coming of the kingdom, is already given to them here and now on this side of the fulfilment of the prayer. Thus to pray the prayer does not excuse them from provisionally rebelling and battling the disorder in their own human thoughts and words and works. On the contrary, they cannot pray the prayer aright without in so doing being projected into this corresponding action of their own which is provisional but nonetheless serious in this particular sphere. (212–13)

Of course, Barth is aware that some action can be wrongly motivated and thus become wrong action; at the same time, I believe that the kind of vacillation that may attend human attempts to clarify motives until a pure one is distilled can lead to terrible inertia and back-pedaling from the serious task of confronting the powers—or living in the offensive/defensive mode. Wisdom attained through discernment within the body—the church—is essential not only for being but also for doing righteous battle in this regard. In the next chapter I will return to precisely how this form of discernment can take place among believers.

The Powers as "Lordless Powers"

But who or what are these renegade powers, and how do they function in the cosmos? Barth uses a two-pronged approach in identifying and describing the presence and functioning of these "lordless lords." He first situates their emergence in the account of the Fall and its consequences for humanity. The attempt by the first human beings to be self-governing (as if that were in any way possible), following the tempter's lie that they could be like God, is the first instance of the presence of these lordless lords. In their attempt to be their own gods and lords, humans slipped into a lordless and godless existence; they found that the very spirits that they produced by their affront to their creator could not be harnessed and controlled. The wayward desires and thoughts of fallen humans have given birth to these various spirits that have in turn gotten away from them: spirits who, like their progenitors, did not want to be under authority (214). Eventually, these spirits that humans have conjured up for their service have become instead the humans' masters (215). But in the same way that humans cannot escape the presence of God, these spirits are incapable of fleeing the presence of God. Their alienation from humans, like that of humans themselves from God, does not necessarily go both ways: that is, God has not therefore ceased to be their God and Lord. Barth goes on to say:

> Indeed, God is not just their frontier; he is at liberty to make use of them in the fulfilment of his will. They may pretend to be absolute, but they cannot be so, nor can they be effectively lordless (even their multiplicity forbids this). For God is their Creator, they are his creatures, and they stand at his disposal. (215)

For Barth, then, these lordless lords, these "powers, abilities, and possibilities of life," are nothing but the spirits behind humans' fierce independence and not in any way suggestive of otherworldly created beings. But that does not suggest that Barth gives no credence to the presence of otherworldly spirit beings that are evil—an oft-assumed position for him. Barth's thinking on the subject is more nuanced than that, even though his dialectical approach at times obfuscates his points on the issue. These lordless lords, notes Barth, "have no real ontology in relation to the reality of God or even humans, and their real purpose is shrouded in obscurity and ambivalence. Furthermore . . . the wraithlike transitoriness with which they manifest themselves, one appearing here and another there, then disappearing or retreating to give place to another, then appearing again" may add to the notion that they do not exist (215). Yet these characteristics do not in any way suggest that they are unreal. To be sure, their shifting form and their differing functions across cultures and eras at both the individual and cosmic levels, the seeming mystery in which they shroud themselves and their activities—appearing simultaneously familiar and unfamiliar—contribute to the inability of humans to concretely name them and thus give them this nefarious aura of unreality. The proper way to address who they are and speak of them is in "consciously mythological ways" (216).

Barth goes on to underscore the need for Christians to avoid being pulled into the position of indecisiveness regarding these powers, based on the seeming nebulous way that he describes their existence and activities, and we do well to note this admonishment.

> We must not be led astray, however, by the reservations just adduced. We have to *speak* about these powers. We have to do so because we *see them* and *know about them* and have to take their reality and efficacy into account. We have to do so because in all their strangeness they are real and efficacious. (216, italics added)

Not only is Barth insistent on taking these lordless powers as real, but he suggests that those in the Western world might look beyond their rational sensibilities to others, who may see more clearly than those ensconced in Western Enlightenment thought.

> In this matter we have one of the frequent cases in which it has to be said that not all people, but some to whom a so-called magical view of the world is now ascribed, have in fact, apart from occasional hocus-pocus, seen more clearly, and come much closer to the reality in their thought and speech, than those of us who are happy possessors of a rational and scientific view of things, for whom the resultant clear (but perhaps not wholly clear) distinction between truth and illusion has become almost unconsciously the criterion of all that is possible and real. (217)

I will take up Barth's point here later (in the discussion of bridging the bifurcation between Western/North Atlantic and Southern views); but for now I will turn to other ideas inherent in Barth's understanding of the lordless powers, ideas that perhaps further complicate how to perceive the elements of the created order—especially his concept of nothingness and evil, which are obvious aspects of his explorations of the spiritual world and the demonic.

Nothingness and Evil

Barth's concept of nothingness associated with evil is found mainly in *CD* III/3, in his section on the "Doctrine of Creation." In fact "nothingness," which is further explicated as "that which is not" (*das Nichtige*), is the general term Barth uses to describe evil.[24] Nothingness "is an element to which God denies the benefit of His preservation, concurrence and rule, of His fatherly lordship, and which is itself opposed to being preserved, accompanied and ruled in any sense, fatherly or otherwise" (289). But we may not ask the question "what is nothingness?" For in the very asking of that question, the presence of the verb "to be" raises Barth's objections, and would, in fact, be an anomaly, because it ascribes existence—being, becoming—to what is in reality nothing. Accordingly, Barth ascribes no ontological reality to this nothingness. Only God and God's creation/creators really are, and nothingness can be neither of these dimensions of existence (349). Nothingness, at the same time, is not nothing. The issue is further complicated by Barth's insisting that all things inhere in Jesus, through whom and by whom all things were created and necessarily owe allegiance (Rom. 11:36).

Two positions must be avoided, says Barth: one is that of the Manichaeans, or Priscillianists, who, in saying either too much (*in excess*) or too little (*in defectu*), were in danger of *a causalitas mali in Deo*, placing the source of evil in the Creator and thus violating the holiness of God (possibly in an attempt to hold to the oneness and unity of God). The other position would be to default to the reasoning of the Pelagians in placing the origin of evil entirely within the bounds of the creature (possibly in order to maintain the holiness of God), in the process undermining the lordship and providence of God (292). The danger is surely always present because the believer is thrust into this dilemma by maintaining the sov-

---

24. Barth, *Church Dogmatics*, III/3, 289. Hereafter, page references to this work appear in parentheses in the text.

ereignty and lordship of God while figuring out the origin and scope of evil or nothingness. The wrong focus here could easily yield what Barth portrays as

> the danger either of an uneasy, bleak and skeptical overestimating of its power in relation to God, or of an easy, comfortable and dogmatic underestimation of its power in relation to us. (293)

At the same time, we are urgently invited to question and to try to resolve—or at least make sense of—the dilemma produced by the conflicting claims Scripture and Christian dogma have produced concerning the powers for millennia. This urgency is filled with the joy of the ultimate victory provided by the Christ event over these lordless powers and over the nothingness from which it is born and to which it gives birth. It is engaged at the same time with the appropriate trepidation of those who know that no real systematic and complete understanding can be brought to bear on these matters, and also of those who know that these powers, while low with respect to God, are high with respect to us (295).

Barth's point and approach to uncovering and assessing and addressing the issue of the powers is the most persuasive and fitting approach because the theological task matches the form in which Barth has presented it. In the same way that these creatures operate outside God's providential parameters, existing within the space between God and creation—at once showing themselves and yet at the same time obscuring—so also does Barth frame and present his insights. He thus engages the powers with equanimity and trepidation (but not uncertainty) and uses an appropriately piecemeal approach, proceeding in fits and starts with the accompanying breaks that mimic the elusive nature of the powers. But we must not shirk the responsibility to pursue understanding these powers, because it is both necessary and achievable (294–95).

We can talk about the powers cogently and assuredly in a consistent way regardless of the veil shrouding certain aspects of our knowing. A first step is to come to terms with what they are or are not. In this regard, the approaches to uncovering their identity and function, explored earlier, coupled with the insights gained from Barth, move us forward in making some formal conclusions about the powers.

On Religion, Revelation, and the Powers

The powers and our relationship with and understanding of them do not occur in a vacuum. They function for us at the level of religion; that is, at the level of our engagement with ourselves, the world, and God (in whatever way we conceive of God), and how we live at the intersections of these engagements. Our religious outlook and practices, and our formation in religious spaces, affect how we approach the principalities and powers. It is thus important that we underscore and probe religion and the various forms in which it is thought out. While a detailed theology of religions is beyond the scope of this work—and Barth himself does not give undue attention to such a theology—nevertheless a few observations are in order. These observations take for granted the normativity of the biblical attestation for our Christian experience and expression as starting points. The Bible is the primary source of our insights about all matters of belief, rather than some doctrines or theologically formulated extrapolations, even if these come from Scripture. In fact, this is Barth's own stance on the subject of theology and biblical interpretation. At the same time, we need to be cautious in how we juxtapose communication and interpretation, especially when we are crediting a text with timeless truth. We need to ask where meaning lies,[25] for we are often in danger (perhaps more as Africans, with an oral heritage, recently introduced to texts) of understanding meaning as lying within the text and as independent of author and reader in a particular historical and cultural context; and this can, in turn, lead to the kind of "proof-texting" often used as a means of guidance in current African pastoral situations.[26] At the same time, as Samuel Ngewa,

25. And, of course, talk of meaning necessarily evokes the second question: "By whose reading?" See Stephen E. Fowl and L. Gregory Jones, *Reading in Communion: Scripture and Ethics in Christian Life* (Grand Rapids: Eerdmans, 1991), and David Kelsey, *Proving Doctrine*, for further elaborations on this question, as well as avenues for thinking through the various scenarios of how Christian communities use and interpret Scripture.

26. I find examples of this phenomenon also in certain postcolonial biblical hermeneutics. For instance, the view of Jesus as liberator, devoid of the meaning of salvation and an understanding of sin as a result of the Fall, easily translates into liberation from colonialism. Or, with regard to our own current explorations of the powers, the tendency to read the meaning and understanding without reference to the practices of the earliest church and its vision of Christian life. Since we understand spoken words in the context in which they are uttered, the same criterion must apply to texts. For further elaboration, see Samuel Ngewa, "The Validity of Meaning and African Christian

following E. D. Hirsch, points out, we need to be vigilant against using the quest for meaning as "a playground for jostling opinions, fancies, and private preference."[27] Therefore, attempts to arrive at "the meaning(s) of texts require that meaning-seekers live faithfully within the text and the context, and because this text is also the revealed word of God (speaking from a Christian perspective), that the conceptual priority and preference be given the text over the context of the reader and interpreter.[28]

The Powers

I start my dialogical interchange on the function and understanding of the powers with Barth, because his treatment of them appears straightforward and less problematic in light of his own thorough processes and presentation of arguments. Of what/whom are the powers, it seems fair to say, that Barth's own dialectical moves allow him to say much and then seemingly almost nothing. They simultaneously *are* and *are not*; they are at once standing against the Lord Christ and subjected to him as created beings; and they are during the same time a warning against underestimating their power in reference to humans. At first blush, one might be tempted to think that Barth's view is not that different in the final analysis from Wink's; the latter seems to vacillate between the notions of the powers as both structural entities and personal beings. It is almost clear that Barth thinks of these powers as both "structuring structures" and personal beings in subjection to Jesus Christ. But it is not quite clear whether he treats them entirely as personal beings who influence the "structuring structures," a position that is markedly different from the

---

Theology," in *Issues in African Christian Theology*, ed. Samuel Ngewa, Mark Shaw, and Tite Tienou (Nairobi: East African Educational Publishers, 1998), 49–55.

27. Ngewa, "Validity of Meaning," 51.

28. It is worth noting that, from a pastoral-theological perspective, such guides for reading apply to the narrative life of the person, what Gerkin terms "the living human document." This "document" is, as it were, sometimes both text and context for reflective engagement in pastoral practice; the individual's or community's own readings of Scripture are always in the mix and relevant for addressing issues of pastoral care. In fact, it is in attention to practices of care that one finds Scripture and the theology that ensues from it illuminated. It is through practice that text(s) and context enter into dialogic encounter and are shaped and reshaped in an ongoing way for the benefit of both. See, e.g., Don S. Browning, *A Fundamental Practical Theology: Descriptive and Strategic Proposals* (Minneapolis: Fortress, 1991).

"inner spirits of external structures" as, for example, Wink proposes (i.e., as autonomous spirit beings that are external to the structures and not what inhabits the structures, as in, e.g., mob violence). Barth seems to walk a very tight rope between seeing these powers as personal beings and as "structuring structures"; but one can sense that he tips toward an understanding of them primarily as personal spirit beings, and he does not speculate about their source, form, and function to any great extent.[29] And he safely overlooks some details that occupy the minds of Wink and other intertestamental scholars.[30] At the same time, a more conservative reading (which Barth himself would welcome since his entire enterprise allows for differing dialogical partner voices in aid of the truth) may require, at the least, that Barth explore the continuing tension between how one comes to understand God as the Lord of "the lordless lords," but not their Creator, yet he remains the creator of all. If God exercises his will positively and negatively, should there not be a corresponding ontological reality that does the same? And could one logically follow with the assumption that the Creator of the whole world would also, in this regard, be the Creator of "nothingness"? Why would pronouncing all creation as good—indeed, very good—have to include a "No" along with the "Yes" from the beginning of creation? Does Barth's dialectic take away from the possibility of a real devil, who was from the beginning (in spite of the fact that such thinking opens him up to the kind of dualism he eschews)? Or is it possible to think of the devil as a real ontological being and yet not walk into the trap of a complete dualism? (That is possibly what lies behind Barth's resistance to attributing ontological dualism to the devil.) How might the African thinking, in its traditional religious form, of Supreme Being and evil spiritual forces and the current African church belief and practice about the reality of evil spiritual powers/devils/demons, interrogate Barth's thinking? In fact, how would it be closer to the experience of Jesus (in his ministry, life, death, and resurrection) as well as that of

29. See, e.g., his use in *CD* of Blumhardt's encounter with the devil and the language in which he describes it. But as I noted in chap. 2, see also the very useful exegetical functional list that Wink's work provides for clarifying the powers and their aid in arriving at meaning.

30. Although we have painstaking details of types and forms of demons, and the origin and development of Satan in other sources, Barth does not find it necessary to offer such information, as if he means to detract from the overvaluing of these created beings. It is enough that the evil of these beings, including Satan, and what they stand for are taken up by the perfect Son and dealt with on the cross.

the earliest churches? As an earlier work by Karl Heim suggests, if we take the reconciling work of Jesus Christ seriously, only two possible avenues are open to us with regard to other evil spiritual forces: 1) that the Satanic power is a reality—and I take this to mean ontological reality—or 2) everything that Christ represented in himself up to the cross and resurrection, and that the biblical witness attests about his destruction of the evil satanic dominion is pure myth in the fairy-tale sense.[31] If the former is the case, it is clear that we cannot understand or address human weakness and frailty in general and explore presenting problems in a holistic and comprehensive way in pastoral practice, without taking seriously the possibility of evil spiritual forces over and against all that is created good. It is fairly obvious that such reality is more present to some than to others, but it might be that intellectual roadblocks contribute to derailing credence in the possibility of the reality of these spiritual powers. But that is an entirely different matter that cannot be addressed at the intellectual level only, since what is spoken of here is largely a matter of faith—perhaps faith seeking understanding. While it does not bypass the intellect, it also does not set too much store by it.

On Religion and Revelation

Attempts to address Barth's perspective on the issue of the relationship between revelation and religion, particularly Barth's strong words against religion, have usually circumscribed the issues at stake. Part of the problem lies in Barth's own comprehensively nuanced and reflexive articulation of the distinctions he lays out, and the playful paradox that brooks no seriously sustainable disagreements with his insights.[32] It might be fair

---

31. Karl Heim, *Jesus, the World's Perfecter: The Atonement and the Renewal of the World*, trans. D. H. van Daalen (Philadelphia: Muhlenberg Press, 1961), 70.

32. See, for instance, summaries of engagements with ardent defenses in Garrett Green, *Karl Barth: On Religion* (London: T & T Clark, 2006), and in John Webster, ed., *The Cambridge Companion to Karl Barth* (Cambridge, UK: Cambridge University Press, 2000). See also Johannes Zachhuber, "Speculative Theology in the Wake of Kant. The Nineteenth Century," undated entry on Zachhuber's website at http://users.ox.ac.uk/cgi-bin/safeperl/trin1631/main.cgi?5+.

Zachhuber's attempt to heal the breach between Barth's discordant notes on revelation and religion walks a tightrope that could make him totter either way. His appeal to rethink Kant's critique (which he believes Barth may have perhaps misunderstood

to say that serious disagreements may be pursued more with the biblical basis of Barth's insights (and this applies to his entire theological project), and that would mean a jettisoning of the inherent logic of the Spirit in Scripture, which provides the warrants for his arguments and conclusions. If my assumption is correct, then Barth might be calling both the theological academy and the church it serves to return to engaging biblical hermeneutics in a different way, that is, to not only read the Bible with the tools offered by the form-critical and narrative-theology approaches, but also devotionally, culling its salutary essence, its ability to form people for life with God. In short, it is thus a way to make doctrine and theology aid in the pastoral work, work that is central to this present project. In this regard, Barth's position is one I am sympathetic with, but as I have noted here, with a caveat.

The protests Barth mounts against taking philosophy too far in theological work may be leveled against him with regard to his understanding of religion as faithlessness, for it seems that his posture gives little room for the benefits of religion and religious effect, even for the apprehension of revelation. Granted that revelation comes from outside, does it still not require a predisposition in the human being toward the religious? As is obvious in my analysis and use of Barth, I concede that he has a valid point. On the issue of religion and its counterpart, philosophy, we can adduce a scripturally normative stance indicating that religions/philosophies could be, on the one hand, divinely providential in guiding us toward apprehending God, and on the other, as having the capacity to be demonically inspired and thus inherently deceptive and deluding, fostering such spiritual poverty that can only be cured by God's mercy. At the same time, it is logical to assume that humans made for fellowship would surely have inbuilt propensities for seeking communion before and even after the Fall.

As I have observed above, several authors have engaged Barth's ideas on religion, especially as they relate to revelation, but frequently the attempts have skirted the main issues.[33] It is important to work out the kinks in the tension between revelation and religion because the work of

---

or misappropriated) and to uplift Hegelian dialectic or a Schellingian turn to positive philosophy seems hardly convincing, in my opinion.

33. See Garrett Green's expositions in *Theology, Hermeneutics, and Imagination: The Crisis of Interpretation at the End of Modernity* (Cambridge, UK: Cambridge University Press, 2000). See esp. the discourse in the debates surrounding a comparison of Barth's thought with Derrida's, as well as interactions with Feuerbach's ideas on semiotics and language.

discernment in pastoral practice requires a passable bridge from one to the other. It is this bridge that allows for the theology embedded in the gospel, "the subject and content of Christian doctrine" that "does not have to do with any such production of the human spirit or human conscience,"[34] to come to the one for whom it is sent out and to confront this one, to touch and transfer this one into a new dimension of self-knowledge—and through a communication of something new—to chart the map for salvation.[35]

There are African and Western historians of Christianity (e.g., Kwame Bediako[36] and, to a lesser degree, Andrew Walls[37]) who have the tendency to valorize African Christianity and its cultural expression. While I do not completely support their arguments—nor do I buy wholesale the role of the primal imagination as preparation for reception of the gospel—a complete negation of it, as in Barth's understanding of the relationship between religion and revelation, is also problematic. His argument (and its basis) seems to constrain even God, for it leaves hardly any room even for a God-human engagement (barring the incarnation, which is, of course, pivotal in his thinking). Barth's concept of religion as faithlessness allows us some freedom to work with the religious thought of both the global Western and Southern churches—but only in a limited way with the latter. For to concede wholeheartedly to the lack of continuity between African primal religious sensibilities and the gospel is to make no room for understanding the gospel and its translatability, as Lamin Sanneh points out.[38] Furthermore, what Walls narrates about the history of Christianity would be moot.[39] While I am not by any means

34. Karl Barth, *Learning Jesus Christ through the Heidelberg Catechism* (Grand Rapids: Eerdmans, 1981 [1964]), 17–18.

35. Barth, *Learning Jesus Christ*, 17–18.

36. See Kwame Bediako, *Jesus in African Culture: A Ghanaian Perspective* (Accra: Asempa, 1990) and *Theology and Identity: The Impact of Culture upon Christian Thought in the Second Century and in Modern Africa* (Eugene, OR: Wipf and Stock, 2011). For as Bediako asserts, there is inherent in ATRs an overt preparation for the gospel. This is a charge that can be sustained against Barth's position.

37. Andrew Walls, *The Cross-Cultural Process in Christian History* (Maryknoll, NY: Orbis, 2002).

38. See Lamin Sanneh, *Translating the Message*, as well as a later article on the same theme: "Gospel and Culture: Ramifying Effects of Scriptural Translation," in *Bible Translation and the Spread of the Church: The Last 200 Years*, ed. Philip Stine (Leiden: Brill, 1990).

39. Walls helps us see that the inevitability of the translation principle is inherently

making a case for natural theology, I may perhaps adduce arguments from Jungian notions of "the collective unconscious" (seen as harboring theological/religious echoes) concerning how people come to believe at all, while at the same time acknowledging the theological assertion that faith is primarily a gift from the triune God.[40] Possible questions that come to the fore in such considerations are: first, would "faithing"—the human capacity to use faith—be also a gift that all humans made in the *imago Dei* possess? At this point it is fair to ask whether Barth's account of religion can be seen as based on elements that characterize its Western form/tradition, particularly among its educated elite. This is because recent texts on Pentecostalism and the sensibilities that attend worship in churches characterized as charismatic, point to the kind of overt dependence on the Holy Spirit that should apply to Christian expressions of faith and suggest that a thicker description of what *is* Christian is required for Barth's point to be sustained.[41] Second, what if "Christian" necessarily implies and can only be accounted for by the kind of dependence on God for revelation/salvation that Barth is able to credit with the noun "non-religion" and the only one that does not come under judgment of God? Barth seems not to have taken full account of the pneumatological factor that bridges revelation and religion, especially a religion that takes over the body with all its sensing faculties.[42] Even in the places of high Protestant church practice, with its emphasis on the Word, the presence of the Spirit makes the words become more than merely words; rather,

---

built into the gospel message and is what propels and allows for transplantation into other cultures. At the same time, we note that translation implies correspondence of objects and signifiers in the other language culture, which complicates and problematizes the argument we are making. Yet one does not need exact, one-to-one correspondence to make adequate translations.

40. C. G. Jung, *The Collected Works* (Princeton, NJ: Princeton University Press, 1966).

41. James K. A. Smith, *Thinking in Tongues: Pentecostal Contributions to Christian Philosophy* (Grand Rapids: Eerdmans, 2010); Asamoah-Gyadu, "Pulling Down Strongholds."

42. Barth's strong emphasis on revelation, which is completely from God about God, stems from the tri-unity of the Godhead (Revealer, Revelation, and Revealedness) as well as the Word (written, incarnate, and proclaimed), and is based mainly on the incarnation. But the charge McGrath and Bonhoeffer level against his thinking has some merit. They suggest that Barth's emphasis on the incarnation brackets the cross because he assumes that man's fault is ignorance rather than alienation. But one could argue with Barth and suggest that ignorance of one's alienation is the prime sin of humanity.

it engages the whole affect. When one troubles these aspects of religion, as it were, would one come away with some semblance of what the incarnation points to—the fact that the divide between revelation and religion (the bodily affective sensibilities intact) is not that wide nor has it been ruptured? How else would revelation occur, since it is always mediated, if there is such a gap between revealer and apprehender? Barth does note that the ability to apprehend at all is itself a gift granted to some, based entirely on God's act alone,[43] and at the same time we are to assume that God grants piecemeal, and at the points of revelation, the capacity for faith and then retracts it; or might we be closer to what is true, following the analogy of gift-giving, that such capacity/receptacle for the gift is already in all individuals? Could Barth's understanding of faith as being granted/renewed at moments of particular encounters with God run counter to Scripture especially if, as Scripture implies, faith is a gift—and further, that gifts are irrevocable (Rom. 11:29)? It is thus a gift of the new creation that begins with repentance and conversion that is by far the entrance to faith most prevalent in the Christian South, where conversions still involve transformation of the whole being. Here, then, "Christian" is a noun and not an adjective that describes certain actions, as we often use it. It becomes the skin (speaking from an African perspective, recalling how culture permeates and undergirds all living such that all thinking and actions are permeated by it) that one lives in rather than garments that are put on and taken off when necessary. It is within this new identity—and as part of the living church, of which Christ is the head—that proper understanding of faith should be understood.

On the one hand, a Christian knows that what has been received is carried by grace and every instance of believing is grace-breathed. There is a spiritual intuiting that one is not acting in these instances but rather acted upon, and God is the actor. In this way the Christian lives in gratitude that she is given grace to believe and receive, but that does not mean that the prior experience dies off and is replaced by a new one in each encounter, which Barth's comments run the risk of implying.

There is an obvious double bind here, because we are invited to know a God who is knowable; at the same time, we cannot claim knowledge in any

43. John Webster notes that "Barth insists that in this event of revelation God is the Subject from first to last" (see Karl Barth, *CD* I/1, 296; *CD* 1/2, 1). "What this means," Webster adds, "is that God acts 'from above' (*CD* I/1, 242) to secure what must happen on both sides of the knowing relation" (Webster, ed., *Cambridge Companion to Karl Barth*, 47 [Kindle edition]).

actual sense, [44]and perhaps that is what Garrett Green refers to as a "herme-neutical vulnerability that Barth displays as he reaches his own conclusion about the knowledge of God."[45] But again, as Green and all theologians will attest, the "hermeneutical imperative" requires that we seek answers not merely for cerebral knowledge but for experiential knowledge; for, af-ter all, it is to a relationship with this God that humans were made and to which they are invited. And the fact that reconciliation is at the heart of the biblical witness propels us to seek understanding in faith that we may know to whom and for what we relate. It means that questions of religion, as they relate to revelation, matter from the human side, and even from the God-human side; religion is the lynchpin in our relating. It is both the practice of God and of human beings coinciding to draw together in particular ep-isodic but concrete reconciling moments until the *parousia*. Furthermore, it is also in the realm of religion that we make the kind of hermeneutical moves that allow us to interpret Scripture one way or the other (for our theologizing is religion), and the relationships between how to conceive of revelation and religion—which offer insight into religion and its prac-tices—are all within the realm of religion qua religion. Doctrines, however pristine, are still born of practice. There is an obvious impasse here, and one needs to be careful not to stray too far in either direction, but rather hold both aspects of the seeming divide in tensive unity and yet not view them as two sides of the same coin. It is the same kind of inseparable unity that attends Barth's own dialectical approach to theology, an approach that takes as its frame of reference the coincidence of divine sovereignty and human freedom and the tensions of which add the noted complexity to Barth's framing of the relationship between religion and revelation, an approach with which I generally sympathize.

44. Here one is invited to think along the lines of George Hunsinger, who pains-takingly parses out the distinctions between actualism and reality in Barth's thought, for Hunsinger makes room for becoming rather than being; see, e.g., *CD* I/2, 226–55. For further explorations, see George Hunsinger, *How to Read Karl Barth: The Shape of His Theology* (New York: Oxford University Press, 1991).

45. Garrett Green notes that Barth made a most remarkable statement in his trea-tise on the knowledge of God in Chapter 5 of *CD* II/1. He goes on further to propose, based on Barth's assertions, that if one were to take seriously the underlying assump-tion of the claim that God's grace distinguishes the *circulus veritas Dei* from the *Deus ex machina*, then, quoting Barth, "we can surely wish to have it no other way than that we cannot in fact defend ourselves in face of that question" (*CD* II/1, 246). Green goes on: "[N]ot only *are* we defenseless as believers, Barth is saying, we should want to be!" (*Theology, Hermeneutics, and Imagination*, 164).

Nevertheless—and more importantly—for the purposes of addressing the correct understandings of the language of the powers in pastoral practice, the church, I have suggested, may need to reclaim and reappropriate the language of myth. But can the church reclaim myth and use mythological language appropriately without paying attention to religion and religious practices? Does it not seem clear that revelation is necessarily carried by the vehicle of religion? Perhaps a relation of religion with revelation, in which the two are not parsed out as neatly and strictly as Barth attempts to do, might help bring his thoughts out of the current idealistic mode and lead us toward the essential existentialist mode that religion allows.[46] Altogether, then, when Barth says that "revelation is God's self-offering and self-presentation" and comes to our religious selves, but he also judges religion, since "religion is resistance to revelation," we can agree with the first part of his statement and not necessarily fully agree with the second part. Could we say, then, that Barth is right in claiming that revelation shows us that religion is "the enterprise by which man anticipates that which God wills to do and does do in his revelation," but it is not always the case that in religion a human contraption has been put "in place of the divine handiwork"?[47] If, as I am suggesting, the existentialist moments that attend to being human (birth, the vicissitudes of life, and death) constitute the real meeting space between God and creatures, as emphasized in creation, then religion and the religious space can be and are utilized by the divine for intervention without repudiation. A prime example is the incarnation, I think. The incarnation opens up that space, one can say, with some latitude, without liminality.[48]

Finally, we should note a warning from Foucault. While it is through language and narratives that knowledge is produced (and thus power, since knowledge is power), serious problems are posed when the vehicle

46. I am thinking here of the numerous ways both the OT and NT emphasize and command ritual, be it the various feasts and structured performances in the OT or the sacraments in the NT, and the assumptions that rituals, as, for example, in the Table of Remembrance or Baptism for belief and formation, are an important part of the life of faith.

47. Garrett Green, "Introduction: Barth as Theorist of Religion," in Barth, *On Religion*.

48. Patricia Ranft's insight into how the church understands the space opened up by the incarnation is apropos in this regard. In that space "humanity is elevated without divinity being degraded." See Ranft, *How the Doctrine of the Incarnation Shaped Western Culture* (Lanham, MD: Rowman and Littlefield, 2012), 83.

of transmission is that of the powerful colonizer; and no matter how thick descriptive research might be done on the ground, much is lost in presenting findings in the language of the academy. In particular, the realm of religion, which in its ineffableness transcends language, loses its rich and multifarious texture with its cultural connotations and complex ambiguities. When we allow African Christian religious practices, for example (barring the problematic extremes I noted earlier), to interrogate Barth's claims about revelation and religion, we might even be surprised. It is possible to say, then, that religion that mars revelation—in spaces like the global South, which is currently teeming with religious fervor, a fervor marked by an affective dimension that takes over the whole person—that could not be the kind of religion that Barth critiques here. For such religion seeks, at the very least, to engage the divine as the only recourse for deliverance in all circumstances.[49]

Reshaping the Conversation

I have offered this discourse on hermeneutics, religion, and revelation as it impinges on our interpretation of the language of the powers and principalities in the New Testament in order to aid us in pastoral practice, and to allow us to approach presenting problems in a holistic way. The approaches to unraveling the language and meaning of the powers discussed in the second chapter—the existentialist approach (Bultmann), the structuralist approach, the functionalist approach (Wink), and the personal/spiritual being approach (Boyd)—all have their promises and limitations for pastoral theology and practice. The several accounts of the powers and principalities as they are conceived of by the primary sources,

49. One has only to witness Africans in worship to experience the sense of utter dependence on the supernatural, with no pretensions that they are worthy but with great expectation that God, the Holy Spirit, will show up and meet worshipers both corporately and individually. See attestations and descriptions of such worship scenes in Asamoah-Gyadu, "Pulling Down Strongholds." It is important to note that such a worship style is not localized but seems to be the ethos of worship in the Diaspora as well. Perhaps it is that their being recent converts and living within the bounds of Scripture as their primary theological source contributes to what is witnessed in African Christianity. And it is precisely this bibliocentrism that marks Barth, who has also been described as a biblicist (of course, there is more to his theology than that, as John Webster notes in his defense of Barth's approach to the biblical text. See Webster, "Introducing Barth," in *Cambridge Companion to Karl Barth*, 59 [Kindle Edition]).

the New Testament itself, lead us to affirm that "the Bible has no single cosmology."[50] Instead, Scripture shows that the powers are both supernatural and structural beings, and that these inhabit not only relational and physical (bodily!) realms, but also the psychological. Barth's approach seems to incorporate and accommodate these varying perspectives while remaining grounded in the scriptural witness, insisting that worldview and its philosophical shoring should not be the primary mode of extrapolating what Scripture teaches on the subject. In short, the scriptural witness does not tie itself to any particular perspective or worldview, but uses and disposes any of them at will, and so should all who would use such an approach in their biblical interpretative task.

Another distinctive feature of Barth's approach is that he rests his arguments on Christological moorings and not on the anthropological considerations found in the dominant existentialist approach of Bultmann. Paradoxically, it is his Christological focus and its promise that frees humanity from the existential angst that troubles and sometimes debilitates; and the existentialist/anthropocentric move of Bultmann somehow does not quite fulfill the expected end of easing the existentialist angst, as one would expect. This is as it should be if the Christ event is what the earliest witnesses and ancient Christianity make it to be: the once-and-for-all-time second Adam through whom humanity is restored to former glory—full weightiness and wealth of being.

The existentialist approach, which focuses on the human and then addresses the human from the human perspective, betrays the kind of speculative philosophical approach that only results in futile attempts to answer an endless circle of questions and in the end does not aid in ameliorating the ravages of being human This approach follows in the line of religion based inside a certain natural theology that Barth eschews. It is not that Barth is unaware of the presence of God in nature or of a kind of revelatory act in other religious traditions, for he speaks of the reality of human beings to have "impressions" of the reality of God in the world that "lay hold of us with serious force,"[51] whereby "we may not speak of an absolute, independent, and exclusive ignorance of God in the world."[52] The tacit opposition to "generalize and to systematize" such phenomena "along the lines of a natural theology" is because it is a next step in making

50. Acolatse, *For Freedom or Bondage?* 123.
51. Barth, *Christian Life*, 122.
52. Barth, *Christian Life*, 127.

religion the basis for Christian theology (that is the subject: human activity including belief, etc.) and thereby also for theological anthropology. For Barth, such a move produces not only an abstract picture of God, but also an abstract and erroneous picture of the human being. This kind of speculative philosophy, says Barth, "arises in the arid place—unspiritual in the biblical sense of 'spirit'—where man has not yet heard the Word of God or *hears it no longer.*"[53] We can obtain no true knowledge of the human being without reference to the relationship between God and human beings, a knowledge that comes to us by revelation, by which Barth means, ultimately, Christ and the Christ event.

In revelation, we are confronted both with the limits and possibilities of the human being in just measure such that the despair of the limits of creaturely existence is affirmed at the same time that the possibilities are encountered in the person of Jesus, the "real man" and "the man for all men."[54] I will take up the anthropological considerations of revelation as encounter and pastoral practice in the next chapter, but it is important to note that revelation is mediated by the Holy Spirit, the communion-fostering person of the triune God.

> The reason, and the only reason, why man can receive revelation in the Holy Spirit is that God's Word is brought to his hearing in the Holy Spirit. For the capacity of man to do this depends upon the fact, and only upon the fact, that it is God's Word which is brought to his hearing in revelation.[55]

Somehow Barth's insistence that apprehension of revelation proceeds only from God to human, based on his reading of Scripture, lends itself to an apparent constricting of religion to the point that if all that is required is from God's side, then the human response, which is also initiated from God's side, becomes moot.[56] Of course, Barth would be the first to disavow such a conclusion because he makes it abundantly clear that what sets the human being aside and makes for true humanity is that there is evidence of the true human. This is because the first mark of being human is that in Christ, God has set upon himself to be the human be-

---

53. Barth, *CD* III/2, 12 (italics added).
54. Barth, *CD* III/2, 46.
55. Barth, *CD* I/2, 247.
56. See Barth, *CD* I/1, 296; see also *CD* I/2, 1.

ing's partner, and the only way to truly be partners is for all to be wholly themselves. In God's election of human beings as covenant partners, they are not thus called to be overwhelmed and overshadowed and minimized by God but rather set "on [their] own feet" for partnership in encounter.[57] It means that we can infer that there would be a response that is human-dependent, what is from the side of human beings. And would that not be what we find in the realm of religion? Whether it is how Barth is read and interpreted that leads to the conclusion of his negation of religion, or whether Barth overstates the case for the priority and precedence of revelation—and especially one that makes no room for the experiencing subject—is debatable.[58] But ultimately, if we believe that Barth's thinking on revelation and religion is either 1) derived from the Protestant German experience of his day, or 2) biblically based, our choice determines how we will approach and implement his thinking. My sympathies are currently with the latter perspective within the bounds of the caveat already expressed. It is likely that if we bracket Barth's rather polemical voice and concentrate on the positive insights that his discourse provides, we might be more inclined to accept his understanding of revelation with respect to religion as normative for theology and the church. But such a posture bespeaks the nature and history of the church, and unless it is viewed as a spiritual reality with an apostolic history, and with a clear eschatological *telos*, the authority of Scripture, to which revelation as we are exploring it points, is irrelevant.[59]

As is becoming clear, much of what I have to say and how I proceed with my interpretative framework for analyzing the language of the powers and its place in the affairs of humanity necessarily rest on revelation and its relationship to religion—that is, on human apperception. And this quest for the correct hermeneutical language is no small task given the divergent views of scriptural interpretation. Therefore,

---

57. Barth, *CD* IV/3, 941.

58. Several debates on the relationship of revelation and religion have occupied the theological and religious landscape. Among the central issues is the epistemological question regarding how one knows what one *knows* as revealed and the ambiguous nature of that knowing—in short, the authority of experience—for revelation occurs at the level of experience and the experiencing subject. See the collection of essays in L. Boeve, Y. De Maeseneer, and Stijn Van Den Bossche, eds., *Religious Experience and Contemporary Theological Epistemology* (Dudley, MA: Leuven University Press, 2005), esp. 269–316.

59. See Barth, *CD* I/1, 214.

the claim I am making for the centrality of revelation via Scripture is a claim that is itself hedged around with difficulties.[60] But for now I need to note particularly that this work of interpretation and hermeneutics is also encompassed with trust-bound elements, with faith as its lynchpin. Accordingly, I will observe some dynamics of revelation as we move on to the anthropological and practical considerations that stem from the discussion so far.

The Dynamics of Revelation in Anthropological Perspective

First, God's self-revealing is particular rather than general: God makes Godself known to some rather than to all in the economy of revelation and redemption, and the revelation is conceived of as an act expressed in the person of Christ, the God-man, and not in some knowledge of the mystery of God.[61] The relationship of revelation to religion thus hangs on Christology, and the question of how Christian understanding of revelation differs from that of other religious traditions comes with it. If the Christian understanding of revelation—and Barth's assessment of it—is correct, then the revelation within other religious traditions must be related to Christ insofar as he is Lord of all, including the "lordless lords."[62] But Christians are the ones who need to be more cautious as they speak and think of revelation, since they possess the written word and run the greater risk of equating the Word of God with the revelation of God as embedded in a set

60. Garrett Green suggests that a possible way of refracting what Barth is saying is to appeal to the language of imagination, since Barth's language in his whole discourse stems from that source. It seems, on the contrary, that while his idea might have promise for preventing us from focusing on the point of contact in the human being for revelation, that imagination also stems from a *point of contact* in the human and may beg the question of validity of properly imagining and receiving imagery. Additionally, could Green merely be replacing religion with imagination since they both, by his analysis, are the loci for revelation? See Garrett Green, *Imagining God: Theology and the Religious Imagination* (San Francisco: Harper and Row, 1989).

61. Barth, *CD* I/1, 140, 329; *CD* I/2, 209.

62. See Barth's exposition on the Word of God and other words (*CD* IV/3, 113–65) and the promise of the Spirit, which applies nevertheless to all regardless of faith (*CD* IV/2, 354–56). For practical theological and interfaith implications of this understanding, see Esther Acolatse, "All in the Family: Recasting Religious Pluralism through African Contextuality," in *Religion, Diversity and Conflict*, ed. Edward Foley and Don S. Browning (Vienna: Lit, 2009).

of texts, especially since they can apply form- and historical-critical tools to analyze and synthesize such texts.

As Trevor Hart points out (following Barth's thinking on revelation), doing so leaves us with the risk of situating God in history—and in my view losing both the revealer and the recipient of revelation—since God transcends the temporal and spatial parameters of history.

> [F]urther, we risk falling under the dangerous illusion that God's "Word" (the biblical category most closely corresponding to that of revelation) is something which has, as it were, become an earthly commodity and been handed over into human custody and control, domesticated and packaged for responsible human use.[63]

In other words, the words in Scripture are not the words of God even though Scripture *is* the Word of God.

Secondly—and stemming from the previous point—because revelation is particular and not general, and since God chooses to reveal Godself to those God wills and not to others, attempts to make revelation accessible to all has no real scriptural basis and finds itself in the realm of religion based on natural theology.[64] Such thinking fosters the idea that the human has inherent capacity for knowing and receiving knowledge of God outside the realm of faith, which is a gift from above. To adjust revelation to accommodate religion, which is what other approaches to unraveling the mythological language of Scripture inadvertently does, is to place the creature above the Creator; as I have pointed out, that represents a loss to the creature on whose account we seek to redress the difficult impasse between revelation and religion. Associated with this selective revelation of God is the fact that one cannot un-know what one has known (regardless of what form that knowing takes) for "in the Holy Spirit we are confronted by what we cannot deny even if we wanted to do so."[65]

What Barth's insistence on not grounding anthropology in philosophy or any other discipline offers, despite the polemical tones in which it is couched, is a way to speak about the human point of contact for revelation

---

63. Trevor Hart, "Revelation," in *The Cambridge Companion to Karl Barth*, ed. John Webster (Cambridge, UK: Cambridge University Press, 2000, 45 [Kindle edition]).

64. Barth, *CD* I/1, 140, 329.

65. Barth, *CD* I/2, 246.

without slipping into error: either the error of undercutting divine sovereignty or one of undervaluing human freedom and participation. The mediating principle between these two extremes is not so much another doctrine to correct for possible anomalies, but the God-man himself, the mediator, "the human for God and the God for humans," on whose life humanity is patterned and undergirded by the Holy Spirit, the communion-creating person of the triune God.

As we can surmise, not only does revelation rest on Christology—that is, that Christ, the act of God's revelation, is the bridge between revelation and religion—but also that anthropology rests on Christology and only in this way is the real human revealed and "affirmed and made new by the revelation of God; and it is man whom the revelation unites with his fellow-men."[66] Not only is Christ the revelation of God, but in acting to bridge revelation and religion in his being—as fully God and fully human—his life and pattern and constitutive form allow us to make inferences about what and how to believe, including how to believe and respond to concepts of the spiritual realm and thus how to navigate the language of powers presented in the New Testament and portrayed in the life of the earliest churches, and also the form of the human on whom these powers impinge. Two avenues for response are predicated on this knowledge: First, we function Christopraxically in both the African and Western contexts, and in that regard we function in ministry where belief in the spiritual world characterizes common life; even when it seems to be peripheral to life, it shows up in fascination with the enchanted world through various media. Second, we pay attention to the constitution of the human, the living human document, as a "besouled body" and "embodied soul" in indissoluble union with a common destiny, for what affects one aspect affects the other aspect equally. Ultimately, we are to understand the effects of these "lordless lords" on humanity, and through this Christopraxical lens we will confront and unmask them as the "impossible possibilities" that they are and delimit their influence in the lives of suffering people. But at the same time we must recognize that any influence they bring to bear on humans affects humans totally and needs to be addressed holistically.

---

66. Karl Barth, "The Christian Understanding of Revelation," in *Against the Stream* (London: SCM, 1954), 235, cited in J. A. Veitch, "Revelation and Religion in the Theology of Karl Barth," *Scottish Journal of Theology* 24.1 (1971): 1–22.

Contextualizing Ephesians 6

CHAPTER 5

How Lived Is Our Theology?

What is the nature of the world picture and the assumed reality Scripture portrays, and how has it been viewed and interpreted in the various eras and contexts of the church? What has been the guiding framework for interpretation of Scripture and the world it portrays in each epoch of the church's life? Has the church always accommodated the culture and its need for understanding Scripture, or have interpretations and interpreters taken their cue from Scripture and ultimately the Holy Spirit, the inspirer of the words and the guide into all truth (John 14–16), about the object of Scripture? Ultimately, it asks, has it taken its hermeneutical cues from the culture it seeks to engage and, in a sense, is it fleeing from the Spirit in its engagement of the world with the Word? This is the larger theological question I address in this book, and thus in this chapter I attempt to give an answer to this question by setting before the reader a description of a biblical view of reality that is expressed in a pastoral context and addressed to ordinary Christians in their everyday lives. In a word, it is an approach to interpretation that, while it seems to be nebulous, is nevertheless the only way to interpret Scripture—biblical realism. This is the distinct and characteristic mode of interpretation that, while utilizing form-critical and literary-critical methods, is careful not to let Scripture become redundant or replaceable for the church. The church lives in the world and yet lives within the confines of another reality presented to it in Scripture, a Scripture that is handed down to it about Israel's testimony of the reality that confronted it in the midst of other peoples and cultures with their own realities. We need to understand and acknowledge that this reality stands apart, over against all other reality, and that what it presents to us in Scripture, and what is attested by the prophets and the apostles, is tangible and real—even if ineffable. The unique characteristic of this reality has been attested in our day in the lives and testimonies of many, and it cannot be jettisoned or run over roughshod by the myriad modern interpretive tools. This is the kind of world described in Ephesians 6:10–20, a text that offers us a glimpse into the beliefs held by the earliest Christians about how to live in light of the reality of the world presented.

Ephesians 6:10–20: A Survey of Interpretations

In the midst of the difficulties of navigating familial relationships, like all humans across the centuries, we receive these words of Paul to the Ephesian Christians:[1]

> [10] Finally, be strong in the Lord and in the strength of his power. [11] Put on the whole armor of God, so that you may be able to stand against the wiles of the devil. [12] For our struggle is not against enemies of blood and flesh, but against the rulers, against the authorities, against the cosmic powers of this present darkness, against the spiritual forces of evil in the heavenly places. [13] Therefore take up the whole armor of God, so that you may be able to withstand on that evil day, and having done everything, to stand firm. [14] Stand therefore, and fasten the belt of truth around your waist, and put on the breastplate of righteousness. [15] As shoes for your feet put on whatever will make you ready to proclaim the gospel of peace. [16] With all of these, take the shield of faith, with which you will be able to quench all the flaming arrows of the evil one. [17] Take the helmet of salvation, and the sword of the Spirit, which is the word of God.
>
> [18] Pray in the Spirit at all times in every prayer and supplication. To that end keep alert and always persevere in supplica-

---

1. While there is debate about the authorship of Ephesians, there is a general agreement on its being in the Pauline tradition, and some go as far as claiming that Paul himself was the author. After extensive study of the conversation about authorship and influence of one text over the other, F. F. Bruce suggests that, when one weighs the dependence of Colossians on Ephesians and vice versa, one may safely ascribe authorship to Paul, with some—however little or much—input from Timothy. See F. F. Bruce, *The Epistles to the Colossians, to Philemon, and to the Ephesians* (Grand Rapids: Eerdmans, 1984), 32.

tion for all the saints. [19] Pray also for me, so that when I speak, a message may be given to me to make known with boldness the mystery of the gospel, [20] for which I am an ambassador in chains. Pray that I may declare it boldly, as I must speak.

How did these early Christians understand these words in light of their situation, and what other extrabiblical clues do we have to help us understand and make a claim on what they heard, assumed, and tried to live into as converts and disciples of this new way of life? In what ways does their context affect not only what they heard but what was communicated to them by the apostle Paul? Was Paul's language in the above verses culturally specific or generically Christian? How has the church understood these words in the past and now? And what, if anything, makes for the hermeneutical continuity or discontinuity we presently note in exegesis and theological writing? Beginning with the church in this Pauline Epistle, I will trace the development of meaning ascribed to the text as we explore what we can know and ascertain about biblical reality.

Beginning with the accounts of the earliest churches as depicted in Ephesians, we are given the idea that they believed in a world teeming with personal spiritual forces accounted for by the language Paul used in his admonition and encouragement to the church. A caution, an invitation for alertness, and a strategy for ensuring victory in the war against the devil are what stand out most in these verses. The struggle is taken for granted: it is always at the doorstep of the believer. The only question that remains is what the believer will do to engage the battle and in so doing be secure and protected and keep going—continuing in the faith.

New Testament exegesis and explanations of what is meant by the language of the powers that Christians engage in their spiritual warfare range from arguing for spiritual, otherworldly personal beings to spirits/essences behind the structural powers.[2] The divided thinking about these powers, however, is as new as the history of progression in interpretation portrays. Scripture has always been conceived of primarily as the book of the church, for reading and engaging the God who still speaks in its pages to those who are in a community of relationship with God. It is only sec-

2. Walter Wink, *Naming the Powers: The Language of Power in the New Testament* (Philadelphia: Fortress, 1984); Wink, *Unmasking the Powers: The Invisible Forces That Determine Human Existence* (Philadelphia: Fortress, 1986); and Wink, *Engaging the Powers: Discernment and Resistance in a World of Domination* (Minneapolis: Fortress, 1992).

ondarily, and more recently, conceived of as literature to be analyzed by the tools of a guild, with a partial aim of making it accessible—by which is meant being made plausible—to modern humans, including churchgoers. The latter aim sometimes seems to overshadow the former; but that was not always the case, as the history of interpretation indicates.

Ephesians 6:10–20: Paul in His Context

Ephesians is often noted as the most influential of New Testament writings and very important for the church's life, thought, and spirituality.[3] It is said to be the first text to have the designation "Scripture,"[4] seems to be addressed as a general letter to a number of Christian congregations, and is believed to be a quintessential Epistle, whether correctly ascribed to Paul or not. Its contents address what can be viewed as the lifeblood of the Christian life and the essentials of Pauline theology, namely, Christian unity, suffering, pneumatology, and eschatology.

Paul's words and the imagery he uses captivate the Christian mind with the picture they paint of the world that Christians inhabit. These words point forward to what is at once in the Christians' present and, with the word "finally," also in their future, thereby dispensing with any ideas that this battle is about conflict at the human level or engaged in on the human plane. It is not a battle with human enemies, but with "rulers and authorities" (v. 12) against "cosmic evil powers" (v. 12), fought not on an earthly plane but in "heavenly realms" (v. 12). Therefore, the admonition is to clothe oneself for battle and be on one's guard. The seriousness of the situation is underscored by the use of imagery of a personal battle, since the fight is in the form of wrestling (v. 12). And while some may try to place the evil spiritual forces in a kind of hierarchy, as Wink does in his trilogy, that is hardly the point. Paul seems to be indicating that attacks by single powers are ineffectual to derail the Christian; their collective power is required for successful attacks, and individually they seem virtually nonexistent. This is a force of evil with amassed combined resources for the battle against Christians, and Paul is careful to make Christians aware that the battle is "against" this one, and "against" that one, and then

---

3. See Jennifer Strawbridge, *The Pauline Effect: The Use of the Pauline Epistles by Early Christian Writers* (Boston: De Gruyter, 2015), 59.

4. Strawbridge, *The Pauline Effect*, 59.

"against" that other one. Each foe is distinctly named to underscore its individuality—and then their collective nature and purpose. Here is no generic evil but *specific* evil, each introduced with a definite article to claim its importance as individual for the work of derailing Christians from the faith in whatever way and by whatever method. This is a battle, hand-to-hand combat, a wrestling match not against one opponent but against a collective opponent. Complete, indefatigable alertness of one's whole being is necessary in order to be standing at the end of each encounter.

In the ancient setting of this text, these words were taken for granted because of the people's belief in a spirit world and in the presence of unseen spirit beings traversing between the world of humans and their own sphere, a location Paul would refer to as the "heavenlies." Further, it was believed that spirit beings operate mainly at night, but are most nefarious during the twilight hours between dusk and dawn, waging battles with the saints during crisis moments and when shifts in spiritual alliances were taking place. Baptism signaled such a shift, as new believers were being symbolically translated from the kingdom of darkness to the kingdom of light, from the control of Satan to that of the righteous king Jesus. So vital are these verses for the Christian life and becoming that they are reported to have been adapted in writings by forty ante-Nicene church fathers—more than 450 times.[5] And as would be the case in the history of the church, because of its belief in the superhuman realm, these verses were recalled especially during baptisms, and until fairly recently were part of the catechism for baptism: they were informing questions posed to the convert, such as whether or not the new convert and catechumen would denounce the devil. There were exorcisms to drive out demons and ward off these malicious spirits, keeping them from tormenting the new believers.

Interpretations Ancient and Modern

Early Christian focus on Ephesians 6 can be seen in the writings of the fathers of the church, especially Origen, Tertullian, and Clement. Each of these fathers used this text in conjunction with other pertinent texts, mainly from 2 Corinthians, Colossians, Revelation, and Isaiah, to interpret these powers as both innerhuman and superhuman spirits intent on doing Christians harm by way of the fiery darts that they throw at Chris-

5. Strawbridge, *The Pauline Effect*, 59.

tians and against which Christians were to be armed with the panoply that Paul describes. It is a divisive world entailing battles with unseen spiritual forces that will marshal evil against Christians. The latter's only safety is to be alert and clothe themselves with God's armor (v. 11) and use the correct weapons—the sword of the Spirit and all kinds of prayer (vv. 17–18)—to engage these unseen enemies, who seem to be operating from a nonearthly plane.

There are nuances in interpretation of the armor, which depended on the cultural imagery that best made sense to the early Christians in their social contexts. The Greco-Roman culture of the day was saturated with military language because of the constant threat of war in the empire and the shadow of persecution, and it made sense for the church fathers to draw on the familiar imagery in order to make Scripture accessible to the hearers and at the same time maintain the inner consistency with the scriptural corpus.

The importance they attached to the Ephesians text shows how crucial it was to the Christians then, and it underscores the need for Christians in our time to pay attention to it as well. It speaks of the heightened sense of alertness essential for the disciplined life but most especially during crisis moments.

The battle was also intense during moments of what could be termed a sideways move, when one switched spiritual allegiance from one master to another, from the kingdom of darkness ruled by these evil spiritual forces to that under the aegis of Christ, the light of the world. Unsurprisingly, then, baptismal vows in the early church were accompanied by exorcisms. John Chrysostom's writing indicates the seriousness with which the belief in spiritual warfare—and the Christian as combatant—was held. Baptism saw its most heightened expression, a ritual Chrysostom describes as "scorning the devil's snares."[6] And the priest has the catechumen say, "'I renounce thee, Satan, thy pomps, thy service, and thy works.' The words are few, but their power is great. "[7] The baptizand thus turns from darkness and evil ways, joining the ranks of Christ, but from that moment the strife between Satan and Christ begins, and it is relentless because the former has lost a subject.[8]

---

6. John Chrysostom, *Baptismal Instructions*, trans. Paul W. Harkins (Westminster, MD: Newman Press, 1963), 23.

7. Strawbridge, *The Pauline Effect*, 51.

8. Strawbridge, *The Pauline Effect*, 52.

These themes are explored with broad strokes, but the sixth chapter of Ephesians reminds Christians of the world they live in, a world that is primarily a spiritual world, teeming with unseen powers intent on doing Christians harm by waging war on them in the heavenlies in order to derail them in their faith. Paul issues a command to Christians, therefore, to be on the alert and to engage in this war in a way that assures them victory. The way to victory is to clothe themselves in the right armor, to fight with the right weapons, and be found still standing after every round of battle.

Who or what are these powers? How and where do they function? What are their aims? Above all, what constitutes the armor Christians need to wage war and be able to stand in the faith? I will turn to how these questions are explored and understood by the early fathers of the Christian church in this first section.

Clement of Alexandria on the Powers

For Clement, the principalities and powers—those innerhuman and superhuman spirits—seek to harm the souls of Christians because the battle is waged in the soul, the seat of the passions. The malleability of the soul allows the forces of good or evil to inscribe their ownership on it, and the embattled Christian must resist the attempt to be co-opted through the passions to join the side of the evil one. Clement builds on the Stoic understanding in which the human senses are what imprint the soul, but he extends it by using the Pauline language of powers, those unseen spiritual forces outside the body, as the culprits who inscribe falsehood on the souls of the Christians.[9] Consequently, Christians were to arm themselves for the task of distinguishing between false and true inscriptions and thus minimize the negative effects on the possibility of salvation[10] and immortality.[11]

In order for the soul to survive the assault, the Christian must follow the injunction of Ephesians 6:11:

9. Ishay Rosen-Zvi, *Demonic Desires: Yetzer Hara and the Problem of Evil in Late Antiquity* (Philadelphia: University of Pennsylvania Press, 2011), cited in Strawbridge, *The Pauline Effect*, 64.

10. Clement of Alexandria, *Stromata*, 7.3 (translation adapted from GCS [*Griechische Christliche Schriftsteller*] 17 and SC [*Sources Chrétiennes*] 428 editions), cited in Strawbridge, *The Pauline Effect*, 64.

11. Strawbridge, *The Pauline Effect*, 11.

[P]ut on the armour of God that we may be able to stand against the wiles of the devil, since the weapons of our warfare are not physical but have divine power to destroy strongholds, cast down arguments and every lofty thing which exalts itself against the knowledge of God, and bring every thought into captivity under the subjection of Christ, says the divine apostle (2 Cor. 10:3–5). There is no doubt a need of one who shall, in a worthy and discriminating manner, treat the things from which passions arise, such as riches and poverty, honour and dishonour, health and sickness, life and death, toil and pleasure. For in order that we may treat indifferently the things that are ethically indifferent, we need within us great powers of discrimination, since we have been previously corrupted by much weakness, and ignorantly enjoyed distortion from bad training and nurture.[12]

The reason is not just that the fight is not against flesh and blood, as Ephesians (6:12) suggests. Clement, in accordance with his treatise on the passions, reaches into another Pauline Epistle to supplement his argument. The additional reason, he argues, is that the weapons (an allusion to the military armory) of the Christian are not physical but ones that are imbued with divine power and are able to bring down and destroy every lofty argument, to hold all thoughts captive, and to bring them in subjection to Christ (2 Cor. 10:3–5). It is this armor of God, parsed as the power of God to bring down lofty arguments, that enables Christians to recognize lies and falsehood and to resist having their souls inscribed by the evil spiritual beings through the passions. These passions arise out of the worldly things with which the soul erroneously and indiscriminately becomes entangled—wealth, health, and pleasure—and the only way to arrive at perfection and overcome the spiritual forces of wickedness is to rid oneself of passions. One must do away with any foothold the evil spiritual forces may use to gain entrance into the soul. This is *apatheia*, the Stoic belief in the perfect state as freedom from emotions. Since the spiritual forces are drawn to and attach themselves to the emotions, a subjugating of and freedom from these passions becomes the way to overcome these spiritual forces. Thus, for Clement, these powers are both innerhuman (the passions, emotions) and superhuman spiritual powers,

---

12. Clement, *Stromata*, 2.20.109 (translation adapted from GCS 52 and FC [*Fathers of the Church*] 85), cited in Strawbridge, *The Pauline Effect*, 64.

working inside and outside the believer. Discriminating between true and false desires, denying the unworthy and the unethical, and making no room for the passions is the way to ensure perfection and movement toward *theosis*.

Origen's Treatise on Ephesians

Like Clement of Alexandria, Origen in his homilies uses images of Christians as embattled; but he has a different perspective on the how and whence of the work of the evil spiritual forces. For Origen, the primary work of fighting the evil spiritual forces comes in using a part of the panoply, the shield of faith, in blocking the fiery darts that the evil spiritual powers throw at the Christian from every direction. In his homilies centered on Ephesians 6, these powers take on both innerhuman and superhuman form as they work within and without the Christian. For Origen,

> the battle of Christians is twofold. Indeed, for those who are perfect such as Paul and the Ephesians, as Paul himself says, it was not a battle against flesh and blood, but against principalities and powers, against the rulers of darkness here in this world, against the spiritual forces of wickedness in the heavenly places (Eph. 6:12). But for those who are weak and those yet not mature, the battle is still waged against flesh and blood, for they are still assaulted by carnal faults and weaknesses.[13]

Here, drawing on 1 Corinthians 2 (thus staying within the biblical corpus)—especially the insights in verses 12–16, in which the things of God are spoken to and understood by the mature, the wise, and thus the perfect, and are unfathomable to the weak, the immature, the unwise, and thus those who are imperfect in the faith—Origen argues that the two kinds of Christians face different forms of the battle.

Attacks from flesh-and-blood adversaries derail the immature since they are still in the flesh, as it were, but the battle of the mature and wise is with the principalities and powers, against the rulers of this world. This is the ultimate battle, a battle that transcends those centered on tempta-

---

13. Origen, *Hom. Jos.* 11.4 (translation adapted from *SC* 71 and *FC* 105), cited in Strawbridge, *The Pauline Effect*, 67.

tions due to the desires of the flesh. It is one in which spirit is locked in a wrestling match with spirit, as Ephesians 6:12 describes.[14] Nevertheless, these powers, whether attacking the weak or the perfect, whether "flesh and blood" or "principalities and powers," are tangible for Origen. The powers are real superhuman powers that are threatening the faithful in their journey, and the closer the faithful move toward godlike perfection, the fiercer the attacks from these demonic forces.[15] Their intent is to stop the progression of Christians at all cost and, in words reminiscent of Clement, to wreak havoc on the soul.

Tertullian

Tertullian sees the evil forces at work in a vastly different way from the two earlier church fathers. Rather than view the fight as emanating from external, superhuman evil forces, as do Clement and Origen, he offers a twist of his own. For him, the evil spiritual powers, these principalities and powers, and these agents of the devil are working overtly and sometimes covertly in the heretical views and writings of some of Tertullian's opponents in the faith, such as Valentinus and Marcion. These opponents

> laid violent hands on [Scripture] with no less a shrewd bent of mind than Marcion. Marcion openly and nakedly used the knife, not the pen, since he cut the scriptures to suit his argument, whereas Valentinus spared them, since he did not invent Scripture to suit his argument, but argument to suit the scriptures; nevertheless, he took away more and added more by taking away the proper meaning of each particular word and by adding arrange-

14. Origen, *Princ.* 3.2.6 (*SC* 268), cited in Strawbridge, *The Pauline Effect*, 68.

15. Of note here is the fact the Christian still needs to be on high alert in this world, but there is a subtle shift in emphasis on the form of the attack, for here we observe the real danger of the Christian under demonic attack and being open to possession with lasting effects on the soul, which in psychological terms is the psyche, and thus the psychological aspects of the embattled life are being explored in these writings. See Rosen-Zvi, *Demonic Desires*, for a fuller account of how the rabbis conceptualize the demonic and rituals against their attacks. See also Dale Martin, *Inventing Superstition: From the Hippocratics to the Christians* (Cambridge, MA: Harvard University Press, 2004), 188–89, where Martin indicates the coming shift in the thought of these early writers in line with the intellectual developments in the period (cited in Strawbridge, *The Pauline Effect*, 67).

ments of systems which have no existence. These are the natures
of the spiritual wickednesses with which we wrestle (Eph 6:12).[16]

The misinterpretation and misappropriation of Scripture, says Tertullian,
are the acts of these spiritual forces of wickedness who offer counterfeit
truth and heresies, with which the Christian must wrestle. They work their
evil will through those who purport to be propagating the word of truth,
while they twist the very words to their own ends—either by additions or
subtractions. In any case, the evil powers falsify the word of truth and use
it to their own advantage.

As the reader can observe so far, the range of imagery that is conjured
up by these three early church fathers—concerning who or what these
principalities and powers are—is quite wide. Though they all are drawing
from the same verses of Ephesians 6, they offer us different interpretations; significantly, though, they each allude to other portions of Scripture
and exercise an intrabiblical focus.

Principalities and Powers in Reformed Thought

While there are other notable epochs within Christian history between the
earliest Christian writers and the Reformation period, the Reformation
does hold a significant place in the history of the church: it is a place from
which to look backward and forward at the same time, and it is in a sense
a holding ground for the traditions that preceded it and those to come.
Following this tradition, I begin the assessments of Ephesians 6:10–20
with the writings of one of the most familiar in the Reformed tradition,
John Calvin. I shall then follow with the insights of Charles Hodge, because of his educational influence in the Reformed tradition in America,
which makes sense because most mainline churches belong within the
Reformed family; it is thus useful to bring the hermeneutical legacy of
the tradition to bear on the interpretation of a text that was held up by the
earliest Christian writers as the most spiritual of texts, especially since we
are probing things of the Spirit.

16. Tertullian, *De Praescriptione Haereticorum* 38–39 (SC 46), cited in Strawbridge,
The Pauline Effect, 66.

Calvin on the Powers: Their Nature and Activities

Calvin's thinking on the powers is confined to his commentary and exhortations on the book of Ephesians. He sees Ephesians as an Epistle of grace: the grace by which the people of Ephesus were first drawn to God through Christ and the grace that sustains them in the face of the numerous adversities they face. The author of the Epistle assures the readers of the protection of the Lord (so that they might not fall away from the faith) and the author's desire to be physically with them. Calvin notes that the writer exhorts them, not in generalities, but with direct and concrete examples: he does not "satisfy himself with describing in general terms how Christians ought to live, but lays down particular exhortations adapted to the various relations of society."[17]

Calvin's insights on Ephesians 6:10–20 follow the same interpretative framework as the earliest Christian writers we have explored above. The evil spiritual forces Christians face are crafty and insidious, and so Christians need to be vigilant. The need for vigilance is underscored by the Epistle's command to take up arms and declare "open warfare," because this enemy "frequently lies in ambush," seeking to trip Christians up with his wiles. So when Paul enjoins us to stand at the ready for the wrestling match, Calvin, drawing on observations by Plutarch on what wrestling entails, says:

> Wrestling was the most artful and subtle of all the ancient games, and the name of it [*palē*] was derived from a word that signifies to throw a man down by deceit and craft. And it is certain that persons who understand this exercise have many fetches, and turns, and changes of posture, which they make use of to supplant and trip up their adversaries.[18]

---

17. John Calvin, *Commentary on Galatians and Ephesians* (Grand Rapids: Christian Classics Ethereal Library Online Version), 157 (hereafter *CGE*). We can attest to the truth of this assertion by simply reading the fifth chapter of Ephesians, a chapter focused on familial relationships, both physical and spiritual (fathers and children, husbands and wives, and the fellowship of believers). Here the dynamics of life in its everydayness are explored, and all are admonished and encouraged to live by the same grace with which they have been found and loved into life with God.

18. Calvin, *CGE*, 286 (citing Plutarch's *Symposiacs*, l. 2). Hereafter, page references to this commentary appear in parentheses in the text.

Following in the same vein—and more like Tertullian, who sees the arts as a stomping ground for evil and the entrance to idolatry—Calvin declares that the evil spiritual powers are as likely to trip up Christians through the arts,

> since many are the arts, arising from the terrors of worldly evil on the one hand, and the natural love which men have to life, liberty, plenty, and the pleasures of life, on the other, that the devil makes use of to circumvent and foil them—that is, the WILES [*tas methodeias*] *of the devil*. (286)

That Paul uses the term "wickedness" to describe the craft of the evil one is to imply the malignancy and utter cruelty and cunning of the devil, and to underscore the need for vigilance against his gaining a foothold and an advantage against the Christians. And it is for a similar reason that he uses the adjective "spiritual" to describe the wickedness with which the entrapment of the devil is named, for that adjective connotes hiddenness, a covertness that makes the danger more acute. The acute danger is further evoked for Calvin by the location of the attack: "the phrase, *in heavenly* places; for the elevated station from which the attack is made gives us greater trouble and difficulty." Further, Calvin is quick to warn any Christians who might, in charging the devil with the responsibility for the deeds of wickedness, be following the Manicheans in their notion of two principles, that is, a dualism in which the devil is "an *antitheos*, an antagonist deity, whom the righteous God would not subdue without great exertion" (287).

It is erroneous to assume that the devil is on a par with God, as though the two were merely similar entities, albeit on different planes. And Calvin goes on to tell us why:

> For Paul does not ascribe to devils a *principality*, which they seize without the consent, and maintain in spite of the opposition, of the Divine Being,—but a *principality* which, as Scripture everywhere asserts, God, in righteous judgment, yields to them over the wicked. The inquiry is not what power they have in opposition to God but how far they ought to excite our alarm, and keep us on our guard. Nor is any countenance here given to the belief that the devil has formed, and keeps for himself, the middle region of the air. Paul does not assign to them a fixed territory, which they

can call their own, but [he] merely intimates that they are engaged in hostility, and occupy an elevated station. (287)

Therefore, the fact that the devil and the evil spiritual forces operate in the heavenly realms and are extremely wicked and unleash such cruelty on the earth indiscriminately is not equal to an assumption that they have free range. Their powers and their operation are delimited by the sovereignty of the will of God.[19] Though these evil spiritual beings, these *"kosmokratores,* that is, *princes of the world"* (further delineated by the phrase "of the darkness of the world") have their activity confined within the parameters of the sovereignty of God; nevertheless, they can exert some force on human beings since they rule in the darkness of the world through the ignorance they have caused in the hearts of people. For this reason, the warning to take up arms is even more urgent. And though the fight is not with humans, the battle is undoubtedly fought in our minds, and thus "we must prepare our minds for the battle"; hence the injunction to take on the whole armor of God (v. 13), not merely for any old day but especially "in the *evil day."* This is in anticipation of the trials and tribulations, the fierce trials yet to come—"hard, painful, and dangerous conflicts." But the anticipated trials also come with anticipated triumphs, for the writer is careful to assure them of the victories at hand; thus he "at the same time, animates them with the hope of victory; for amidst the greatest dangers they will be safe" (287). The victory is assured by the armor of God that the believer is enjoined to put on.

The Armor in Calvin's Thought

To begin his exploration, Calvin encourages his readers to eschew dabbling in vain attempts to ascertain and comprehend the minutest details of what exactly Paul means by the choice of articles that comprise the Christian's armor for the battle against these evil spiritual forces. It is enough to allude to a military image, says Calvin, and wondering whether righteousness is conceived of, for example, as a breastplate rather than, say, a girdle is nei-

19. There is no doubt that this interpretation, a very Reformed way of thinking, poses its own inherent problems relating to where the principalities and powers come from and their function in the economy and purpose of God, especially when Col. 1:16, or even Eph. 3:10, is considered.

ther here nor there—indeed, is just idle speculation. For "Paul's design was to touch briefly on the most important points required in a Christian, and to adapt them to the comparison which he had already used." Truth, the most essential element in the armor, is seen here as the sincerity of mind produced by the right reception of the gospel, which should engender the purity that drives out "all guile, and from our hearts all hypocrisy" (289). I see this as indicative of Jesus's own words about being single-minded and letting our yes be yes (Matt. 5:37). It is a call to a determined attitude about the Word of God that holds all aspects of faith up, and without which our faith fumbles during hard times.

Regarding the breastplate of righteousness and its importance to the armor, says Calvin, we must not only think of the imputed righteousness of Christ via the atonement, but more "a blameless life," for Paul "enjoins us to be adorned, first, with integrity, and next with a devout and holy life" (290). Thus, like the earliest Christian writers before him, Calvin draws on other parts of Scripture for his interpretation of these verses. Here one clearly hears the injunction to work out our own righteousness with fear and trembling (Phil. 2:12).

Calvin includes a very interesting twist in his view of the meaning of having one's foot shod with the gospel (Eph. 6:15). He says:

> The allusion, if I mistake not, is to the military *greaves*; for they were always reckoned a part of the armor, and were even used for domestic purposes. As soldiers covered their legs and feet to protect them against cold and other injuries, so we must be shod *with the gospel*, if we would pass unhurt through the world. It is *the gospel of peace*, and it is so called, as every reader must perceive, from its effects; for it is the message of our reconciliation to God, and nothing else gives peace to the conscience. (290; italics in original).

It seems paradoxical that Calvin takes great lengths to protect a people who are to follow God in the work of reconciliation in a world in which God suffers to procure reconciliation. Furthermore, the very fact of donning the armor as the way of safety, and of "passing unhurt through the world," may sound countercultural from a Christian perspective, since suffering is in many ways the crucible of our refining and sanctification. But the Christian is not to court suffering. This peace as a protector is given to and acquired and maintained by the Christian; and the idea of the "military greaves" used even for domestic purposes, I believe, goes to underscore the need for constant vigilance both at home and outside.

The Christian life is not to have an on/off switch, nor is it an act that one puts on: it is not lived at the level of a persona but is part of the core self, as one is transformed and daily integrated into a whole person formed in the image of Christ in demonstrating that conversion and regeneration have been received. Either we are this identity at all times, or we are not. The preparation that describes the readiness for this gospel, further noted as the gospel of peace, likewise need not be overthought, says Calvin, as some—like Erasmus, for example—have tried to explain it. It is not to be conceived of as a preparation for the reception of the gospel—its effect, the product of the new life. It is an invitation "to lay aside every hindrance, and to be prepared both for journey and for war," since by nature we are likely to give up when the going gets tough, and the message of the gospel is the only means of grace to help us endure (290). Here again we see the tendency to interpret Scripture by Scripture: Calvin refers to the passage in Hebrews about running the race in order to win, and laying aside every weight and sin, to help us understand what is at stake in this aspect of the armor (Heb. 12:1).

These interpretations may not, at first blush, suggest that Calvin is thinking of these evil spiritual powers as personal beings, for it reads like attending to temptations in the everydayness of life. But this is what "wiles" are all about, and the tendency in our day is to bifurcate the Christian life into private and public, or even to think of gradations of sin and assume some are accounted for just by our own weakness, without paying attention to the reality of the enemies, who are exploiting that weakness to their advantage and our demise. Thus Christians must take up the shield of faith that, for Calvin, is coterminous with the Word of God—even though Paul assigns them two separate domains.

> I call them one, because the word is the object of faith, and cannot be applied to our use but by faith; as faith again is nothing, and can do nothing, without the word. But Paul, neglecting so subtle a distinction, allowed himself to expatiate at large on the military armor. In the first Epistle to the Thessalonians he gives both to faith and to love the name of a *breastplate*—"putting on the breastplate of faith and love" (1 Thess. 5:8). (291)

As faith is needed to effect the Word in the Christian, so is the Word needed to arouse faith, and the one cannot exist without the other. With the Word, the sword of the Spirit, in tandem with faith, Christians are able to quench the fiery darts of the evil one. Calvin notes the efficacy and appropriateness of the word "quench," as opposed to "*ward off* or *shake off*, or some such word. *Quench* is far more expressive; for it is adapted to the epithet applied to *darts*. . . . [F]aith will be found capable, not only of blunting their edge, but of *quenching* their heat." And Calvin adds to these insights words from the Epistle of John: "'This,' says John, 'is the victory that overcometh the world, even our faith'" (1 John 5:4). (291; italics in original)

The approach to interpretation here again is the use of other parts of Scripture to clarify and shed light on a more opaque passage of Scripture, so that in all cases one is operating within the parameters of Scripture. In this way, when interpretation takes note of particular contexts, the pitfall of allowing the context to crowd out Scripture's meaning and import is more easily avoided. Thus, even though Calvin's context is different from that of the earliest Christian writers, his approach to interpretation maintains the internal consistency of Scripture and its salutary significance.

Charles Hodge on the Powers, Their Works, and the Armor of God

Charles Hodge's reflections on Ephesians 6:10–20 suggest that the exhortative words are the pinnacle of what Paul has to say: they are "so full of elevated views, and so rich in disclosures of the mysteries of redemption, with directions as to the struggle necessary to secure salvation."[20] Given that conflict is inevitable, the question is whether Christians will "muster strength" and seek it from the Lord. Using the analogy of the vine and the branches that Jesus uses to underscore the dependence of the disciples on him and on each other (John 15:5), Hodge notes:

> As a branch separated from the vine, or as a limb severed from the body, so is a Christian separated from Christ. He, therefore, who rushes into this conflict without thinking of Christ, without putting his trust in him, and without continually looking to him for strength and regarding himself as a member of his body, deriving all life and vigour from him, is demented. (193–94)

20. Charles Hodge, *A Commentary on the Epistle to the Ephesians* (Grand Rapids: Christian Classics Ethereal Library, 2009 [1856]), 192. Hereafter, page references to this commentary appear in parentheses within the text.

While the salvation of Christians has been secured by the Christ event at no cost to Christians, they are ushered into conflict and have to contend with enemies to maintain that salvation. Hodge warns of the foolhardiness of assuming that the conflict is merely intrapsychic or moral and thus can be fought at the moral level with enough philosophical verve. It is more than that. It is "a protracted conflict. This is not a figure of speech. It is something real and arduous" (193). The Christian is seen as embattled and invited from the inception of life with God in Christ to a conflict that is

> not only real, it is difficult and dangerous. It is one in which true believers are often grievously wounded; and multitudes of reputed believers entirely succumb. It is one also in which great mistakes are often committed and serious loss incurred from ignorance of its nature, and of the appropriate means for carrying it on. Men are apt to regard it as a mere moral conflict between reason and conscience on the one side, and evil passions on the other. They therefore rely on their own strength, and upon the resources of nature for success. (193)

To rely on one's own strength and assume that one is fighting at the natural, human level is to lose the battle before it starts. Because humans "belong to a spiritual, as well as to a natural world, and are engaged in a combat in which the higher powers of the universe are involved," and since humans "have superhuman enemies to contend with," the only surety for safety and victory is "not only superhuman strength, but divine armour and arms" (193), says Hodge, paraphrasing Paul. The strength for the battle does not come from frail human arms but only from the arms that are joined to the body of Christ; otherwise, they fail. Christians are invited to think about their new position and identity in Christ and understand that they are united with Christ. Thus, joined with Christ, they take the life and power of Christ as theirs, for "it is not we that live, but Christ that liveth in us; and the strength which we have is not our own but his. When we are weak, then are we strong. When most empty of self, we are most full of God" (194). The reference to Galatians 2:20 is obvious here in this analogy of putting on the armor as putting on Christ, being part of his body and, as it were, having Christ do battle for the Christian.

While being hidden in Christ is the beginning of the battle with these spiritual forces, taking up one's place and being on the offensive is a necessary requisite for navigating the conflict as well. Therefore,

Endysasthe tēn panoplian tou Theou, put on the whole armour of God. *Panoplia, panoply*, includes both the defensive and offensive armour of the soldier. The believer has not only to defend himself, but also to attack his spiritual enemies; and the latter is as necessary to his safety as the former. It will not do for him to act only on the defensive, he must endeavour to subdue as well as to resist. (194)

What, then, is the manner and method of this defending and subduing? To Hodge, this simple truth has been "overlooked" and misunderstood over the lifespan of the church, resulting in injury to many, because people are either using their own resources—wits, that is—or failing that, escaping from the world.[21]

Seclusion from the world (i.e. flight rather than conflict), ascetic and ritual observances, invocation of saints and angels, and especially, celibacy, voluntary poverty, and monastic obedience, constitute the panoply which false religion has substituted for the armour of God. (194)

Our own efforts, regardless of how well intentioned they are, will fail every time—that's the warning here. And more dangerous still is the fact that such efforts may well wear the clothes not only of puffed-up pride but humility, as in the kind of ascetic behaviors he delineates. All these allusions are to Colossians 2:18–23, where Paul warns the Christians at Colossae not to be led astray by fancified fluff in the garb of new esoteric knowledge consisting of do's and don't's. Here is the reason nothing else would work and why it is foolhardy to assume anything else would:

But as we have to contend with Satan, we need the armour of God. One part of the Bible of course supposes every other part to be true. If it is not true that there is such a being as Satan, or that he possesses great power and intelligence, or that he has access to the minds of men and exerts his power for their destruction; if all this is obsolete, then there is no real necessity for supernatural power or for supernatural means of defence. If Satan and satanic influ-

---

21. I also suggest that today that injury may be felt in the lament of the church as it mourns the dwindling numbers and shrinking budgets because of the casualties of this conflict.

ence are fables or figures, then all the rest of the representations
concerning this spiritual conflict is *empty metaphor*. But if one part
of this representation is literally true, the other has a corresponding depth and reality of meaning. (195; italics in original)

To persist in doing it ourselves, as if this were a battle of wits against natural beings, is to make nonsense of the whole commandment expressed
in the simple phrase "put on the armor of God." It is as though one were
being invited to quench a little fire with the ocean, and if that is so the
instruction can be ignored because of it. What is at stake is whether we
believe in the existence of Satan and other evil spiritual beings or not. And
as Hodge notes, the reality of one part of the command implies the reality
of the other, and the only reason for inaction is a lack of belief in one and
thus the other reality, it seems.

The urgency with which the Epistle writer sends out the call to arms,
and the description of the foe, point to the fact that the embattled Christian is not dealing with human foes but with superhuman beings. "The
signification of the terms here used, the context, and the analogy of Scripture, render it certain that the reference is to evil spirits," notes Hodge.
And with reference to the further descriptions based on 2 Peter 2:4 and
Jude 6, where the evil powers are called *daimonia*—"demons, who are de-
clared to be fallen angels"—he interprets Ephesians 6:12 as referring to
hierarchies and functions of evil spiritual powers that "are now subject
to Satan their prince" (195). The epithet "wickedness," ascribed to these
spirits, also needs to be understood not in the abstract but in the reality of
their existence, for the grammatical use of the adjective is similar to what
is used to describe real entities, such as the cavalry.

> But *ta pneumatika tēs ponērias* cannot be resolved into *pneumatikai
> ponēriai*. *Ta pneumatika* is equivalent to *ta pneumata*, as in so many
> other cases the neuter adjective in the singular or plural is used
> substantively, as *to hippikon*, the cavalry; *ta aichmalōta*, the captiv-
> ity, i.e., captives. *Spirits of wickedness* then means *wicked spirits*.
> The beings whom the apostle in the preceding clauses describes
> as principalities, powers, and rulers, he here calls wicked spirits,
> to express their character and nature. (196)

In nature and character, Hodge wants to make clear that these powers
be thought of as spirits, spirits with extensive control over the cosmos—

the domain they have been assigned to rule over—this darkness, thus the darkness of the world in its entirety (*tou skotous tou aiōnos toutou*). He further points to the ways in which the minds of humans have been polluted by these evil spiritual beings because the minds of humans are subject to these spirits (196). Here Hodge makes an obvious allusion to the descriptions of Satan and his works in 2 Corinthians 4:4 and John 16:11 that is a key to following his interpretation. Humans for now occupy a domain assigned to Satan and his minions, and there is no way to get around that. Taking up defensive and offensive arms provided by God is the only way to ensure safety in this fight.

The stakes for which the Christian is embattled and needs to stay alert are not so much for "heavenly things"—that is, a reward—which is the way Calvin and other interpreters explain the purpose of the warfare. For Hodge, there is no reason to think that "heavenly things" refers to a prize instead of a location, because "*en tois epouraniois* always means heaven in this Epistle; and . . . *en* does not mean 'for'" (196). The apostle is clear about the fact that these beings are "in heaven"—in the heavenlies, as Scripture phrases it. What "in heaven" exactly means may continue to exercise the minds of people, as it has done through the ages. Some speculation as to the abode of these spirits, or where heaven is, becomes the focus for some on how to interpret these words. The assumptions about location and whether the spirits are in the heavenlies as in the atmosphere are also erroneous, the way Hodge sees it. The proper way to think of the term "in the heavenlies" is just that: all cogent beings belong to heaven or earth; these are not earthly beings; therefore, they are automatically heavenly beings. Heaven, then,

> is very often used antithetically to the word *earth*. 'Heaven and earth,' include the whole universe. Those who do not belong to the earth belong to heaven. All intelligent beings are terrestrial or celestial. Of the latter class some are good and some are bad, as of the angels some are holy and some unholy. These principalities and potentates, these rulers and spirits of wickedness, are not earthly magnates, they belong to the order of celestial intelligences, and therefore are the more to be dreaded. (197)

Since believers have such formidable adversaries to contend with, they are to take up arms that God provides, and as the belt in the Roman attire allows for garments to stay in place so that one might exercise freedom in actions, so is the word of truth vital here. And this word of truth is not even so much as revealed truth, since that is what the apostle refers to as the "sword of the Spirit"; or even a sincere heart, since that would be merely human tendency and effort; rather, it "means truth subjectively considered; that is, the knowledge and belief of the truth. This is the first and indispensable qualification for a Christian soldier" (198). One's self-reflexive belief about the truth that has been encountered, which is the support system for the armor, is what Hodge is suggesting. In other words, personal faith that has been integrated into one's life tested and tried. So important is what he says about how to wear the word of truth to the arguments I present in this book that I quote his insights here at length and without comment partly because his words are self-explanatory, and partly because I will return to them in the concluding chapter.

> Let not anyone imagine that he is prepared to withstand the as-saults of the powers of darkness, if his mind is stored with his *own theories or with the speculations of other men*. Nothing but the truth of God clearly understood and cordially embraced will enable him to keep his feet for a moment, before these celestial potentates. *Reason, tradition, speculative conviction, dead orthodoxy, are a gir-dle of spider-webs.* They give way at the first onset. Truth alone, as abiding in the mind in the form of divine knowledge, can give strength or confidence even in the ordinary conflicts of the Chris-tian life, much more in any really "evil day." (198; italics added)

The other parts of the armor, *ton thōraka tēs dikaiosynēs*—the breast-plate of righteousness and the footwear, the gospel of peace—are indis-pensable to victory in this warfare. Righteousness here is not the Chris-tian's own, because no human conscience can resist accusations, but what is imputed by Christ, the righteous one, which the believer acquires through faith (Phil. 3:8–9).[22] Putting the gospel of peace on one's feet (be-cause sturdy feet are needed to support the legs in a wrestling match) is un-derstood by Hodge to mean that "the Gospel is the *hetoimasia* with which the Christian is to be shod," whether the aim is to be ready to defend the

---

22. Hodge also draws on Isa. 59:17, where God rouses himself and puts on righ-teousness as a breastplate and salvation as a helmet as he goes out ahead of Israel—a way of suggesting that this is how God himself fights foes, and 11:5, where the coming Messiah would appear girded with faithfulness around his loins.

gospel or to propagate it (199).[23] That is to say, a steadiness, a sure footing on its apposition truth rather than wishy-washiness is required to stand, to fight, to win the battle, and to keep standing when all is done.

Finally, Christians are enjoined to take up *ton thyreon tēs pisteōs*, the "shield of faith." This *thyreos* (literally, a door) "was essential to the safety of the combatant" (199).[24] This is the shield of faith that is used to ward off the fiery darts thrown by the enemy. For Hodge, this faith is to be thought of simultaneously as that which justifies the believer and also that of which "Jesus is the object," that is, belief in Jesus as who he claims to be. In addition, it is a faith equated with trust and hope and is capable of sustaining one through the vicissitudes of life as captured in Hebrews 11.

Faith being in itself so mighty, and having from the beginning proved itself so efficacious, the apostle adds, *en hō dynēsesthe panta ta belē tou ponērou ta pepyrōmena sbesai*, whereby ye shall be able to quench all the fiery darts of the evil one . . . .

These fiery darts that the enemy throws at the Christians are seen as representative of those in ancient battles, with the arrows surrounded by combustible material that is lit and thrown at the enemy. Further analogy is found in the illustration from Psalm 7:13. It is of special note to Hodge that the reader not miss the significance of the source of this attack, for what the apostle mentions is not "wicked," but darts from the evil one, here assumed to be a direct reference to the devil (199).[25]

He showers arrows of fire on the soul of the believer; who, if unprotected by the shield of faith, would soon perish. It is a common

23. Hodge offers an adequate explanation as to why *euangeliou* in the phrase "your feet shod with the preparation of the gospel of peace" should be viewed as the genitive of apposition and is to be preferred over the meaning of *euangeliou* as the genitive of the object. For it is not the feet that are being shod with alacrity, it is the Gospel itself that is providing the foundation and the certainty with which the one with alacrity of mind prepares to share it.

24. Hodge describes this as a "large oblong shield, which is four feet long by two and a half broad, it completely covered the body," and the picture it conjures for us is from the images we see of Roman soldiers in movies such as *Gladiator*, or even films about Jesus.

25. In addition, Hodge alludes especially to Matt. 13:19 and 38, and passages on the wicked one, whom he equates with the devil, the one who wreaks havoc on the field in which the good word is sown for the kingdom.

experience of the people of God that at times horrible thoughts, unholy, blasphemous, skeptical, malignant, crowd upon the mind, which cannot be accounted for on any ordinary law of mental action, and which cannot be dislodged. They stick like burning arrows; and fill the soul with agony. They can be quenched only by faith; by calling on Christ for help. These, however, are not the only kind of fiery darts; nor are they the most dangerous. There are others which enkindle passion, inflame ambition, excite cupidity, pride, discontent, or vanity; producing a flame which our deceitful heart is not so prompt to extinguish, and which is often allowed to burn until it produces great injury and even destruction. Against these most dangerous weapons of the evil one, the only protection is faith. (200)

All these aspects of the armor are, however, ineffectual without the two vital pieces that tie all the pieces together: the helmet of salvation and prayer (all types of prayer, as Paul commands). For Hodge, the helmet of salvation (thought the most decorative part of the armor) is also the most significant since it is the certainty of one's standing with God that allows for Christians to hold their heads up high in this warfare. In addition is the indispensable prayer to which the Christian is called, because in spite of the protection of the armor, the Christian still needs help. The Christian prays for aid in battle while wielding the sword of the Spirit, and the only defensive weapon is how the embattled Christian fights and stands at the end of the fight.

What emerges in the analysis of Reformed thought on the interpretative approach to the powers—who they are and how to engage them—is a pattern similar to what we encountered in the earliest Christian writers. Each writer speaks to his age but refracts what he is, first through scriptural lenses and then through the prism of the culture for understanding. In that way the purpose of Scripture—that people might hear and understand and in so doing have faith—is fulfilled without sacrificing the context, and contextualization takes place without losing the Scripture for the church.

Principalities and Powers: A Puritan Treatise

In *The Christian in Complete Armour*, a classic that is scarcely referred to today, William Gurnall (1617–79), who was writing during about the same period when Bunyan, Brooks, Charnock, Owen, Flavel, Howe, and Watson were active, notes that the cosmic war fought for the souls of humans is the "gruelest" fought by men."[26] Compared to spiritual warfare, he says, all wars, regardless of their intensity or casualties, are total "child's play." This is because spiritual warfare, which has no beginning point nor a foreseeable endpoint in human time and terms, engulfs the entirety of the Christians' earthly existence (xv). I will now explore how Gurnall's treatise and evaluation of our central biblical text represents the Puritan and immediate pre-Enlightenment approach to belief, and to an understanding of the powers and warfare in which Christians are engaged.

Gurnall was a little-known minister in the Church of England who, unlike two thousand of his fellow nonconformist ministers, did not secede from that body on St. Bartholomew's day.[27] He continued as the rector of Lavenham, and because of his nonconformist stance, he was left behind, not only in the new direction taken by his fellow Puritan nonconformist ministers, but also in the actual historical account of the great theologians of his era, including Baxter,[28] Manton, Owen, Goodwin, and others (xv).

Gurnall kept his Puritan doctrines and practices but remained in the Church of England, and thus he was looked on with great suspicion by both sides of the religious divide of the day. The very neutral stance of this Cambridge-trained cleric—nonconformist in sentiment but in actuality a minister in the Church of England—is perhaps what makes him a good choice for the representative voice in this regard. His three-volume treatise is also a very comprehensive theological and pastoral work that seeks to be faithful to what he notes as the intent and goal of Paul's words. The shape of the work was like many of his time, based on sermons and lectures on

26. William Gurnall, *The Christian in Complete Armour: A Treatise to the Saints' War against the Devil* (London: Banner of Truth Trust, 1964), xv. Hereafter, page references to this work appear in parentheses in the text.

27. From J. C. Ryle, "A Biographical Account of William Gurnall," reprint of article dated April 23, 1864, available at http://www.isom.vnsalvation.com/Resources%20En glish/Christian%20Ebooks/JC%20Ryle%20A%20Biographical%20Account%20of%20 William%20Gurnall.pdf.

28. Richard Baxter (1615–91), whom I shall consider later, is one who shares with Gurnall a similar history of nondefection.

a theme (here Ephesians 6:10–20), and my concern here is with the first half of the text. The brief biographical statement that prefaces the book contains this statement about Gurnall's work:

> One grand peculiarity of the *Christian in Complete Armour* is the soundness of its doctrinal statements. There is nothing extravagant or overstretched in Gurnall's exhibition of any point, either in faith or practice. Nothing is glaringly over-coloured, nothing is completely thrown into the shade. In this respect it is eminently like Bunyan's *Pilgrim's Progress*, a work so beautifully proportioned in doctrine, that Calvinist and Arminian, Churchman and Dissenter, are alike agreed in admiring it. (xlii)[29]

Gurnall: Exegesis on Ephesians 6

According to Gurnall, Paul constructs his Epistle to the Ephesians as a structural engineer at work, pulling beams together to build a "powerful exhortation" for his readers that would sustain their Christian faith and their walk as worthy people called of Christ. They were to walk in holiness and with the transparency that does not shine occasionally, only to darken sometimes, but a light that is constant and permeates every facet of their lives.

Paul's words of exhortation to the Ephesian Christians, says Gurnall, are appropriately words of coverage, an invitation to cover themselves with courage. This is a commonly used word in Scripture (Isa. 35:4; 2 Chron. 32:7; Josh. 1:7) indicating the need to prepare oneself, not so much for

29. Ryle also compares the illustrative vividness of Gurnall's writing with that of the "Divine Master," who uses similitudes in teaching. John Newton is purported to have said that if he had a choice of just one book, barring the Bible, it would be *The Christian in Complete Armour*. By comparison, other more modern theological books stemming from a "broader and kinder system" show themselves to be vague, shallow, indistinct, and full of "a superficiality, an aimlessness, a hollowness," indicating them to be of the earth. A page of Gurnall's *CCA* was seen to be of surpassing worth compared to "such books as the leaders of the so called Broad Church School" put forth—no doubt an indictment of modern theology as far back as the seventeenth century and perhaps even of premodernity today. It is worth noting that this sentiment is one Barth notes when he speaks about postmodernity preceding and embedded in modernity, so that our enchantment with postmodernity as a novel ideal to which we might aspire is really dated.

war, but for obedience to God—a much more difficult engagement, as any Christian knows well. The warfare, in a sense, hinges on whether one would irrevocably be with and for God or be with and for Satan. No neutral positions are possible or envisioned. Courage is needed to live into this obedience (but it is predicated on believing the reality of the warfare), and Gurnall turns to explaining the steps to engaging and winning the fight laid out in Paul's explicit directions.

Paul's instructions in these verses can be broken down into what Gurnall observes as various branches. The ultimate branch—and the reason it is the ultimate branch—is that the Christian must be armed to enter into the battle. Paul notes that it is foolhardy for Christians to presume that they are appointed by God and should thus rush in to do battle without "the whole armour of God," expecting to return from the battle unscathed. They would be placing their trust in God and hoping in his mercy to no avail; as long as they are without the "whole armour," they will be naked and open to the wiles and attacks of Satan.

> It is not a man's morality and philosophical virtues that will repel a temptation, sent with a full charge from Satan's cannon, though possibly it may the pistol-shot of some less solicitation; so that he is the man in armour that is in Christ. (45)

To put on the armor, then, is to put on Christ himself, for in him inhere the graces and virtues sufficient to deflect the attacks of the evil one, Satan, and to keep the Christian safe. Note that this safety is not just about possible bodily harm; the emphasis is on the possibility of falling into sin via temptation, a worse outcome. Without Christ (the Christians' armor), one is naked and thus "unfit to fight Christ's battles against sin and Satan" (45). Gurnall here uses wordplay with the word "nakedness," as the primal pair first encountered it after the Fall into sin: it is the nakedness and the resulting inability to fight against the evil one that Christ's righteousness covers. To go into battle without putting on Christ is to remain in that unregenerate mode of sin—and that is to lose the battle.

The armor that the Christian is to wear must be of God, in "institution and appointment and constitution" (50). Yet one is not to place one's hope in the armor of God but "rather in the God of armour." Furthermore, while praying and repenting of sin and believing are important, they avail little if one places trust in their efficacy rather than in the one to whom they are professed (53). Such is the relentlessness of the war the evil one presents that the armor must be constantly worn: "We must walk, work and sleep in them or else we are not true soldiers of Christ" (64). The task of ministers, Gurnall suggests, is primarily to exhort the Christian in the work of armor bearing (69) to fight against the spiritual wickedness.

How, then, is this "spiritual wickedness" conceived? How are we to understand "spiritual"? Here again, Gurnall points out the importance of interpreting the word as both referring to "the spiritual nature of the devil and the wickedness thereof . . . but also to . . . the nature and kind of sins which these wicked spirits" lure people, including Christians, into committing. As to the nature of these sins, they are not fleshly sins to satisfy carnal lusts, "but sin spiritualized." This is the most accurate interpretation, "because it is not *pneumata* but *pneumatika*, not spirits but spirituals" (176). From this understanding he draws three doctrinal conclusions: 1) "the Devils are spirits"; 2) "the devils are spirits extremely wicked"; and finally, 3) they irk believers and provoke them into committing "spiritualized sin" (177).

To say of the devils that they are spirits is to suggest that their essence is immaterial as opposed to corporeal (Luke 24:39: Jesus's postresurrection dialogue). It is the immateriality of devils that allows them entrance into bodies, since a body cannot enter into another body. To ascribe spiritual substance to the devil is not to speak of him in terms of "qualities or evil emotions arising from us as some have absurdly conceived." That is not to say that it is a figment of the imagination or some part of our unconscious projection. Gurnall notes that such disbelief was found in Jesus's own days among the Sadducees and their followers, adding that if one refuses to believe in the reality of the devil and angels because they are unseen spiritual beings, one must "deny the being of God himself, because invisible" (177).[30] Not only is the devil conceived of as a personal being; one must know something about how this being functions and where, and how exactly this warfare against which the Christian is asked to be on guard is waged. The warfare is said to be waged *en tois epouraniois*--in the heavenlies. There is a certain ambiguity that is inherent in this phrase, says Gurnall, which has lent to its being erroneously translated as "in high" or "heavenly places." However, that interpretation raises issues for him because it goes in doctrinal directions that are antithetical to Scripture.

30. Note also that Jesus addresses the devil as a person. Gurnall also points to a particular address of the devil—"Father of lies"—as an apt descriptor for an originator of a trade, emphasizing that he is conceived of as a person.

"In high" or "heavenly places" should not be seen as suggesting location, especially if it coincides with heaven—a space the devil can never enter (213). He prefers the referent to be the prize—the heavenly reward, the reward on high—for which the devil is in contention with the Christian. These are the weightier matters. Citing Occumenus, who thinks that Paul could have said that "we wrestle not for small trivial things but for heavenly," Gurnall clinches his point by adding the view of Chrysostom and Musculus, both of whom affirm the interpretation of things, that is, prize over place, that is, the heavenlies.

What, then, are we to conclude from Gurnall's treatises on the belief in the devil and his works in the Puritan age? The summaries speak for themselves, but it is worth noting that the era and context in which he lived and for which he speaks has a great deal to do with how his hermeneutics developed. I note one particular point here: the warfare is waged largely over spiritual dispositions, over the soul/spirit rather than over the body as such. It is the soul, the spiritual life of the Christian, that is at stake: it is sin that might trip the Christian up, particularly sin coming from within rather than from without. And even within, it is the innocuous sins that would be the Christian's downfall. What kind of biblical realism is being painted within this particular context, and how truly biblical is it?

Baxter on Spiritual Beings and the Fate of Christian Souls

While Richard Baxter does not write directly about the Ephesians passage that we are exploring in this chapter, he offers us an opportunity to engage the work of another Puritan on how to navigate the language of the powers in the New Testament. Baxter's background as one familiar with the Reformed tradition—and often thought of as Presbyterian, while he was being tutored by and functioning within the Church of England—makes him an interesting interlocutor.[31] His reputation is as an independent thinker who nevertheless toed a centrist line among dissenters and separatists because he chose unity over doctrinal differences that would fracture the church of God. That was a testimony to his steadfastness. His centrist approach to resolving difficult church issues that no doubt involve

31. Although the Presbyterian form of government appealed to him, he was fairly comfortable with a modified form of Anglicanism, but was never one to be tied down by any form and preferred the purpose of religion over its regulations.

interpretation of texts and contexts, gives him a room at this table where my focus is clearly on how the church can maintain its organic unity in the face of disagreements about core passages of Scripture regarding spiritual reality that speak to what it actually believes about God. In addition, though his treatises focus on belief in otherworldly spiritual beings, they stem from and draw on the assumptions about spiritual warfare encapsulated in Ephesians 6.

In the twentieth volume of Baxter's *Practical Works*, under the section on "Unpardonable Sins against the Holy Spirit," Baxter deals with the Christian life and the states of souls, as well as with spiritual beings and Satan's temptations. He sees these spiritual beings and Satan's temptations as actualities, and he wonders about how people may not believe that such beings are real. In his dealings with evil spiritual beings, Baxter juxtaposes the being and action of Jesus with Satan, pointing out that the two are clearly contrary in every regard and emanate from two very different sources. As he rightly notes, it is pointless to get into any kind of argument with people about whether the evil one exists or not, since it would be nonsense to attribute to the devil the source and power of the miracles of Jesus if he were not believed to exist and be real, as the Jewish authorities did.[32] The larger context of his deliberations consists of proving "that souls of believers, when departed hence, shall be with Christ" (253). He attempts to prove this thesis by looking to several different particular aspects of the Christian life, one of which is spiritual warfare, obviously the contention over the souls of humans. In this regard, he provides what he sees as incontrovertible proof of the reality and existence of Satan by inviting us to consider the presence of evil in the world, what I have earlier referred to, in the words of English poet Tennyson, as "nature, red in tooth and claw," meaningless evil that makes us gawk and tremble at the same time and to which we involuntarily assign causation beyond what we term nature's rampant destructive act. These acts, says Baxter, stem from evil spiritual beings; and if further proof were required, he would suggest that we look no further than "their nature and works, to make short of it," for these were creatures created by God and in excellent form for the performance of good, and the extent of the evil that they wield is equal to the good for which they were intended (254). In

---

32. William Orme, *The Practical Works of The Rev. Richard Baxter with a Life of the Author and a Critical Examination of His Writings*, vol. 20 (London: James Duncan, 1830), 253. Hereafter, page references to vol. 20 of this work appear in parentheses in the text.

other words, the perfection and extent of the evil we see are attributable to the perfection of the creatures that effect it—proof of sentient beings originally created for perfect goodness by God.

These creatures, having turned against God and as a result being disinherited and unable to win back their former relationship, are against humans because they are able to possess what the evil ones will never be able to acquire: God and the pleasure of his company. Thus they have become "natural haters of virtue and holiness who . . . hate all mankind and wish their ruin; but especially the saints, with their deepest hatred" (254). Herein are echoes of Ephesians 6:10–20 and the call to Christians to take up arms against the enemy, whose aim is to "hinder the kingdom of God" (254–55) by distracting and destroying the saints who work for the kingdom.

If the scriptural proofs and Jesus's encounters with demons are not enough to convince us of the reality of Satan and his demons—and we would behave like the Sadducees of Jesus's day, requiring further the proof that "the devils have such inclinations, interests and designs"—the answer lies simply in this:

> that we that believe in God's supernatural revelations in his word, do know it thereby: but for those that do not, they may know it by the evil actions and spirits, which are so agreeable to these natures, interests, and designs. (255)

In addition to the above reasons, Baxter's pastoral experiences led him to the conviction of the presence of evil spiritual beings through the diabolical acts of witches. He mentions that he has had many convincing proofs of witches and the contracts they have made with devils (255), a theme he has explored in earlier writing and which he reiterates here, as well as the many testimonies of haunted houses (284). And to those

> that would not believe that there is such a thing but would suppose that all the talk about witches to be delusory, and that they are but fantasms that delude the persons themselves, or forced confessions by which they have deluded others, if they be not so proud as to scorn to hear reason, nor so lazy as to refuse the easy means of better information, nor so mad as to be incapable of understanding plainest, satisfactory evidence, I would tell them how they can be cured of their error. (255)

The point is clear: not believing in the existence of witches and transactions with them may continue even in our day, especially in the North Atlantic. But as Baxter notes (and I agree with him), reasons for that lack of belief might satisfy the sophisticated mind, but the evidence across the globe, then and now, does not bear the weight of such reasoning.[33] Not only is Baxter convinced of the existence of evil spiritual powers through the testimony of witches, but he declares that he has "both read, and partly seen, convincing evidence. . . of diabolical powers as we commonly call possession," and has "felt, and heard, and known from others, of such sorts of temptations, as show themselves to be the acts of malicious spirits, enemies to mankind" (284–85). To ignore these and live ignorantly and "insensible and regardless of the full nature of our spiritual and corporal dangers . . . makes us the more dull and formal in that necessary daily prayer 'Deliver us from the evil one'" (271).[34]

Baxter continues this same theme on the nature and works of evil spiritual beings in his theme on unpardonable sin against the Holy Ghost, stating the obvious fact that the experiences of these witches and demonic possessions he testifies to at length, demonstrate the enmity between Christ and Satan. He writes in familiar terms about cosmic war in the spiritual realm, about the two armies formed under two generals, and the various ways the devil, general of one army, frustrates the army of Christ. This army is employed to hinder the rescue and redemption of Satan's captives and to fight against Christ and against all those who are

33. I have made references to similar personal experiences with otherworldly spiritual beings in my previous work, and I have, like Baxter, anticipated the assumptions of either autosuggestion with demonic activity or false confessions regarding witchcraft. I have also cautioned against the extremes of valorizing such experience as a source of proof for belief, and I have suggested possible psychological explanations of some of these paranormal activities; see Esther Acolatse, *For Freedom or Bondage? A Critique of African Pastoral Practices* (Grand Rapids: Eerdmans, 2014). Furthermore, missionary reports from the field in the past and in recent times demonstrate at the very least the need to pay attention to these phenomena and the belief in them. See Paul Hiebert, "The Flaw of the Excluded Middle," *Missiology: An International Review* 10, no. 1 (1982): 35–47, for an account and analysis of this concept and its implication for missions then and now.

34. Orme, *Practical Works*, vol. 20, 271. And he is correct that in our day we intone these prayers in church as part of worship. The Lord's Prayer is the most popular prayer the world over, but it is often said without credence, without any attention to the import of what it means, or, as Baxter continues to show, with ignorance of what Satan is up to and "God's daily restraining him, and saving us from his rage."

employed by Christ for the recovery of souls. He is "called the prince of devils. His companions in sin, are the first and chief part of his army," and here Baxter makes reference to the verse in Job where Satan is depicted as "walking to and fro, compassing the earth" (Job 1:7; 2:2) (323).

The other army is commanded by the Son of God. The soldiers of this army are both the good angels and the regenerate men, and Baxter goes on in earnest about the role of angels in ministering to humans, which is beyond the scope of this present work but well worth exploring as further treatises on the spirit world. What is of utmost importance are his reflections on the Christian's part in the conflict. He says:

> And the way of our conquest is not always nor principally in a visible prosperity and worldly greatness and dominion: but ordinarily by patience and contentedness in our sufferings; it being a grace and the prosperity of the soul that we fight for, it must be done by that way that has the true and certain tendency to these ends and not by carnal pleasures and prosperity which are ordinarily our greatest adversaries. In patience we must possess our souls, if we would secure them against the storms of Satan. (326–27)

In addition, Baxter proceeds to analyze the conflict between Christ and Satan as recorded in the New Testament. Part of this analysis includes Baxter's claim that Christ gave laws to his people so that they could stand against the devil's wiles. As he puts it:

> Christ planteth against it [the works of Satan] the ordinance of his word, and tells the sinner he must change his master or burn in hell; there is no remedy; it must be one of these two. He fitteth his ministers who are to make this battery, with a holy skill for his work, and giveth them his Spirit, which is, as the gun-powder in our battering-pieces, the chief cause of all the execution; so that, as they fight against principalities and powers, and spiritual wickedness in high places (Eph. 6:12), so are they furnished with spiritual ordnance for that end. (342)

This spiritual ordnance is the whole armor of God found in Ephesians 6:10–20, which he quotes in its entirety, indicating the seriousness with which he holds the insights spelled out in the instructions by Paul. For him the main battle regards the proper knowledge of God and a proper life of godliness, against which Satan fights, the very souls of Christians as they live Godward and make their journey to be with the resurrected Christ.

Ephesians 6:10–20: The Powers in African Perspective

The muted tones, that is, the paucity of resources and exegesis and writings on these verses in the African perspective is telling. But it raises two questions that underscore part of the problem I am dealing with in this book, a problem expressed in the title. What we notice is that the cultures that are most vociferous and have the most to say exegetically and theologically about the language of the powers and their meaning are also the ones for whom it is absent in lived religious experience and expression. The ones for whom it takes center stage in experience and expression in liturgy and worship are ironically the ones who give little attention to writing about the phenomenon and its importance for theological reflection. While it is possible that a largely oral traditional system of communication may be the reason for the paucity of literature on the subject from the majority world, I believe that it is more likely that scholarship for that part of the world lags behind that of the North Atlantic. This is even more true when scholars have written about the subject: they are not invited to the larger conferences of theological discussion, as though they were not on par with their peers. This happens, I believe, partly because a certain suspicion still surrounds the work of scholars who open up the realm of the Spirit in ways that invite attention to it as *real* rather than unreal. The preference in definition and exegesis is to either see the powers as pertaining to an outmoded worldview and thus to be demythologized (as in Rudolf Bultmann and, to some extent, Markus Barth and Timothy Gombis); or to see them as structuring structures, angelic and sociopolitical forces behind world powers (as in the works of Walter Wink or Wesley Carr); or to see them as real and personal spirit beings (Arnold, Dickason). The differences among the three approaches are not just a matter of varying worldviews determined by geographical location and culture, but of differing attitudes toward Scripture that either see the word as a specimen to be analyzed with the tools of historical criticism or advocate the use of such tools while at the same time allowing room for enchantment and devotion. Furthermore, theological discourse about religion, religious belief, experience, and expression is still dogged by the age-old belief in a hierarchy of religions, to the extent that writings from perspectives that are not, so to speak, "respectable" are removed.

There are various works in biblical scholarship in the North Atlantic and beyond that I referred to in chapter 2, and especially in African biblical scholarship, that deal with the principalities and powers, their definition and meaning, and how to interpret the language of the powers to which we can point as exemplars.[35] Keith Ferdinando's work on demonology in Africa and its implications for the whole Christ event, especially redemption,[36] and numerous other writings in the African Pentecostal and charismatic genre, invite Christians to read these passages in communion with the whole Christian corpus. When Clinton Arnold reminds us to take into account, in our interpretations, the historical setting of the book of Ephesians in Asia Minor, he may as well be describing the African contexts. Of course, I need to note the caveat that such a statement requires as we consider kinship between the biblical context and the African one.[37] In opposition to modern interpretations that follow Bultmann in degrees of demythologizing, African readers and interpreters of these verses are more keenly aware of the supernatural in spite of inroads into modern technological advancements, and they do not feel the need to shy away from interpreting the language of the powers as real spiritual beings, as Paul would have meant it. For there is no substantial argument as yet to sustain the view that Paul meant otherwise, considering the world that he and the early Christians inhabited, a point Clinton Arnold argues persuasively.[38] These African scholars have painted the meaning and interpretation of these powers in broad strokes; and though they have not offered us a blow-by-blow dissection and analysis of every verse under consideration in the Ephesians 6 passage, as did the earliest Christian interpreters that we have explored, their insights echo the conclusions of these earliest Christian

35. C. Fred Dickason, *Demon Possession and the Christian* (Chicago: Moody Press, 1987); Merrill F. Unger, *What Demons Can Do to Saints* (Chicago: Moody Press, 1991).

36. See Keith Ferdinando, *The Triumph of Christ in African Perspective: A Study of Demonology and Redemption in the African Context* (Carlisle, UK: Paternoster Press, 1999).

37. See, e.g., Acolatse, *For Freedom or Bondage?*; Kwesi Dickson, "Continuity and Discontinuity between Old Testament and African Life and Thought," in *African Theology en Route: Papers from the Pan African Conference of Third World Theologians*, December 17–23, 1977, Accra, Ghana, ed. Kofi Appiah-Kubi and Sergio Torres (Maryknoll: NY: Orbis Books, 1979); and Kwesi Dickson and Paul Ellingworth, eds., *Biblical Revelation and African Beliefs* (London: Lutterworth, 1969).

38. Clinton E. Arnold, *Ephesians: Power and Magic: The Concept of Power in Ephesians in Light of Its Historical Setting* (Grand Rapids: Baker, 1992).

writers. For both groups, the language of Ephesians is to be interpreted within the biblical corpus, within the current context of the readers, but without missing the intention of Scripture, in this case the need for Paul to assure the Christians of Ephesus and beyond of the all-encompassing victory of Jesus over all the powers for all time, and how they can live into and maintain and retain that victory in the everydayness of life.

Thus Annang Asumang, in his writing on evil forces in Ephesians that explores three different hermeneutical approaches to comprehending the language of powers in the New Testament, says that, given the work of Paul in Ephesus that is narrated in Acts, and the context in which the letter to the Ephesians is being written, the only way to understand Paul's meaning is to think of the beings he mentions as personal spiritual beings. Hence Paul's use of *archai*, for instance, can only rightly be thought of as meaning

> superhuman forces, which are antagonistic to Christ and his people (e.g., Rom. 8:38; Col. 2:15). Certainly, in Ephesians 3:10, where the apostle again refers to these powers, they are in the "heavenly realms"—a phrase used by Paul on five occasions in this epistle for "the realm to which Christ has been raised."[39]

Similarly, J. Ayodeji Adewuya, engaging with the Pentecostal readings of Ephesians, points out, like Clinton Arnold, that readers should not ignore the sociocultural context of Paul in his writings, and that his readers will understand these powers as personal superhuman beings. He adds:

> [T]he idea here is the same as in 2 Cor. 10:3–4. "For though we walk in the flesh, we do not war according to the flesh." It is irrelevant if the particular opponent we face is a principality, a power, or a ruler of the darkness of this age. Collectively they are all members of the hosts of wickedness in the heavenly places.[40]

For Paul to say that we are living on the level of flesh, *sarx*, but warring on a different level, is to make an obvious distinction between what is flesh

---

39. Annang Asumang, "Powers of Darkness: An Evaluation of Three Hermeneutical Approaches to the Evil Powers in Ephesians," *Conspectus* 5, no. 1 (online) (2008): 4.

40. J. Ayodeji Adewuya, "The Spiritual Powers of Ephesians 6:10–18 in the Light of African Pentecostal Spirituality," *Bulletin for Biblical Research* 22. no. 2 (2012): 256.

and of this world and whatever level the war is taking place on. No matter how many ways we parse the words we use to describe those who contend against us, we are being pointed to the realm that is not fleshly and is obviously of the spirit. To agree on the terminology and acknowledge that the war is at the level of spirit and then explain "spirit" in natural terms, even when we talk about the spirit behind world powers and structures—"structuring structures," as Bourdieu invites us to call them, and in line with Wink's comprehensive thinking on the powers—is to reduce spirit to a this-worldly existence and strip it of the supernatural. If it were merely this-worldly, then the invitation to shore oneself up with the whole armor of God would be an act of overdressing!

It is long overdue to rethink the position that Bultmann touts and that continues to be the direction in which interpretation of the world picture painted by Scripture is headed. The idea that it is impossible to hold the biblical understanding of belief in the supernatural side by side with the scientific and technological advancements in the modern world is simply not true. Kwesi Dickson says of the African context:

> Africans are coming to terms with the new technological and other developments without sacrificing their traditional presuppositions. Africans are using modern agricultural implements and avail themselves of the facilities offered by modern medicine; nevertheless, the traditional religio-cultural world view persists, simply because that and the scientific approach ask different questions and seek for different answers, and Africans see the two approaches as complementing each other.[41]

It would be erroneous to assume that this is the case only in a less sophisticated context like Africa, which is merely on the cusp of technological advances and modernity, while the West is decidedly postmodern. The only difference in the two contexts, it seems to me, is that the West is suppressing and repressing such belief and living it vicariously through other media forms—mainly entertainment, with its pornography of evil and otherworldly spiritual beings, even in the more Christian examples of the genre. In the West we are becoming purveyors of the life and acts of this supernatural world as if they were alien to our lives; and yet they are

---

41. Kwesi Dickson, "African Theology: Origin, Methodology, and Content," *The Journal of Religious Thought* 32, no. 2 (1975): 38.

constantly on our doorsteps in the myriad criminal acts that are drawn to our attention in the media and prosecuted daily by our judicial system.[42] Evil has become entertainment and we can appropriately be said to be, in Neil Postman's words, "amusing ourselves to death." This is death not only of an individual's soul but of a whole culture, marked by people dying for something to believe in and give their lives to, people searching for a language other than what is provided by the scientific worldview.

Today's world is much like the world of Ephesus, which had its numerous gods and charlatans promising a good life, its magicians, astrologers, and occultism in every corner, and the temple of Diana towering over the city (not to mention the failed exorcism of the sons of Sceva), where Paul spoke with power about the extraordinary victory wrought by the cross, death and resurrection of Christ over the forces that held many captive.[43] There are numerous testimonies by Western missionaries to the so-called majority world, whether in the nineteenth, twentieth, or twenty-first centuries, who have encountered something of the demonic or supernatural world characterized in the African worldview along the lines of the Greco-Roman world described by Paul.[44] Not only has the West excluded

42. Some of the horrific mass murders, school shootings, and bombings cannot be explained mainly through the mental illness of the perpetrators, for they are too heinous to be so described. The work of psychologist M. Scott Peck offers important insight: his book *The Road Less Traveled* (1978) is often celebrated, while his evidence of having stared into the abyss of hell when he has looked into the eyes—and souls—of certain patients, has not earned him a soft spot in the minds and hearts of earlier fans. See also Peck, *People of the Lie: The Hope for Healing Human Evil* (New York: Simon and Schuster, 1983).

43. Our airwaves are loaded with invitations to the occult, with promises to tell our future through psychic advisors networks, and young ones experimenting with Ouija boards in hopes of encountering otherworldly beings or at least a sense of whether they exist or not. These and the level of increased Spiritism, even in the innocuous "spiritual but not religious," are all indications of the search for meaning in the transcendent realm.

44. See Hiebert, "Flaw of the Excluded Middle." His experiences, first as a missionary child in India and then as a missionary and professor in that same country, later caused him to come to terms with the exclusion of this vital middle arena of human life, a place where God acts intentionally in human history. As he notes, "[I]t is no coincidence that many of the most successful missions have provided some form of Christian answer to middle level questions" (46). Additionally, Walter Wink, who has written most extensively and comprehensively on the language of the powers in the NT, has had his own run-ins with this "excluded middle," and I believe this accounts for the kind of vacillation that shows in his interpretation of the powers. And so we take seriously his

the middle tier of experience, clinging only to the separate sphere of religion on its terms and science on its terms (even though the scientific encroaches and tries to determine the religious), but it has also excluded the theological voices of those who believe in the middle, the place where God intersects with human life, and a theology that offers explanations of life's mysteries and inexplicable sufferings in terms of the spirit world in consonance with Scripture.

If the theology of the church has historically been born in its thriving centers (and we have already sounded a caution for the description "thriving"), then what Africans—and indeed many theologians and Christians in the global South—are pointing to in their reading of Scripture needs to be taken seriously. Writing on Ephesians 6:10–18, Adewuya names this attitude and its implications for the theological enterprise in general and underscores why reading in communion is important.[45] He notes that "in order to validate its claim to universal validity, the biblical text is dependent on the appropriation of readers with different orientations in different contexts."[46] In a certain sense, the need to make scriptural claims universal requires that the Bible be read with the past and present believers in view and with an eye toward the future, what Anderson terms an "eschatological preference."[47] Not only is reading in communion important for the work of interpretation, but the context matters as well. Ultimately, it is not so much about redeeming interpretation from worldview—not even when it is used to strong-arm theological interpretation—but about arriving at meaning that speaks to the church in all its epochs, without the bifurcated tongue that worldview and its near valorization affords us today. When we overemphasize worldview, we elide not only Scripture but its author, the Holy Spirit. It is in this way that we can be seen to be fleeing from the Spirit, the giver of all truth who also leads into all truth, even if we think we are being faithful interpreters.

---

insight that we "pilgrimage away from a rather naïve assurance that the 'principalities and powers' mentioned in the NT could be 'demythologized,'" and that "always there was this remainder . . . that would not reduce to physical structures—something invisible, immaterial, spiritual, and very, very real" (Naming the Powers, 5).

45. Adewuya, "Spiritual Powers of Ephesians."

46. Adewuya, "Spiritual Powers of Ephesians," 251, citing Bernard C. Lategan, "Scholar and Ordinary Reader—More than a Simple Interface," Semeia 73 (1996): 254.

47. Ray Anderson, The Shape of Practical Theology: Empowering Ministry with a Theological Praxis (Downers Grove, IL: InterVarsity, 2001).

Biblical Realism

CHAPTER 6

The Demands of Contextual Hermeneutics

It is commonly accepted in hermeneutics that there is necessarily an epistemological distance between the text and the interpreter, not only because of time and space but because of the cultural distinctions between the current interpreter and the text. Therefore, a proper approach to the text requires an acknowledgment of this distance, and at the same time the interplay between the culture of the interpreter and of the text, even as one seeks to offer a faithful interpretation, what Gadamer calls the "fusing of horizons."[1] Moreover, such faithful interpretation should also facilitate the reception of the text into the new community to which it is given. That is to say, the context of the hearer needs to be taken into account for scriptural interpretation to have meaning and currency for each context. It means, to a large extent, that metaphors and allusions in interpretation must be easily accessible to the imagination of the new recipients of Scripture. The new recipients must be able to enter imaginatively into the sociocultural world of the authors and first recipients. Since it is possible to enter imaginatively into the sociocultural world of the author and primary recipients, it stands to reason that there are aspects of the text that transcend and traverse cultural boundaries; or perhaps the cultural distance is not as wide as was suspected to begin with, especially if one considers

---

1. Hans-Georg Gadamer, *Truth and Method* (New York: Continuum, 1997), 302. Hans de Wit invites us to see this as a meeting between the self and the other, and a recognition of the otherness of the text, and to be cognizant of the fact that two contexts are always at stake: the text's original context and our cultural contexts as interpreters. See Hans de Wit, "Exegesis and Contextuality: Happy Marriage, Divorce, or Living (Apart) Together?" in *African and European Readers of the Bible in Dialogue: In Quest for a Shared Meaning*, ed. Hans de Wit and Gerald O. West (Boston: Brill, 2008), 4–5.

what pertains in the social imaginary in contemporary culture as depicted in film and other media. Otherwise, we would have an unsurmountable hermeneutical challenge, for how would we even conceive of the possibility of how to interpret old texts in new contexts?

Yet, according to Bultmann and theologians of his persuasion, to live in the present scientifically and technologically rich times, in what we assume to be the "real" world, Scripture presents a challenge to modern humans. Consequently, he invites us to demythologize Scripture, strip it of the myth that bogs it down so that we can get to what we want it to convey: the kerygma without the virgin birth of Jesus,[2] the miracles that Jesus performed,[3] his resurrection—in short, a credible gospel for modern humans.[4] The vehicle is not as important to the goods in it as one might assume, he suggests, and it can be easily refitted for modern roads of knowledge. Yet, as I tried to demonstrate in the first chapter, the Bultmannian approach is hardly sustainable in itself as a viable alternative to what Bultmann sees as a naïve reading of Scripture and its picture of the world picture. His project to rehabilitate Scripture for modern consumption, however, allows us to run from the content and intent of Scripture and replace it with a form of humanism that in the long run is antithetical to Scripture, at variance with traditional Christian thought, and anemic for pastoral practice. We see this trend across the board in most liberal theological interpretations of Scripture—and sometimes even when the slant is toward more orthodox understandings of inspiration. Therefore, in interpretation, when it comes to Scripture's world picture, spirit beings (the devil, demons, and what to make of the principalities and powers), exousiology—what is often referred to as "the spirit world" and, in a broader sense, "pneumatology"—there is often the retreat to rationalism and, at best, an unhealthy monism.

Though the contextual presuppositions of the interpreter are commonplace in all hermeneutics as we try to make sense of the authorial intent of ancient texts in a contemporary setting, with new epistemic commitments and standards of truth, we must always ask to what end we are making our interpretative moves. As Brian Blount, drawing on sociolinguistic theory, reminds us, the fact that what we find in Scripture is not

2. Rudolf Bultmann, *Jesus Christ and Mythology* (New York: Charles Scribner's Sons, 1957), 16.

3. Rudolf Bultmann, *Jesus Christ and Mythology*, 61.

4. Rudolf Bultmann, *New Testament and Mythology and Other Basic Writings* (Philadelphia: Fortress, 1984), 32.

so much meaning but "meaning potential" does not preclude a search for meaning, which is always dialectical and not hierarchical. It does not mean that the interpersonal relationship between the text and the interpreter has the final say always in the interpretative endeavor; meaning is not arbitrary. It is never to each his or her own. Each attempt at interpretation should take into account the fact that hermeneutics should be done in communion, assuming all interpreters of Scripture as part of one's interpretation.[5] This way, as Blount learned firsthand, "the text—indeed, all of the New Testament text—must have a meaning that is not confined to the reality of a single interpretative ideology."[6] Encapsulating interpretation in one single ideology, making one cultural context speak for all contexts, is a sure way not only to constrict the liberating ethos of the texts, but also to suggest that one method of interpretation, precisely the Eurocentric literary-critical method, is the only viable way to find the meaning or *meaning potential* in the text. Encapsulating interpretation and meaning in only one method results in Scripture's serving the limited needs of only a few—and maybe even suppressing others.[7]

When it comes to the issue of reading and interpreting the language of the powers and the Spirit, however, what is at stake is more than a disagreement about which we can agree to disagree, feeling comfortable allowing disparate meanings to exist side by side. The realm of the spirits and the Spirit is entirely different because the core belief that sets Christian faith apart from non-Christian belief systems is at stake in how we interpret the passages of Scripture that describe the powers and the Spirit.

---

5. Stephen E. Fowl and L. Gregory Jones explore this concept in *Reading in Communion: Scripture and Ethics in Christian Life* (Grand Rapids: Eerdmans, 1991). Fowl and Jones demonstrate the benefits of reading and interpreting texts with diverse Christian communities by way of socially embodied traditions that illuminate Scripture. I am stretching this idea to include not just scholarly readers but lay readers across epochs and geographical regions at the same time.

6. Brian Blount, *Cultural Interpretation: Reorienting New Testament Criticism* (Minneapolis: Fortress, 1995), 3.

7. Blount recalls his own attempts to offer what he assumed to be a liberating interpretation of Luke 6:33 for all peoples because he had found it freeing and empowering, only to find out that it undercut freedom and a sense of relevance for others. The invitation to seek God's Kingdom, the emphasis to focus on spiritual things and watch God work out material needs, might well work for some middle-class people and actually be empowering; but to the struggling person in the housing projects, at the bottom of the economic ninety-ninth percentile, such emphasis is an invitation to become "nothing" in the future (see Blount, *Cultural Interpretation*, 2–3).

This is because eventually, and ultimately, we are making an inference about the divinity of Christ and about the existence of God—about things unseen. In other words, there is an internal inconsistency in a position that acknowledges one kind of unseen realm, that of God, and not another, that of spirits. We cannot label one aspect as myth without relegating all aspects to myth.

Moreover, as I have explored at length above, myth is the most elusive and yet the most irresistible aspect of culture: it is the medium of communication as well as the repository of wisdom. The irresistibility of myth shows in the failed centuries-old attempts to suppress enchantment by promoting rationalism, aided by marketplace economies that direct people to focus on the here and now. Unexpectedly, the agenda and drive toward disenchantment and the total crippling of what was seen as myth— unreal superstition and arcane knowledge—hardly put a dent in the path of myth's forward march. What we see is the constant veering of people into those restricted places, the eschaton and the otherworldly sphere— especially in film. In addition, the rise of New Age and Eastern mystical religions, the new monasticism within Christianity among mainly the Millennium cohort, the flirting with spirituality through the occult by many Generation Xers, and the resurgence of charismatic Pentecostal religion—these religious impulses all show not only that we have reached the limits of disenchantment but that secularism and rationalism never derailed myth, nor did those impulses quite evaporate from the religious sphere.[8] And why or how could they?

Myth is always intertwined with religion because myth aids in refracting the essential themes and hidden dimensions of religion, expressing the ineffable and indescribable with the everyday linguistic tools at our disposal. In the case of Christianity, whether in Israel's encounter with the *Real*, expressed in the Old Testament, or its ultimate culmination in the Christ event in the New Testament, myth is central to how the faith is transmitted. To speak of God's act in the world and to speak of humans in relationship with this God who acts in the world—and to make meaning of how to speak about both—require myth. And myth, as we have explained, is more than fable. Myth becomes how we make meaning of the world, explain occurrences and inexplicable phenomena, and especially religious life, which is carried out mainly through symbol and ritual. To jettison

---

8. Raymond Lee and Susan Ackerman, *The Challenge of Religion after Modernity: Beyond Disenchantment* (Aldershot, UK: Ashgate, 2002), vii.

myth, especially from religion and, in this case Christianity, is to cut off the tongue and yet attempt to speak.

However, that has been the invitation of demythologizing, and no wonder that the conversation within that framework stutters along and becomes sometimes unintelligible, fraught with numerous internal inconsistencies and contradictions, invariably at variance with received biblical teaching. I have already pointed out how the rejection of myth or holding it at bay shows up in the interpretation and theology of Bultmann and Wink, respectively. Bultmann's view has often been taken as the liberal perspective in New Testament studies, and Wink's view, because he calls attention to the reality of myth (though refracted sociologically and sometimes psychodynamically), is seen as offering a centrist approach to looking at myth in our engaging of the powers and, by extension, the Spirit. It is surprising—or perhaps not so surprising—that within this milieu, where the suspicion of myth threatens to make skeptics of the best of us, even in the work of a theologian whose account of the Spirit receives acclaim from evangelicals and Pentecostals alike, we find lurking the seeds of demythologizing. Such is the implied posture found in the work of John Levison, who in the last decade has written a number of books on the Holy Spirit in Christian thought.

The New Theological Aesthetics of the Spirit:
Engaging the Work of John Levison

John Levison is by all standards what one might describe as a straight-ahead evangelical, because in most minds, nothing spells evangelical like Wheaton. Educated at Wheaton College, where his fascination with Scripture began, Levison would go on to complete his academic formation at Cambridge and Duke universities. He has taught at Seattle Pacific University and currently occupies the X.X.Y. Power Chair in Perkins School of Theology at Southern Methodist University. Of his ten books, which have received wide acclaim and international recognition, four are devoted to a theology of the Holy Spirit: *The Spirit in First-Century Judaism*; *Filled with the Spirit*; *Fresh Air: the Holy Spirit for an Inspired Life*; and *Inspired: The Holy Spirit and the Mind of Faith*.[9] Beyond his writing on the Holy Spirit,

---

9. John R. Levison, *The Spirit in First-Century Judaism* (New York: Brill, 1997); *Filled with the Spirit* (Grand Rapids: Eerdmans, 2009), which Scot McKnight, author

he is a founding editor of a new book series, entitled *Ekstasis: Religious Experience from Antiquity to the Middle Ages*.

Levison's work on the Holy Spirit is largely a correction of current misunderstandings of the literature about—and, in some sense, Christian belief and practice regarding—the third person of the Trinity. Who the Holy Spirit is, and how the Spirit has been conceptualized in Christian history and thought—perhaps especially how the Spirit has been misconceptualized in evangelical and Pentecostal experience and writing—is the focus of Levison's project. I mention the praise for his insights on the Holy Spirit and their importance for Christian theology to underscore the importance of his work in the theological academy—mainstream neoliberal, evangelical, and Pentecostal—and by extension their influence in the church in the North; it means that he is someone who commands the attention of a broad spectrum of theological positions. But this should also prompt us to ask how people on various sides of the debate about the Holy Spirit might find a home, as it were, in his company as a conversation partner on such a controversial aspect of Christian theology. Can it be that he has spoken to every issue with such clarity and persuasion that scholars all along the spectrum of pneumatology, Pentecostal and non-Pentecostal alike, can agree with his assessment of the Spirit as it is expressed within the biblical corpus? Or is it more likely that here we have an account that is so accommodating and expansive that all find a landing place? In what way could there be a subtle fleeing from the Spirit from even a bibliocentric evangelical pen such as Levison's?

Levison's Pneumatology: A Corrective or a Problem?

It is difficult to paint an adequate picture of the Holy Spirit, and perhaps appropriately so, because we have been forewarned in Scripture about the seeming elusiveness of the third person of the Trinity. The Spirit blows where it wills and shows up in various ways, shapes, and forms in both Scripture and, in our day, in the work of various theologians. Surprisingly,

---

of *The Jesus Creed*, describes as "the benchmark and starting point for all future studies of the Spirit"; Walter Brueggemann has hailed it simply as "inspired"; *Fresh Air: The Holy Spirit for an Inspired Life* (Brewster, MA: Paraclete, 2012), which Eugene Peterson has called "a rare and remarkable achievement"; and *Inspired: The Holy Spirit and the Mind of Faith* (Grand Rapids: Eerdmans, 2013).

many theologians insist, in their pneumatologies, on discovering and describing exactly how one should or should not think about the Spirit while at the same time noting the ineffable nature of the Spirit and the Spirit's work. Levison is one theologian who, in his various writings for both academic and lay readers, has cast a wide net for grasping who the Holy Spirit is and what the Spirit does both in private and public life. His work is accessible to many Christians, and many may thus take their cue from his description of the Spirit.

At first blush, Levison's account of the Spirit resounds with the biblical description of the third person of the Godhead—that is, until we test what he says against the expansive descriptions in the book of Acts. Some have suggested that this biblical book should be, properly speaking, entitled the Acts of the Holy Spirit rather than the Acts of the Apostles. When we compare his descriptions and accounts of the Spirit to those testified to and witnessed to in Acts, Levison's characterization falls short of a comprehensive picture of the manifestation of the Spirit at Pentecost, through the missionary journeys and formation of the church and its growth, and its direction through the life of the apostles, who are imbued with power for the propagation of the gospel, from "Jerusalem to the uttermost parts of the earth" (Acts 1).

The Holy Spirit, Human Life, and History in Levison

Filled with the Spirit, a four-hundred-plus-page book by Levison, is a very valuable contribution to the theology of the Holy Spirit, and there is not sufficient space for me to offer a thorough analysis of it in its entirety here. But here I shall trace key aspects of his arguments. The contours of Levison's description of the Holy Spirit, which he offers via a painstaking exploration of both Old and New Testament texts and extrabiblical historical accounts, he conveniently breaks down into three eras. This allows the reader to follow the trajectory of his thinking but also the development of thought and understanding of the Holy Spirit over time—from the earliest Hebraic understanding to what it is now. He offers us a lengthy and comprehensive history and comparison of the Jewish and Greco-Roman literature and argues that what we see in the Jewish literature, especially in its account of ecstatic experience, was an influence of Hellenistic culture. Earliest Christian writings, he argues, were influenced by Hellenistic literature and then incorporated into the Jewish writings, an influence that would diminish the earlier Hebraic understanding of the Spirit as the same spirit of life breathed into the human at creation.

Levison's analysis of the Holy Spirit and his exegesis of key passages, in which he describes the work of the Spirit, is often troubling. For example, he posits that the life-giving Spirit at creation, the breath God places into the human made from the dust of the earth and out of which the human became a living being (Gen 2:7), is the very breath of God. "This inbreathing is not merely a 'life principle' or 'soul,' which cannot be identified with the Spirit of God."[10] To assume otherwise is to dismiss Hebraic teaching on and understanding of the Spirit and to lapse into what he sees as antithetical to the evidence in Israelite literature. He cites well-known biblical characters who had unique gifts and who performed miraculous feats—such as Daniel and Joseph and their rare gift of dream interpretation, and the differing, but also great, prophetic gifts of Micah and Isaiah—as exemplars of this fact. In his explorations of the kind of wisdom wielded by Daniel and Elihu, for example, Levison suggests that the "God-given spirit" identified as breath is the same "font of wisdom" that allowed Daniel, for instance, to have understanding beyond his years (81). This Spirit, which was demonstrated in Daniel for three generations, should not be distinguished from what is encountered in episodic charismatic bursts sprinkled throughout Scripture—in, for example, Samson's feats. In many ways the sustained presence of the Spirit in someone like Joseph, whose wisdom preserved Israel for generations, far outshines the prowess of Samson, in whom the spirit was more visibly expressed (81). The presence of the spirit (and it is not quite clear whether he is referring to human spirit or the Holy Spirit) in these characters, Levison declares, is not something that comes from outside of them. Rather, it is a reifying of what always existed in them when the occasion called for it. The difference between Daniel and Joseph and other humans is the extent to which those individuals have allowed for the cultivation of the particular skill they have been given and the spirit (sometimes "holy spirit" with a lowercase h and s) stirs in them. Levison writes:

> Those who were filled with the God-given spirit, with intelligence, knowledge, and wisdom, may have had an ineluctable,

---

10. Levison, *Filled with the Spirit*, 15. Hereafter, page references to this work appear in parentheses in the text.

albeit less dramatic, impact upon Israel, even more so than its elders, its judges, and even its first king.

> *The qualities of this spirit—wisdom, knowledge, and insight— are to be cultivated.* Perhaps better than all others, Elihu expresses the Israelite conviction that "truly it is the spirit in a mortal, the breath of the Almighty that makes for understanding" (Job 32:8). (81–82; italics added)

Moreover, Levison adds, these individuals—including

> Micah . . .Joshua, Oholiab. . .—are distinguished because they have God-given spirit within to a lavish degree. This spirit is imbued with acquired qualities—justice, power, wisdom, skill, and knowledge—that distinguish these Israelites from false prophets and foreign diviners alike, from others of Israel's artisans and potential leaders. (105)

The above quotes and the implications of the thrust of Levison's analysis raise two related questions at the very minimum. Is the narrative describing two different moments of the same phenomenon, when the God-given Spirit shows in wisdom and knowledge, say, in the cases of Daniel and Joseph, or in charismatic feats, as in Samson and some of the other judges of Israel? Could it also be that the narrative is describing two separate encounters with the Spirit? If this is the breath of life given to all humans, are we to assume that some have this in unequal measure and, if so, what are the implications for life and death? Is the breath of God in humans the same as the Holy Spirit, the third person of the triune God? What exactly is this "Spirit," sometimes described as holy with a lowercase *h*? How far may we follow Levison when he says that the Holy Spirit—very much against popular understanding—is the same as the life-giving spirit at creation, a point that he argues is evident in Israelite literature, which makes no distinction between the Holy Spirit and the spirit that inhabits all life forms; spirit is spirit.

In a postscript to the section in which he explores the spirit at creation and in the lives of the key characters noted above, Levison continues to underscore this crucial point, that is, not making a stark distinction between the Spirit and the breath of God given at creation. These notable characters are full of the vitality of the spirit, so full of the spirit that even in the face of death-dealing situations, one such as Ezekiel faced, they are able to live toward hope. In fact, in the valley of dry bones, where death lurks, the spirit can be said to do its most artful work, calling people to nation-building, which is the primary vocation of Israel. Again, in the words of Levison:

> This is the new spirit and new heart that God promised. This is the new creation, the rescuing of life from death, the raising of the dead from their graves . . . . A new national body. A new spirit. . . . [A] new creation altogether. . . the spirit accomplishes its most lavish task of re-creation, it would seem, in a grotesque valley of death. (105)

The story here is the familiar one of the dry bones that come to life at the command of God, who sends the wind to blow through the valley and bring back human life. But here is the confusion: at times we are sure Levison is speaking of the human spirit that stands tall in the face of adversity, and the bigger measure of this spirit a person has (God-given though it be), the more such a person is able to do. As to why some have this spirit (the same life breath at creation, if we are reading him right) in more measure than others do is not clear. It seems that Levison is vacillating here. There is no clear explanation or succinct argument for how, if this is the same breath that enlivens humans (which implies all humans at creation), a number of people or a group has more and others more sparingly of the same spirit. Alive is alive, dead is dead. We cannot have a case in which some are more alive than others. Unless, of course, we are talking about an entirely different spirit, one who resides outside the person with spirit, that is, a living Superbeing/Spirit who works extraordinary works through that human.

When one travels with Levison down his chosen path of reasoning from the Old Testament through the Israelite literature to the New Testament analysis of the contours of the spirit in humans, one is left wondering whether his account, in the end, gives us a biblical picture of the human spirit and, more importantly, the Holy Spirit. When he speaks of being filled with the spirit, is he referring to the promised gift in Jesus's farewell discourse (John 14–16) or the outpoured spirit at the church's inception at Pentecost (Acts 2)? Or is he speaking about the power that raised Christ from the dead (Rom. 8:11; Eph.1:19–20) and vivifies the church and is the "earnest of the salvation," the inheritance of the believer as a foretaste of the glory to come (2 Cor. 1:22; Eph. 1:14)? Some of the extraordinary works that Levison points out in the characters he uses as examples seem like the result of the in-filling or empowering of the Holy Spirit. A look at the stories in Acts would further spell out this anomaly, this tension between what Levison proposes as the proper way to conceptualize the human spirit vis-à-vis the Spirit, and how Scripture paints and distinguishes between the human spirit and the Holy Spirit. Let me examine a clear example that Levison explores in his chapter in *Filled with the Spirit* entitled "Filled with the Spirit and the Book of Acts."

Levison on Being Filled with the Spirit in the Book of Acts

Here Levison examines Luke's account of some important encounters with the Spirit that he thinks have been misinterpreted by Christian exegetes and apologists. He refers to four narratives of the Lukan account in Acts to make his point by means of a history of religion approach, coupled with intertextual and contextual exposition. The first is the pericope about Paul and the slave girl, which he calls "The Salience of a Slave Girl" (321–35); the second, "The Allure of Ecstasy at Pentecost," signals the first outpouring of the Holy Spirit (336–47); while the third, "Speaking in Tongues" (347–63), suggests what that actually signifies. The fourth passage is "Spirit and the Inspired Interpretation of Scripture" (318). While each of these four deserves attention in this discussion, two will suffice for our purposes.

The Salience of a Slave Girl

According to Levison, the account in which Paul encounters a slave girl in the marketplace at Philippi, the ensuing confrontation with her owners, and the subsequent imprisonment of Paul and Silas (Acts 16:16–25) has been misread. The history of interpretation has suggested that this pericope is about the confrontation between two powers: the Holy Spirit at work in Paul and the demonic/evil spirit of divination at work in the slave girl—and how those powers are not the same. Levison, however, believes that traditional interpretation has focused on obscure aspects of the pericope. Therefore, he seeks to show by textual analysis the error in this interpretation and invites us to rethink our assumptions about the narrative. Rather than see Paul's action as an expulsion of the spirit of divination from the slave girl because the source of her spirit was in opposition to the one that operates in him (i.e., Paul), we are to understand the exorcism of the slave girl as a result of Paul's being "ticked off" by her screaming for days. The spirit at work in both Paul and the slave girl is thus the same life-giving and power-conferring spirit.

For Levison, our misreading here is due to the fact that we read what is a transitional tale through the prism of the Pentecost event in Acts 2:1–41, the template for our reading of the Lukan account in Acts. Here, in "this short transitional tale," says Levison, "is an . . . indispensable prism through which we can begin to distinguish the hues of Luke's conception of being filled with the Spirit" (318). According to Levison, we should not hear in the slave girl's words a threat to Paul's mission or a different source for her inspiration, but rather should perceive her message as "the most concise encapsulation of the message of salvation in Acts" (321). Yet there are tensions and problems with Levison's interpretation of the pericope, not least of which relate to what Scripture teaches about divining spirits. There are numerous warnings about divination in the Old Testament (e.g., Deut. 18:9–11; Lev. 19:26; Num. 22–24): the passage in Numbers about Balaam's divinations, which are condemned in the Old Testament, and again in the New Testament, where divination is referred to as a sin (2 Pet. 2:15; Jude 11; Rev. 2:14).

Levison's suggestion that Paul was merely expecting the slave girl to muffle her spirit or enthusiasm is problematic enough; but for Levison to further see her calling attention to Paul and Silas as "servants of the most high God" as an affirmation of the gospel because it prepares the way for the work of proclamation to come is seriously faulty. In the first place, Scripture acknowledges that the devils know who God is and yet do not believe; which is to say that they are not on God's side doing kingdom work (James 2:19). Tacit—and even overt—acknowledgment is obviously not enough; as the scriptural allusions above regarding divination indicate, diviners were effective in their craft; otherwise, they would not have been dangerous.[11] Furthermore—and the more important point—the demons knew and pointed to who Jesus was, and each time his response was outright rejection of their acknowledgment, sharp rebuke, and expulsion

11. Of course, such a declaration opens up a can of worms about gifts of grace given by God to all humans. Gifts of intuition and sensing, which can be honed by practice but which can, nevertheless, be misdirected and misappropriated and open the individual to spirits other than God's spirit—these should be acknowledged as well. At the same time, we do not want to slip into a form of Manicheism, with its extreme dualistic cosmology, and posit two equal gods at work in the world.

(Mark 1: 34; Luke 4:41). And the fact that Paul's actions mimic Jesus's indicates that Paul saw the girl's spirit as one in opposition to his own and an affront, rather than an ally, to the gospel.

Levison's premise on the "salience of the slave girl" and his assumption that the spirit at work in the slave girl is not in opposition to the spirit in Paul reaches far back into the events at Pentecost and the outpouring of the Holy Spirit. Levison overplays the evidence of the outpouring of the Holy Spirit, the glossolalia that was mistaken as drunkenness on the part of the disciples, in his analysis of the events. For Levison, one needs to read the scene Luke paints for us within the background of ecstatic phenomenon, what he terms "the allure of ecstasy with the dominant presence of Delphic priestesses ... who fired the imagination" of all those who dwelt in that region, Jewish and Christian alike, "with her oracles and mysterious processes that led to them" (326). Not all ecstatic phenomena need to be seen as deriving from an "evil *pneuma*," Levison points out. Plutarch distinguishes four kinds of inspiration, and Levison invites us to consider one of the options as the plausible basis of the occurrence at both Pentecost and the Delphic oracle, and, in a sense, the salience of the slave girl. Following Plutarch, he notes:

> There is a second kind, however, which does not exist without divine inspiration. It is not intrinsically generated but is, rather, an extrinsic afflatus that displaces the faculty of rational inference; it is created and set in motion by a higher power. This form of madness bears the general name of "enthusiasm." It is precisely the form of inspiration whose allure many authors of the Greco-Roman era were unable to resist . . . discovered in the word *ekstasis* (Gen 15:12). . . . what regularly befalls the fellowship of prophets. The mind is evicted at the arrival of the divine spirit [*tou theiou pneumatos*], but when that departs the mind returns to its tenacity. Mortal and immortal may not share the same home. (327)

From the prophetic ecstasies of the band of Old Testament prophets, the Delphic oracle—and even with the event at Pentecost—argues Levison, the pattern here is the same. What occurs at Pentecost is indistinguishable from inspiration in other narratives of inspiration (328–30). For one thing, borrowing from the insights of Plutarch and Philo, who describe forms of ecstasy usually confused with intoxication in the Greco-Roman world (332–35), Levison posits that the Lukan account derives from Greco-

Roman understandings of ecstasy, since there are no Hebraic antecedents for such descriptions of the in-filling of the spirit. "There is simply no scriptural reservoir that can explain this coalescence of fire, in-filling, and apparent intoxication in Luke's story of Pentecost" (334). It is erroneous to read Luke as pointing to inspiration after the manner of Hebrew prophets for these Jesus followers and not to what pertains in the Greco-Roman world, and, for Levison, this fact clinches why Paul was only mildly irritated with the slave girl with the pythonic spirit. He goes on:

> Was there a latent appreciation for mildly illicit Greco-Roman conceptions of inspiration? Perhaps there was. At Pentecost, that appreciation lies embedded in the texture of the narrative. Beneath Luke's penchant for order—apostolic hegemony, the authority of the Jerusalem church, clear proclamation that convinces and convicts—lies an appreciation for the less tidy and more passionate experience of possession, with its fiery face and chaotic qualities, which could raise the status of the early believers because such ecstasy was understood as the direct gift of the divine world. (335)

The point of all this—to put a generous read on Levison's assertion—is an exaggeration on the part of Luke, so that the Greco-Roman world, which had by then lost its oracle-telling luster, would now turn to Jerusalem as the new home of oracles. Pentecost displaces Anthesteria as Jerusalem supplants Delphi (335). While this might be plausible, there are too many problems following Levison to the logical conclusion of his analysis and comparisons. That the earlier followers of Jesus who, like their forebears, are a people who have been primed to be unlike any other people, and who are called to separate from the world around them, would so intentionally mimic their surrounding culture in order to preach a gospel antithetical to the receiving culture is highly improbable and problematic. Suggesting that Luke exaggerates the narrative at this point to, as it were, win points for the ecstatic phenomenon by letting the filling of the spirit mimic the pythonic phenomenon of Delphi comes dangerously close to blasphemy against the Holy Spirit. This is because, in the final analysis, most of Levison's insights depend on his overemphasis of the charge of drunkenness, against which Peter defends the earlier Jesus followers. There is also too much in the Gospels and in the account of the Spirit and the church in the book of Acts that underscores its difference from the normal ecstatic tradition of Delphi and even that of the prophets in the Old Testament. I can also not help wondering what kind of comparison Levison might make if he were considering ecstasy in the African or other "first nations" settings. Beyond the charge of drunkenness, the words with which Luke portrays the response of the crowd, the amazement, the bewilderment, the perplexity (Acts 2: 5–12)—not to mention the many who became believers on account of the inspired word that day (Acts 2:41)—make his assertions difficult to accept.

We could go on to explore the other two examples Levison uses in his exploration of "being filled by the spirit in Acts," but the above two suffice to demonstrate his line of thinking and his conclusions about the spirit. Whether in the "salience of the slave girl," the spirit in Paul that effectively "excoriates" rather than expels the spirit, or the outpouring of the spirit at Pentecost, what we have at the end, according to Levison, is the same spirit at work in all cases. Moreover, it appears that he would say that the main characters in the various pericopes are aware of this fact.

Levison's Proposal: Retrospect and Prospects

In the end, Levison's proposal is fraught with challenges, if one views it from a biblical perspective and from the received teaching of the church about the spirit. Of course, Levison is right to caution against the tendency toward both rationalism and extreme supernaturalism. We have to be vigilant against falling into either of the traps that are set for those navigating the hermeneutical issues concerning what Scripture means by "the work of the Spirit." Yet the way Levison frames the questions, and the vision he casts for theological engagement with the world picture painted in the strange world of Scripture, is in real danger of expelling the supernatural completely from the character and account of the Holy Spirit. He is thus in some ways closer to Durkheim than even to Bultmann (whose demythologizing I have explored at length above).

Ultimately, Levison's account offers us an ordinary notion of the Spirit, at once common, real, and indefinable, leading to a domesticated, ordinary mysticism—generic and thus problematic. As I have been arguing, it is at the bar of practice, in the pastoral and theological moments, whether in private or public theology, in personal or corporate care, as in some of the community and national crises experienced in recent times, that such a theology falls far short of a thoroughgoing biblical account of the Spirit.[12] It seems appealing and gentrified to fit the mood of the age. It allows people to be "spiritual and not religious," and especially to eschew the demands of the gospel in their lives and yet to hold themselves out as Christians in the public sphere if need be.[13] Yet, despite how close Levison stays to the biblical narrative in his analysis of the Spirit, he demonstrates that he is a product of his times. After walking us through foundational, postfoundational, nonfoundational, and postmodern approaches to Scripture, Levison lands right back at modernity, with its insistence on weeding out the supernatural from the biblical accounts by reifying the Spirit within a natural form. In the end, his analysis demonstrates an affinity for the modern agenda at several points. While the account of the Spirit, the Spirit's aid in human endeavors, and the supporting data (as presented in *Filled with the Spirit*), at first blush help us overcome the extreme dualism of the Holy Spirit's work in and through humans, they actually stop short of a thoroughgoing biblical understanding of the Spirit. In the end, he conflates the two moments of the work of the Holy Spirit, an indwelling energizer of the Christian community as well as a sanctifier who purges what should properly be termed grace-given gifts and draws those gifts out into the world as a foretaste of the kingdom. More importantly, he eventually conflates the human spirit and the Holy Spirit, the third person of the Godhead.

The tendency to skew interpretation toward the modern agenda, I think, is in part due to the fact that there are many who believe in something akin to Levison's portrait of the Holy Spirit. In that sense, an overemphasis on anthropomorphizing without sufficient alternative images in play contributes to a Spirit who is easily reducible to human powers and skills. Such a Spirit is an impotent image in the face of injustice, especially structural evil, because the Spirit is so nonthreatening that it can accommodate all human lives and stratagems. In other words, the reification of the Holy Spirit in the form of the human spirit compromises its prophetic function. When worldview overshoots its bounds in the hermeneutical task, the result is usually an interpretation that does not serve the church and its mission in the world because part of its identity—which stems from

12. Columbine, CO; Sandy Hook, CT; Dallas, TX, and 9/11. These crises, as the polls and religious leaders confirmed, brought many people and communities seeking answers and comfort and hope to houses of worship all over the nation.

13. Consider the many political candidates, especially those with assumed conservative leanings, whom the evangelical leadership have endorsed and encouraged Christians to support.

reading Scripture in communion with the faithful in the past and even the future and in all locales—is lost.

The answer, however, is not to avoid worldview, because, as I have argued, all meaning is context-bound. In addition, Scripture itself demands contextualization in the interpretative task, and the text-context dance is wedded to the appropriation of Scripture in the life of Israel (Old Testament), as well as the earliest churches (New Testament). And as Hans de Wit notes, and readers of Scripture can attest, Scripture itself is context-bound. Thus "allegory, typology, midrash haggada, and halacha are nothing more than terms that refer to this happy bond . . . a way of living together *traditum* and *tradition*." We find their offspring in patristic commentaries, Mishna, Midrash, Talmud. Inherent in Scripture and these hermeneutical steps is the fact of Scripture's expansiveness to accommodate new contexts that prevent it from being chained to its past.[14]

These same characteristics of text/context in hermeneutics are observed in how the church has dealt with interpretation in its past. The kind of happy marriage between exegesis and appropriation in hermeneutics that existed in premodern times, and that was fractured during the Enlightenment because it was assumed that the text could be explained without reference to appropriation in the new context, contributes to the current state of hermeneutics viewed as a neutral task of theologians (4). And though it might seem as if there were thus no merit to a project such as mine, because in reality both demythologizing and the remythologizing I am advocating are heavily worldview-bound (which may constitute a fleeing from the Spirit), the emphasis and purpose of using the worldview and the extent of it are different in the two instances. In tracing the history of interpretation in the preceding chapter, however, I have offered examples of how the church has embodied the interpretative task within its particular context while staying close to Scripture. It was able to do this because the interpretation was in aid of the church and the building up and care of the faithful, rather than a theological task to fit a laid-down form or to follow an acceptable approach. The approach used by the church to explore the depths of things hidden from the foundation of the earth (Ps. 78:2)—and in our case the language of the powers—is one that keeps in its view a vital fact: that what is at stake is not so much principalities and

---

14. De Wit, "Exegesis and Contextuality," 8. Hereafter, page references to this essay appear in parentheses within the text.

powers, but what in the final analysis is the miraculous in-breaking of the triune God through the power of the Holy Spirit.

That approach has always allowed the critical tools to shed light on Scripture for the church, and never to be at variance with Scripture—which was consistently the same until the period of the Enlightenment. But hermeneutics is as old as Scripture itself and continues within and among various Scripture texts, as text meets context in the life of Israel and the church, and as the relationship that we observe as a "happy marriage" between exegesis and appropriation exists during premodern times. There was no perceived disjunction between text and context, reading, and application. Premodern readers obviously perceived texts to be coming from a different culture, but this "difference" was not something to be feared, not something that inhibited the interpretation of Scripture. It was assumed that appropriation in a new context was the proper way to deal with the text. Texts were meant to speak to new places.

With the Enlightenment came the new way of seeing the world with a critical-historical consciousness: "[R]eason and rationality become the arbiters of meaning" and the happy marriage began to disintegrate (8). Disintegration came about precisely because lay readers, without the sophisticated tools of inquiry (what de Wit calls the appropriation camp of the text-context dance of interpretation), would be left behind. From the Enlightenment, with its historical consciousness, onward, "no matter how colourful the development of Western biblical studies will further be, historical orientation, coherence, consistency and reason would be its most important instruments for a long time" (8). But is there a way to return to the marriage, not within the precise terms but with the primary aim—that of exegesis and hermeneutics in aid of the church—and where the text is invited to enter the lives of readers and effect change in their lives? A characteristic of this happy marriage was also that appropriation into new contexts led the way, and thus lay readers were an important and integral part of interpretation. Surprisingly, de Wit notes, it is these "lay-contextual readers" who read with emphasis on appropriation, who are the lifeline and provide the lifeblood to the church—those who were seen as the cause of the problem leading to the breakup. The problem was largely due to a diversity and divergence of methods and, as de Wit rightly observes, less about geographic location than about what the exegesis serves. Perhaps, even though we may not return to the marriage with the same parameters—and it is not feasible to "live happily apart," as it were—we might find common ground in the approach embedded within Scripture itself: biblical realism.[15] In this approach the stringent methodology and tools that exegesis mandates are not required as such, even though they are utilized. Therefore, holding loosely to methodology allows many to come to the hermeneutical table. I believe that this can allow North and South, lay congregant and academic theologian alike, to explore and interpret Scripture together.

The Promise of Biblical Realism for Hermeneutics in Context

What will occur if we allow a return to biblical realism, Scripture's own way of interpreting itself? Biblical realism allows for biblical interpretation, with context in mind and without sacrificing the text. The key is its fluidity in use, its resistance to "faddishness" and to the limitation of being deemed a "school" of thought, and its gaze beyond a purely academic approach. So, as the theologian missiologist Hendrik Kraemer says:

> The Bible offers no religious or moral philosophy, not even a theistic or Christocentric one. It is rebellious against all endeavours to reduce it to a body of truths and ideals about the personality of God, the infinite value of man, the source of ethical inspiration. To be sure, a personal God, a very personalistic idea of man, and a vigorous ethos are conceptions and ideas *derived* from the Bible and the Christian faith, and as such have their great significance. It is, however, an adulteration of the concrete and radical religious realism of the Bible and Christian faith to take these derivations as the essential and abiding invariables of the Gospel. This intense religious realism of the Bible proclaims and asserts realities. It does not intend to present a worldview, but it challenges man in his total being to confront himself with these realities and accordingly take decisions. It does not ask for agreement with world-and-life views, not even Christian views of life and the world.[16]

15. A concept found in Hans de Wit's explorations as a possibility and reflected in the title of his essay.

16. Hendrik R. Kraemer, *The Christian Message in a Non-Christian World* (New York: Harper and Brothers, 1938), 64–65 (italics in original).

There is a freedom in reading the text here, a fluidity captured in the words of one of its main proponents, John Howard Yoder, who describes it as "a position, a tendency, a stance, a way of reading," more or less literary acumen, it seems, for intuiting what is being born of each verse in tandem with the other verses.[17] It is a hermeneutics that takes account of all the tools of literary-historical criticism without any traditional scholasticism, yet without letting Scripture be taken away from the church.[18] It is, as proper exegesis ought to be, appropriating old texts in new contexts in the interest of the text even in the context. Thus the way the text is appropriated in the context needs to come with a hospitality to the text. As de Wit might say, it is a way to recognize the text's "otherness" from the interpreter and to view the reading as a meeting between the text and the interpreter (de Wit, 4). In such a reading of the text, a gesture of hospitality is allowed to take the lead and disclose itself to the reader. That is the contextual task, a task in which the text is appropriated within the new context and made to feel at home, as it were, in the context in which it now lives. More than that, it seeks both a critical and existential attitude— which is the dialectic between exegesis and appropriation—so that the result is that the reader is led into new life, which is the aim of Scripture (5). These are the core characteristics of the approach used in biblical realism and in many ways constitute the approach most implemented by lay readers in the global South.

There is a warning that we must heed in using biblical realism as an interpretative framework, an approach that, it is hoped, will return the church to itself and will allow Scripture to aid in interpreting Scripture. This is more pertinent regarding those passages of Scripture about the spirit(s). It is to avoid the fallacy of comparison and a defensive attitude about any approach to interpretation between North and South (24). At the same time, we have to acknowledge that the playing field has been skewed toward exegesis rather than toward appropriation, and toward attention to the context and the voices from the periphery. The long reach of Western theological education that seeks to keep exegesis apart from appropriation and to protect the gospel is a trend that endures as the North continues to be the primary locale for theological education

17. See John Howard Yoder, *To Hear the Word* (Eugene, OR: Cascade, 2010): position (74, 89, 177); mood (190); tendency (87); stance (76); style (182); perspective and point of view (160–62, 171).

18. John Howard Yoder, *The Politics of Jesus: Vicit Agnus Noster* (Grand Rapids: Eerdmans, 1972), viii.

(9).[19] For even people trained elsewhere are largely taught by Western-educated theologians. And so even in the African context, where belief in the spiritual and the supernatural is assumed to be normal and not an infringement of scientific laws, I find the following observation by T. A. Beetham to be illustrative of an obvious anomaly:

> The curriculum (of African theological colleges) is in most cases too much tied to a traditional Western pattern. Students can still come away from their lecture-room after studying the first two chapters of Mark's Gospel—with its account of the touch of Jesus of Nazareth on different kinds of illness, including mental sickness—without having come to grips either with the failure of their church, despite its hospitals and clinics, to exercise a full ministry of healing or with the success of some Independent Churches in this respect.[20]

Conclusion

The ultimate question, then, is: Why does the theological enterprise continue to follow in the wake of Bultmann and not Dickson, when it is the latter who helps us think comprehensively about both testaments and thus brings both Christian North and South to the hermeneutical table to engage in the interpretive task? Why do we follow after Bultmann and his demythologizing, which, as I see it, continues to have theology and the church talking about talking about God, what has been called "theologology," instead of following after Dickson, who allows us to probe spiritual reality in a way that is careful to keep the whole biblical account of reality in view—and does not remove the Old Testament from the New Testament?

Accordingly, while we avoid the pitfall of defensiveness and the fallacy of comparison, we also own that there is a method with an "epistemological fit" for exegesis and hermeneutics for the global church.[21] And in

19. As de Wit notes, in the unhappy quarrel between exegesis and appropriation that is contextual readings, "The Europe of Descartes says: all those arbitrary and capricious appropriations are destroying us and the Gospel."

20. T. A. Beetham, *Christianity and the New Africa* (London: Pall Mall, 1967), 106-7.

21. William Abraham argues persuasively that theology needs to quit hiding be-

terms of fitness, then, we are looking at what makes for internal consistency. Since in religion we deal with myth as a matter of course, as I have argued throughout this book, we do not need to jettison it at the bar of modernity; but we may hang in there, engaging other disciplines that are coming to us on their own terms and within the paradigm that fits with their way of conceptualizing reality—as do we. Thus we stay with biblical realism as the way forward for the method most fit for crippling the long reach of demythologizing, which serves neither theology nor the church it is meant to serve, and which gave birth to it. Thus we may be persuaded to pay attention to Dickson's analysis and program for engaging biblical reality vis-à-vis the culture, and we may take seriously his contribution to a hermeneutics in which the global North and South can engage in theological discourse about the powers and the Holy Spirit with coherence, and will not need to break down into North/South, Pentecostal/Mainline strands. We can have a robust conversation without fleeing from either the Spirit or from one another, and without attempting to coexist in a marriage apart, thereby fracturing our communion.

There are enormous implications for pastoral theology, care, and counseling for our day when migrant churches from the South are springing up everywhere in the North Atlantic/West, many promising to vivify the church in their new homeland and, in turn, needing spiritual care and theological education in a way that makes sense to the way they refract Scripture. As the academy forms students for a global church, especially in contexts with a high view of Scripture and the Holy Spirit/spirits, such an approach to exegesis and appropriation in union—what is termed "biblical realism"—will prove beneficial. This will happen only if and when the demands of the context impinge on our exegesis and we do not flee from the Spirit—into either extreme supernaturalism (South) or rationalism (North). It is my hope that the approach I have recommended in this book helps us find our way to a thoroughgoing biblical account of the spirits— the principalities and powers—and the Holy Spirit.

---

cause it sees itself as disparaged at the bar of science and required to provide evidence for its assertions. Yet theology ought to be able to hold its head high at the bar of science, because there is such a thing as "epistemic fit," whereby disciplines are judged according to their internal fitness. Theologians are as welcome to expect to be judged according to fitness of their discipline, when they are called upon to defend their claims, as, e.g., the scientist and the historian are; and so, like all disciplines, theology can demand epistemic equity. See Abraham, *Crossing the Threshold of Divine Revelation* (Grand Rapids: Eerdmans, 2006), 29.

Bibliography

Abraham, William J. *Crossing the Threshold of Divine Revelation*. Grand Rapids: Eerdmans, 2006.

———. *Divine Revelation and the Limits of Historical Criticism*. Oxford: Oxford University Press, 1982.

———. "Turning Philosophical Water into Theological Wine." *Journal of Analytic Theology* 1, no. 1 (2013): 1–16.

Acolatse, Esther E. "All in the Family: Recasting Religious Pluralism through African Contextuality." In *Religion, Diversity, and Conflict*, edited by Edward Foley and Don S. Browning, 261–71. Vienna: Lit, 2011.

———. *For Freedom or Bondage? A Critique of African Pastoral Practices*. Grand Rapids: Eerdmans, 2014.

Adewuya, J. Ayodeji. "The Spiritual Powers of Ephesians 6:10–18 in the Light of African Pentecostal Spirituality." *Bulletin for Biblical Research* 22, no.2 (2012): 251–58.

Anderson, Allan. *To the Ends of the Earth: Pentecostalism and the Transformation of World Christianity*. New York: Oxford University Press, 2013.

Anderson, Neil T. *The Bondage Breaker*. Eugene, OR: Harvest House, 1990.

———. *Victory over the Darkness*. Grand Rapids: Bethany House, 1994.

Anderson, Ray. *The Shape of Practical Theology: Empowering Ministry with Theological Praxis*. Downers Grove, IL: InterVarsity Press, 2001.

Appiah-Kubi, Kofi, and Sergio Torres, eds. *African Theology en Route: Papers from the Pan African Conference of Third World Theologians, December 17–23, 1977, Accra, Ghana*. Maryknoll, NY: Orbis, 1979.

Arinze, Francis A. *Sacrifice in the Ibo Religion*. Ibadan, Nigeria: Ibadan University Press, 1970.

Arnold, Clinton E. *Ephesians: Power and Magic: The Concept of Power in Ephesians in Light of Its Historical Setting*. Grand Rapids: Baker, 1992.

———. *Power and Magic: The Concept of Power in Ephesians*. Eugene, OR: Wipf and Stock, 2001.

———. *Powers of Darkness: Principalities and Powers in Paul's Letters*. Downers Grove, IL: InterVarsity, 1992.

Asad, Talal. *Formations of the Secular: Christianity, Islam, Modernity*. Stanford, CA: Stanford University Press, 2003.

Asamoah-Gyadu, J. Kwabena. "Pulling Down Strongholds: Evangelism, Principalities, and Powers and the African Pentecostal Imagination." *International Review of Mission* 96 (2007): 306–17.

———. *Sighs and Signs of the Spirit: Ghanaian Perspectives on Pentecostalism and Renewal in Africa*. Eugene, OR: Wipf and Stock, 2015.

Asumang, Annang. "Powers of Darkness: An Evaluation of Three Hermeneutical Approaches to the Evil Powers in Ephesians." *Conspectus* 5, no. 1 (2008).

Athanasius of Alexandria. *The Life of Antony: The Coptic and the Greek Life*. Translated by Tim Vivian and Apostolos N. Athanassakis. Kalamazoo, MI: Cistercian, 2003.

Augsburger, David. *Pastoral Counseling across Cultures*. Philadelphia: Westminster Press, 1985.

Avis, Paul. *God and the Creative Imagination: Metaphor, Symbol, and Myth in Religion and Theology*. New York: Routledge, 1999.

Awulalo, J. O. "Sin and Its Removal in African Traditional Religion." *Journal of the American Academy of Religion* 44, no. 2 (1976): 275–87.

Barr, James. "The Meaning of Mythology in Relation to the Old Testament." *Vetus Testamentum* 9, no.1 (1959): 1–10.

Barth, Karl. *The Christian Life: Church Dogmatics IV, 4: Lecture Fragments*. Grand Rapids: Eerdmans, 1981.

———. "The Christian Understanding of Revelation." In *Against the Stream*. London: SCM, 1954.

———. *Church and State*. Translated by Ronald Howe. London: Student Christian Movement Press, 1939.

———. *Church Dogmatics*, III, *Doctrine of Creation*. Edinburgh: T. & T. Clark, 1960.

———. *Church Dogmatics*, IV/3. London: T. & T. Clark, 2009.

———. *The Epistle to the Romans*. Translated by Edwyn C. Hoskyns. 6th ed. Oxford: Oxford University Press, 1975 (1933).

———. *Learning Jesus Christ through the Heidelberg Catechism*. Grand Rapids: Eerdmans, 1981 (1964).

———. *On Religion*. Translated by Garrett Green. London: T. & T. Clark, 2006.

Bediako, Kwame. *Christianity in Africa: The Renewal of a Non-Western Religion*. Maryknoll, NY: Orbis, 1995.

———. *Jesus and the Gospel in Africa: History and Experience*. Maryknoll, NY: Orbis, 2004.

———. *Jesus in African Culture: A Ghanaian Perspective*. Accra: Asempa, 1990.

———. *Theology and Identity: The Impact of Culture upon Christian Thought in the Second Century and in Modern Africa*. Eugene, OR: Wipf and Stock, 2011.

Beetham, T. A. *Christianity and the New Africa*. London: Pall Mall, 1967.

Beilby, James K., and Paul R. Eddy, eds. *Understanding Spiritual Warfare: Four Views*. Grand Rapids: Baker Academic, 2012.

Bell, Richard H. *Deliver Us from Evil: Interpreting the Redemption from the Power of Satan in New Testament Theology*. Tübingen: Mohr Siebeck, 2007.

Blount, Brian. *Cultural Interpretation: Reorienting New Testament Criticism*. Minneapolis: Fortress, 1995.

Boeve, L., Y. De Maeseneer, and Stijn Van Den Bossche, eds. *Religious Experience and Contemporary Theological Epistemology*. Dudley, MA: Leuven University Press, 2005.

Bourdieu, Pierre. *The Logic of Practice*. Stanford, CA: Stanford University Press, 1990.

Boyd, Gregory. *Satan and the Problem of Evil: Constructing a Trinitarian Warfare Theodicy*. Downers Grove, IL: InterVarsity Press, 2001.

Browning, Don S. *A Fundamental Practical Theology: Descriptive and Strategic Proposals*. Minneapolis: Fortress, 1991.

Bruce, F. F. *The Epistles to the Colossians, to Philemon, and to the Ephesians*. Grand Rapids: Eerdmans, 1984.

Brumfiel, Geoff. "Einstein, a Hunch, and Decades of Work: How Scientists Found Gravitational Waves." National Public Radio, February 12, 2016. http://www.npr.org/sections/thetwo-way/2016/02/12/466559439/einstein-a-hunch-and-decades-of-work-how-scientists-found-gravitational-waves.

Bubeck, Mark. *The Adversary: The Christian versus Demon Activity*. Chicago: Moody Publishers, 1975.

―――. *Overcoming the Adversary: Warfare Praying against Demon Activity*. Chicago: Moody Publishers, 1984.

Bultmann, Rudolf. *Jesus Christ and Mythology*. New York: Charles Scribner's Sons, 1957.

―――. "Karl Barth's Epistle to the Romans in Its Second Edition." In *The Beginnings of Dialectic Theology*, edited by James Robinson, 117–20. Richmond, VA: John Knox, 1968.

―――. *New Testament and Mythology and Other Basic Writings*. Philadelphia: Fortress, 1984.

―――. *Theology of the New Testament*. 2 vols. New York: Charles Scribner & Sons, 1951.

―――. *Theology of the New Testament*. Vol. 1. Translated by Kendrick Grobel. Waco, TX: Baylor University Press, 2007.

Calvin, John. *Commentary on Galatians and Ephesians*. Grand Rapids: Christian Classics Ethereal Library Online Version. Available at: https://www.ccel.org/ccel/calvin/calcom41.i.html.

Campbell, Charles. *The Word before the Powers: An Ethic of Preaching*. Louisville: Westminster John Knox, 2002.

Cassian, John. *The Conferences*. Translated by Boniface Ramsey, OP. Mahwah, NJ: Newman Press, 1997.

Charry, Ellen. *By the Renewing of Your Minds: The Pastoral Function of Christian Doctrine*. New York: Oxford University Press, 1999.

Charyton, Christine, ed. *Creativity and Innovation among Science and Art: A Discussion of the Two Cultures*. London: Springer, 2015.

Childs, Brevard S. *Memory and Tradition in Israel*. London: SCM, 1962.

―――. *Myth and Reality in the Old Testament*. London: SCM, 1960.

Chrysostom, John. *Baptismal Instructions*. Translated by Paul W. Harkins. Westminster, MD: Newman Press, 1963.

Congdon, David. *The Mission of Demythologizing: Rudolf Bultmann's Dialectical Theology*. Minneapolis: Fortress, 2015.

Cox, Harvey. *Fire from Heaven: The Rise of Pentecostal Spirituality and the Reshaping of Religion in the Twenty-first Century*. Reading, MA: Addison-Wesley, 1995.

Cullmann, Oscar. *Christ and Time: The Primitive Christian Conception of Time and History*. Translated by Floyd V. Filson. Philadelphia: Westminster, 1950.

Cyril of Jerusalem. *The Works of Saint Cyril of Jerusalem*. Vol. 1. Translated by Leo P. McCauley, SJ, and Anthony A. Stephenson. Washington, DC: The Catholic University of America Press, 1969.

Danquah, J. B. *Akan Doctrine of God*. London: Cass, 1968.

Dawn, Marva. *Powers, Weakness, and the Tabernacling of God*. Grand Rapids: Eerdmans, 2001.

De Wit, Hans. "Exegesis and Contextuality: Happy Marriage, Divorce, or Living (Apart) Together?" In *African and European Readers of the Bible in Dialogue: In Quest for a Shared Meaning*, edited by Hans de Wit and Gerald O. West, 1–30. Boston: Brill, 2008.

Dickason, C. Fred. *Demon Possession and the Christian*. Chicago: Moody Press, 1987.

Dickson, Kwesi A. "African Theology: Origin, Methodology, and Content." *The Journal of Religious Thought* 32, no. 2 (1975): 34–45.

———. "Continuity and Discontinuity between Old Testament and African Life and Thought." In *African Theology en Route: Papers from the Pan African Conference of Third World Theologians, December 17–23, 1977*, edited by Kofi Appiah-Kubi and Sergio Torres. Maryknoll, NY: Orbis, 1979.

———. *Theology in Africa*. Maryknoll, NY: Orbis, 1984.

———. *Uncompleted Mission: Christianity and Exclusivism*. Maryknoll, NY: Orbis, 1991.

Dickson, Kwesi A., and Paul Ellingworth. *Biblical Revelation and African Beliefs*. London: Lutterworth, 1969.

Dorrien, Gary. *The Barthian Revolt in Modern Theology: Theology without Weapons*. Louisville, KY: Westminster John Knox, 2000.

Douglas, Mary. *Purity and Danger: An Analysis of Concepts of Pollution and Taboo*. New York: Praeger, 1966.

Edinger, Edward F. *Ego and Archetype: Individuation and the Religious Function of the Psyche*. New York: G. P. Putnam's Sons, 1972.

Ela, Jean-Marc. *My Faith as an African*. Maryknoll, NY: Orbis, 1988.

Elliott, Neil. *Liberating Paul: The Justice of God and the Politics of the Apostle*. Maryknoll, NY: Orbis, 1994.

Evans-Pritchard, E. E. *Theories of Primitive Religion*. Oxford: Clarendon Press, 1965.

———. *Witchcraft, Oracles, and Magic among the Azande*. Clarendon: Oxford, 1976 (1937).

Farley, Edward. *Theologia: The Fragmentation and Unity of Theological Education*. Philadelphia: Fortress, 1983.

Feldman, B., and R. D. Richardson. *The Rise of Modern Mythology, 1680–1860*. Bloomington: Indiana University Press, 1972.

Ferdinando, Keith. *The Triumph of Christ in African Perspective: A Study of*

Demonology and Redemption in the African Context. Carlisle, UK: Paternoster Press, 1999.

Fishbane, Michael A. *Biblical Myth and Rabbinic Mythmaking.* Oxford: Oxford University Press, 2003.

Fowl, Stephen E., and L. Gregory Jones. *Reading in Communion: Scripture and Ethics in Christian Life.* Grand Rapids: Eerdmans, 1991.

Frazer, James. *Man, God, and Immortality: Thoughts on Human Progress.* New York: Macmillan, 1927.

Freud, Sigmund. *The Future of an Illusion.* New York: Norton, 1961.

———. *Totem and Taboo.* Greentop, MO: Greentop Academic Press, 2011.

Friedman, Michael. "Ernst Cassirer." In *The Stanford Encyclopedia of Philosophy* (Spring 2011 Edition), edited by Edward N. Zalta. http://plato .stanford.edu/archives/spr2011/entries/cassirer/.

Fukai, Tomoaki, ed. *Paul Tillich: Journey to Japan in 1960.* Berlin: De Gruyter, 2013.

Gaba, C. R. "Anlo Traditional Religion: A Study of the Anlo Traditional Believer's Conception of and Communion with the 'Holy.'" PhD diss., University of London, 1965.

———. "Sacrifice in Anlo Religion." *Ghana Bulletin of Theology* 35 (1968): 10–15.

Gadamer, Hans-Georg. *Truth and Method.* New York: Continuum, 1997.

Geertz, Armin W. "Can We Move beyond Primitivism? On Recovering the Indigenes of the Indigenous Religions in the Academic Study of Religion." In *Beyond Primitivism: Indigenous Religious Traditions and Modernity,* edited by Jacob K. Olupuna, 37–70. New York: Routledge, 2004.

Gerkin, Charles. *The Living Human Document: Re-visioning Pastoral Counseling in a Hermeneutical Mode.* Nashville: Abingdon Press, 1984.

Gifford, Paul. *Ghana's New Pentecostalism: Pentecostalism in a Globalizing African Economy.* Bloomington: Indiana University Press, 2004.

Grant, Colin. *Myths We Live By.* Ottawa: University of Ottawa Press, 1998.

Green, Garrett. *Imagining God: Theology and the Religious Imagination.* San Francisco: Harper and Row, 1989.

———. *Karl Barth: On Religion.* London: T & T Clark, 2006.

———. *Theology, Hermeneutics, and Imagination: The Crisis of Interpretation at the End of Modernity.* Cambridge, UK: Cambridge University Press, 2000.

The Guardian, July 27, 2010, https://www.theguardian.com/commentis free/belief/2010/jul/27/religion-witches-africa-london-exorcism.

Gurnall, William. *The Christian in Complete Armour*. London: Printed for Ralph Smith, 1658.

———. *The Christian in Complete Armour: A Treatise to the Saints' War against the Devil*. London: Banner of Truth Trust, 1964.

Guy, Harold A., ed. *Our Religions*. London: Dent, 1973.

Gyadu, Asamoah. "Pulling Down Strongholds: Evangelism, Principalities and Powers, and the African Pentecostal Imagination." *International Review of Mission* 96 (2007): 306–17.

Haldon, John F. *A Tale of Two Saints: The Martyrdoms and Miracles of Saints Theodore 'The Recruit' and 'The General.'* Liverpool: Liverpool University Press, 2016.

Hart, Trevor. "Revelation." In *The Cambridge Companion to Karl Barth*, edited by John Webster. Cambridge, UK: Cambridge University Press, 2000.

Hartlich, Christian, and Walter Sachs. *Der Ursprung des Mythosbegriffes in der modernen Bibelwissenschaft*. Tübingen: J. C. B. Mohr, 1952.

Heelas, Paul, ed. *Religion, Modernity, and Postmodernity*. Oxford: Blackwell Publishing, 1998.

Heim, Karl. *Jesus, the World's Perfecter: The Atonement and the Renewal of the World*. Translated by D. H. van Daalen. Philadelphia: Muhlenberg Press, 1961.

Hiebert, Paul. "The Flaw of the Excluded Middle." *Missiology: An International Review* 10, no.1 (1982): 35–47.

Hodge, Charles. *A Commentary on the Epistle to the Ephesians*. Grand Rapids: Christian Classics Ethereal Library, 2009 (1856).

Horton, Robin. "African Traditional Thought and Western Science. Part I. From Tradition to Science." *Africa: Journal of the International African Institute* 37, no. 1 (1967): 50–71.

Hunsinger, Deborah van Deusen. *Theology and Pastoral Counseling: A New Disciplinary Approach*. Grand Rapids: Eerdmans, 1995.

Hunsinger, George. *How to Read Karl Barth: The Shape of His Theology*. New York: Oxford University Press, 1991.

Idowu, E. B. *Olódùmarè: God in Yoruba Belief*. Plainview, NY: Original Publications, 1995.

"Irreligion." Wikipedia. https://en.wikipedia.org/wiki/Irreligion.

Israel, Jonathan. "Enlightenment! Which Enlightenment?" *Journal of the History of Ideas* 67, no. 3 (2006): 523–45.

Jenkins, Philip. *The Next Christendom: The Coming of Global Christianity*. Oxford: Oxford University Press, 2011.

Jennings, Willie. "Baptizing a Social Reading: Theology, Hermeneutics, and Postmodernity." In *Disciplining Hermeneutics: Interpretation in Christian Perspective,* edited by Roger Lundin, 117–27. Grand Rapids: Eerdmans, 1997.

Josephus. *Antiquities.* In *Josephus: The Complete Works*, translated by William Whiston. Nashville: Thomas Nelson, 1998.

Jung, C. G. *The Collected Works.* Princeton, NJ: Princeton University Press, 1966.

———. *The Psychology of the Transference.* London: Ark, 1983.

Justin Martyr. *First and Second Apologies.* Translated by Leslie William Barnard. Mahwah, NJ: Newman Press, 1997.

Kellermann, William Wylie. "Naming the Powers: William Stringfellow as Student and Theologian." *Student World* 247 (2003): 24–35. http://www.koed.hu/sw247/william.pdf.

Kelsey, David. *Proving Doctrine: The Uses of Scripture in Modern Theology.* Harrisburg, PA: Trinity Press International, 1999.

Klein, William W., et al. *Introduction to Biblical Interpretation.* Dallas: Word, 1993.

Knox, John. *Myth and Truth: An Essay on the Language of Faith.* Charlottesville: University Press of Virginia, 1964.

Koskenniemi, Erkki. *The Old Testament Miracle-Workers in Early Judaism.* Tübingen: Mohr Siebeck, 2005.

Kraemer, Hendrik R. *The Christian Message in a Non-Christian World.* New York: Harper and Brothers, 1938.

Kurtz, William S. "Naming the Powers: The Language of Power in the New Testament." *The Catholic Biblical Quarterly* 48, no. 1 (1986): 151–52.

LaCugna, Catherine. *God for Us: The Trinity and Christian Life.* San Francisco: Harper, 1992.

Lang, Andrew. *The Secret of the Totem.* London: Longmans, 1905.

Lategan, Bernard C. "Scholar and Ordinary Reader—More than a Simple Interface." *Semeia* 73 (1996): 243–55.

Lee, Raymond, and Susan Ackerman. *The Challenge of Religion after Modernity: Beyond Disenchantment.* Aldershot, UK: Ashgate, 2002.

Levison, John R. *Filled with the Spirit.* Grand Rapids: Eerdmans, 2009.

———. *Fresh Air: The Holy Spirit for an Inspired Life.* Brewster, MA: Paraclete, 2012.

———. *Inspired: The Holy Spirit and the Mind of Faith.* Grand Rapids: Eerdmans, 2013.

———. *The Spirit in First-Century Judaism.* New York: Brill, 1997.

Lévy-Bruhl, L. *How Natives Think*. London: Allen & Unwin, 1926.

———. *Primitive Mentality*. London: Allen & Unwin, 1923.

Lewis, C. S. *Screwtape Letters*. Uhrichsville, OH: Barbour, 1990.

Loder, James E. *The Knight's Move: The Relational Logic of the Spirit in Theology and Science*. Colorado Springs, CO: Helmers and Howard, 1992.

Malinowski, Bronislaw. *The Foundations of Faith and Morals: An Anthropological Analysis of Primitive Beliefs and Conduct with Special Reference to the Fundamental Problems of Religion and Ethics*. London: Oxford University Press, 1936.

———. *Myth in Primitive Psychology*. Westport, CT: Negro Universities Press, 1925.

Martin, Dale. *Inventing Superstition: From the Hippocratics to the Christians*. Cambridge, MA: Harvard University Press, 2004.

Mbiti, John. *African Religions and Philosophy*. Oxford: Heinemann, 1990.

———. *Concepts of God in Africa*. Nairobi, Kenya: Action Publishers, 2012.

McKenzie, John L. *Myths and Realities: Studies in Biblical Theology*. Milwaukee, WI: Bruce, 1963.

Meyerowitz, Eva L. R. "Concepts of the Soul among the Akan of the Gold Coast." *Africa* 21 (1951): 24–31.

Moltmann, Jürgen. *The Spirit of Life: A Universal Affirmation*. Translated by Margaret Kohl. Minneapolis: Fortress, 1992.

Moses, Robert. *Practices of Power: Revisiting the Principalities and Powers in the Pauline Letters*. Minneapolis: Augsburg Fortress, 2014.

Mugambi, J. N. Kanyua. "Challenges to African Scholars in Biblical Hermeneutics." In *Text and Context in New Testament Hermeneutics*, edited by J. N. Kanyua Mugambi and Johannes A. Smit. Nairobi: Acton Publishers, 2004.

Mugambi, J. N. Kanyua, and Nicodemus Kirima. *The African Religious Heritage*. Nairobi: Oxford University Press, 1976.

Newbigin, Lesslie. *The Gospel in a Pluralist Culture*. Grand Rapids: Eerdmans, 1989.

Ngewa, Samuel. "The Validity of Meaning and African Christian Theology." In *Issues in African Christian Theology*, edited by Samuel Ngewa, Mark Shaw, and Tite Tienou. Nairobi: East African Educational Publishers, 1998.

Niebuhr, Reinhold. *Moral Man and Immoral Society: A Study in Ethics and Politics*. New York: Scribner, 1960.

Oakley, Francis. *The Conciliarist Tradition*. Oxford: Oxford University Press, 2003.

Oden, Thomas. *The African Memory of Mark: Reassessing Early Church Tradition*. Downers Grove, IL: InterVarsity Press, 2011.

———. *Early Libyan Christianity: Uncovering a North African Tradition*. Downers Grove, IL: InterVarsity Press, 2011.

———. *How Africa Shaped the Christian Mind: Rediscovering the African Seedbed of Western Christianity*. Downers Grove, IL: InterVarsity Press, 2007.

Omenyo, Cephas N. "Charismatic Renewal Movements in Ghana." *Pneuma* 16, no. 2 (1994): 169–85.

———. "A Comparative Analysis of the Development Intervention of Protestant and Charismatic/Pentecostal Organizations in Ghana." *Svensk Missionstidskrift* 94, no. 1 (2006): 5–22.

———. "From the Fringes to the Centre: Pentecostalization of the Mainline Churches in Ghana." *Exchange* 34, no. 1 (2005): 39–60.

Opoku, Kofi Asare. *West African Traditional Religion*. Accra, Ghana: FEP International, 1978.

Orme, William. *The Practical Works of The Rev. Richard Baxter with a Life of the Author and a Critical Examination of His Writings*. Vol. 20. London: James Duncan, 1830.

Pannenberg, Wolfhart. *Anthropology in Theological Perspective*. Louisville, KY: Westminster John Knox, 1985.

Parrinder, Geoffrey. *West African Religion*. London: Epworth Press, 1961.

Pearson, David. "How Churches Fight Belief in Witchcraft: African Churches in Britain Are Learning How to Safeguard Children's Rights against Exploitative Pastors." *The Guardian*, July 27, 2010. https://www.theguardian.com/commentisfree/belief/2010/jul/27/religion-witches-africa-london-exorcism.

Peck, M. Scott. *People of the Lie: The Hope for Healing Human Evil*. New York: Simon and Schuster, 1983.

Pierson, Arthur. *In Full Armour, or the Disciple Equipped for Conflict with the Devil*. New York: Fleming H. Revell, 1893.

Pinnock, Clark H. "Theology and Myth: An Evangelical Response to Demythologizing." *Bibliotheca Sacra* 128, no. 11 (1971): 215–26.

Pobee, John S. "African Instituted (Independent) Churches." In *Dictionary of the Ecumenical Movement*, ed. Nicolas Lossky, 12–14. 2nd ed. Geneva: World Council of Churches, 2002.

———. *Towards an African Theology*. Nashville: Abingdon, 1979.

Polanyi, Michael. *Personal Knowledge: Towards a Post-Critical Philosophy*. New York: Harper & Row, 1964.

———. *The Tacit Dimension*. Gloucester, MA; Peter Smith, 1983.

Price, Daniel. "Karl Barth's Anthropology in Light of Modern Thought: The Dynamic Concept of the Person in Trinitarian Theology and Object Relations Psychology." PhD diss., University of Aberdeen, Scotland, 1990.

Radcliffe-Brown, A. R. *Method in Social Anthropology: Selected Essays*, edited by M. N. Srinivas. Chicago: University of Chicago Press, 1958.

Radcliffe-Brown, A. R., and C. D. Forde, eds. *African Systems of Kinship and Marriage*. London: Oxford University Press, 1950.

Ranft, Patricia. *How the Doctrine of the Incarnation Shaped Western Culture*. Lanham, MD: Rowman and Littlefield, 2012.

Rattray, R. S. *The Ashanti*. Oxford: Clarendon Press, 1923.

Ricoeur, Paul. *The Conflict of Interpretations*. Evanston, IL: Northwestern University Press, 1974.

Rogerson, J. W. "Slippery Words v. Myth." *The Expository Times* 90 (1978): 10–14.

Rosen-Zvi, Ishay. *Demonic Desires: Yetzer Hara and the Problem of Evil in Late Antiquity*. Philadelphia: University of Pennsylvania Press, 2011.

Ryle, J. C. "A Biographical Account of William Gurnall." Unsourced reprint originally dated April 23, 1864, available at: http://www.isom.vn salvation.com/Resources%20English/Christian%20Ebooks/JC%20 Ryle%20A%20Biographical%20Account%20of%20William%20Gur nall.pdf.

Sanneh, Lamin. "Gospel and Culture: Ramifying Effects of Scriptural Translation." In *Bible Translation and the Spread of the Church: The Last 200 Years*, edited by Philip Stine. Leiden: Brill, 1990.

———.*Translating the Message: The Missionary Impact on Culture*. Maryknoll, NY: Orbis, 1989.

Sawyerr, Harry. *Creative Evangelism: Towards a New Christian Encounter with Africa*. London: Lutterworth, 1968.

———. *God: Ancestor or Creator*. Harlow: Longmans, 1970.

Shore, Chris. "Myth." In *The Blackwell Dictionary of Modern Social Thought*. Edited by William Outhwaite. Malden, MA: Blackwell Publishing, 2002.

Smith, Archie, Jr. "Alien Gods in Black Experience." *Process Studies* 18, no. 4 (1989): 294–305.

Smith, James K. A. *Thinking in Tongues: Pentecostal Contributions to Christian Philosophy*. Grand Rapids: Eerdmans, 2010.

Spero, Shubert. "Sons of God, Daughters of Men?" *Jewish Bible Quarterly* 40 (2012): 15–18.

Spieth, Jakob. *Die Religion der Eweer in Süd-Togo*. Leipzig: Dieterich'sche Verlagsbuchhandlung, 1911.

Stott, John R. W. *God's New Society: The Message of Ephesians*. Downers Grove, IL: InterVarsity, 1979.

Strawbridge, Jennifer. *The Pauline Effect: The Use of the Pauline Epistles by Early Christian Writers*. Boston: De Gruyter, 2015.

Stringfellow, William. *Free in Obedience*. New York: Seabury, 1964.

Taylor, Charles. *Modern Social Imaginaries*. Durhan, NC: Duke University Press, 2004.

Theissen, Gerd. *Psychological Aspects of Pauline Theology*. Philadelphia: Fortress, 1987.

Thiemann, Ronald F., and William C. Placher. *Why Are We Here? Everyday Questions and the Christian Life*. Harrisburg, PA: Trinity Press International, 1998.

Thiselton, Anthony C. *New Horizons in Hermeneutics: The Theory and Practice of Transforming Biblical Reading*. Grand Rapids: Zondervan, 1992.

Thurneyson, E. *A Theology of Pastoral Care*. Richmond, VA: John Knox, 1962.

Torrance, Thomas F. *The Ground and Grammar of Theology: Consonance between Theology and Science*. Edinburgh: T & T Clark, 1980.

Troeltsch, Ernst. *The Absoluteness of Christianity and the History of Religion*. Atlanta: John Knox, 1971.

Twelftree, Graham. *In the Name of Jesus: Exorcism among Early Christians*. Grand Rapids: Baker Academic, 2007.

Tylor, E. Burnett. *Primitive Culture: Researches into the Development of Mythology, Philosophy, Religion, Language, Art, and Custom*. New York: Brentano's, 1924.

Unger, Merrill F. *What Demons Can Do to Saints*. Chicago: Moody Press, 1991.

Van Huyssteen, J. Wentzel. *The Shaping of Rationality: Toward Interdisciplinarity in Theology and Science*. Grand Rapids: Eerdmans, 1999.

Veitch, J. A. "Revelation and Religion in the Theology of Karl Barth." *Scottish Journal of Theology* 24, no. 1 (1971): 1–22.

Walls, Andrew. *The Cross Cultural Process in Christian History: Studies in the Transmission and Appropriation of Faith*. Maryknoll, NY: Orbis, 2002.

———. "Towards Understanding Africa's Place in Christian History." In

Religion in a Pluralistic Society, edited by John S. Pobee. Leiden: Brill, 1976.

Ward, Graham. "Barth, Modernity, and Post Modernity." In *The Cambridge Companion to Karl Barth*, edited by John Webster. Cambridge, UK: Cambridge University Press, 2000.

Wariboko, Nimi. *Nigerian Pentecostalism.* Rochester, NY: University of Rochester Press, 2014.

———. *The Pentecostal Principle: Ethical Methodology in New Spirit.* Grand Rapids: Eerdmans, 2012.

Webster, John, ed. *The Cambridge Companion to Karl Barth.* Cambridge, UK: Cambridge University Press, 2000.

———. "Introducing Barth." In *The Cambridge Companion to Karl Barth*, edited by John Webster. Cambridge, UK: Cambridge University Press, 2000.

Wierzbicka, Anna. *Emotions across Languages and Cultures: Diversity and Universals.* Cambridge, UK: Cambridge University Press, 1999.

Williams, David. *Saints Alive: Word, Image, and Enactment in the Lives of the Saints.* Montreal: McGill-Queen's University Press, 2010.

Williams, J. J. *Hebrewism of West Africa: From Nile to Nigar with the Jews.* London: Allen and Unwin, 1930. Available at https://archive.org/details/HebrewismsOfWestAfricaFromNileToNigarWithTheJews.

Wink, Walter. *Engaging the Powers: Discernment and Resistance in a World of Domination.* Minneapolis: Fortress Press, 1992.

———. *Naming the Powers: The Language of Power in the New Testament.* Philadelphia: Fortress Press, 1984.

———. *The Powers That Be: Theology for a New Millennium.* New York: Doubleday, 1999.

———. "Principalities and Powers: A Different Worldview." *Church and Society* 85, no. 5 (1995): 18–28.

———. *Unmasking the Powers: The Invisible Forces That Determine Human Existence.* Philadelphia: Fortress Press, 1986.

———. "William Stringfellow: Theologian of the Next Millennium." *CrossCurrents* 45, no. 2 (1995): 205–16.

———. "The World Systems Model." In *Understanding Spiritual Warfare: Four Views*, edited by James K. Beilby and Paul R. Eddy. Grand Rapids: Baker Academics, 2012.

Yoder, John Howard. *To Hear the Word.* Eugene, OR: Cascade, 2010.

———. *The Politics of Jesus: Vicit Agnus Noster.* Grand Rapids: Eerdmans, 1972.

Yong, Amos. *The Spirit of Creation: Modern Science and Divine Action in the Pentecostal-Charismatic Imagination*. Grand Rapids: Eerdmans, 2011.

———. *The Spirit Poured Out on All Flesh: Pentecostalism and the Possibility of Global Theology*. Grand Rapids: Baker Academic, 2005.

———. *Spirit-Word-Community: Theological Hermeneutics in Trinitarian Perspective*. Eugene, OR: Wipf and Stock, 2006.

Zachhuber, Johannes. "Speculative Theology in the Wake of Kant. The Nineteenth Century." Forthcoming publication, currently available at: http://users.ox.ac.uk/cgi-bin/safeperl/trin1631/main.cgi?5+.

Zündel, Friedrich. *The Awakening: One Man's Battle with Darkness*. Farmington, PA: Plough, 1999.

Subject Index

Scripture Index